The logic of bureaucratic conduct

The logic of bureaucratic conduct

An economic analysis of competition, exchange, and efficiency in private and public organizations

ALBERT BRETON
University of Toronto

RONALD WINTROBE
University of Western Ontario

CAMBRIDGE UNIVERSITY PRESS

Cambridge
London   New York   New Rochelle
Melbourne   Sydney

Published by the Press Syndicate of the University of Cambridge
The Pitt Building, Trumpington Street, Cambridge CB2 1RP
32 East 57th Street, New York, NY 10022, USA
296 Beaconsfield Parade, Middle Park, Melbourne 3206, Australia

© Cambridge University Press 1982

First published 1982

Printed in the United States of America

Library of Congress Cataloging in Publication Data
Breton, Albert.
The logic of bureaucratic conduct.
Includes bibliographical references and index.
1. Bureaucracy.   I. Wintrobe, Ronald.
II. Title.
HD38.4.B73   302.3'5   81–21722
ISBN 0 521 24589 3   AACR2

For
CATHERINE, NATALIE, FRANÇOISE, AND ROBERT
and for
DIANA BIRKENHEIER

Contents

Preface   *page* ix

  1   Preliminary survey   1
1.1   Introduction   1
1.2   The structure of the model   4
1.3   Implications   11

  2   Public and private policies   13
2.1   Introduction   13
2.2   The characteristics of policies   17
2.3   Economic and accounting budgets   20
2.4   The production of public policies   22
2.5   The interests of bureaucrats   26
2.6   Conclusion   29

  3   A theory of selective behavior   30
3.1   Introduction   30
3.2   Classical theories of bureaucracy   33
3.3   Selective behavior illustrated   37
3.4   Inefficient behavior   42
3.5   The theory   46
3.6   The cost of public policies   54
3.7   Conclusion   60

  4   The accumulation of trust   61
4.1   Introduction   61
4.2   Why trust?   62
4.3   The production of trust   64
4.4   A digression inspired by the literature
       on trust and related phenomena   73
4.5   Networks and the equilibrium volume of trust   78
4.6   Notes on sundry topics suggested by the
       theory of trust   87

5   The compensation of bureaucrats   89
5.1   Introduction   89
5.2   Monopoly models of bureaucracy in the
      public sector   91
5.3   Competition   94
5.4   Selective behavior and managerial competition   99

6   The size distribution of bureaus   107
6.1   Introduction   107
6.2   Schumpeterian competition   108
6.3   Schumpeterian competition in the public sector   111
6.4   The allocation of resources among bureaus   113
6.5   Entrepreneurial capacity   121
6.6   Restrictions on competition   127
6.7   Conclusion   130

7   Some applications   132
7.1   Introduction   132
7.2   Organizational structure and productivity   133
7.3   The Japanese firm: an ideal bureaucracy?   140
7.4   Income and price controls   146
7.5   Parkinson's Law   154

8   Concluding observations and agenda   162
8.1   Departures   162
8.2   The way ahead   164

Notes   *167*
Index   *189*

Preface

The motivation for writing this book came from our dissatisfaction with existing economic theories of bureaucracy. In his 1974 monograph *The Economic Theory of Representative Government*, Breton adopted Niskanen's general approach to bureaucracy. Therefore, he had nowhere to turn for a hypothesis about the relationship between public bureaucrats and politicians. To solve this problem, he assumed that whenever there was a conflict between these two groups, the one with greater power would win. Without a theory of accumulation of power by bureaucrats and politicians, that assumption was, of course, unsatisfactory.

In 1975, Breton and Wintrobe published a note on Niskanen's theory seeking to provide the beginnings of a model on the relationship of bureaucrats and politicians.[1] In that paper, it was suggested that bureaucrats must be viewed as subordinates even if they are also someone's superiors. It was argued that the power of bureaucrats lies not in their formal position but in their control of information, that is, in their ability to distort and conceal it. Further, to the extent that governing politicians can police or counteract the distortions of bureaucrats through the use of redundancy, external data checks, and direct monitoring,[2] the power of bureaucrats would be checked, and they would revert to their formal status as subordinates.

In 1976 Wintrobe completed his doctoral dissertation on bureaucracy.[3] Building on an idea of Tullock,[4] he sought to break with the tradition of modeling bureaucracies – public or private – either as pure systems of authority or as pure voluntary associations such as teams. In his analysis, an organization is defined as "bureaucratic" to the extent that its employees act according to rules and instructions from above and do not use their own discretion or authority. Wintrobe developed a model showing that the efficient level of *bureaucratization* in this sense could be predicted to vary systematically with such variables as the cost of control, the wages of employees, the organization's division of labor, and its size. He further recognized that whenever subordinates are allowed discretionary authority, they

ix

can use it in two ways: to pursue their own interests at the expense of their superiors', or to act in ways that promote their superiors' objectives. However, in that model the only controls available to superiors are those associated with the formal structure: rewards, sanctions, and monitoring. So, Wintrobe's 1976 model still pertained to the uses and limitations of the formal structure.

The present study begins with the recognition that one cannot fully understand bureaucratic behavior nor model the workings of bureaucracies by looking only at the formal structure or at variables associated with it, such as budgets, formal rewards and sanctions, and formal relationships of authority (policing).

The questions we address are the following: Can subordinates pursue their own objectives when these are at variance with those of their superiors? If so, under what conditions, and to what extent? In seeking to answer these questions, we developed a theory of trust and networks as the basis of a theory of selective behavior. This book, then, describes the development and application of a theory of selective behavior, which is at the same time a logic of bureaucratic conduct.

Research monographs such as this one are usually many years in the making. One inevitable consequence is that the authors become indebted to many friends and colleagues for comments and criticisms. Another consequence, attributable also to faulty memory and less than perfect note taking, is that in expressing our gratitude, we can never be certain that we did not forget someone who was particularly helpful, especially in the earlier days of research.

We must, however, mention Thomas Borcherding, Raymond Breton, and Harry Nishio, who have been particularly helpful at critical points in our work; without their help, this monograph would be very different. Our thanks go also to all those who in seminars and workshops in Blacksburg, Virginia; London, England; London, Ontario; Interlaken; and Toronto have helped us to clarify our ideas and to avoid unseen pitfalls. We have also benefited from the helpful comments of two referees.

Finally, we thank the Canada Council, which, through its Killam Awards Program, has allowed us to take off a year from teaching and the menial tasks of academic life to work full-time. As a form of research support – especially theoretical research – the Killam Awards Program is unique. We are honored and grateful to have been its recipients. Without it, this monograph would never have been completed.

All the chapters in this book were typed and retyped – some as many as eight times. We are most grateful to Louise Dalhouse for doing that work with efficiency and dedication.

A. B.
R. W.

CHAPTER 1

Preliminary survey

1.1   Introduction

What has come to be known as public choice rests on the basic intuition – initially sketched by Schumpeter – that the methodology of neoclassical economics can be used to analyze decisions and adjustments of participants in the public sector, and in other areas where decisions and adjustments are collective, just as it can in the market sector of modern economies. The working out of this intuition, one imagines, would narrow the awesome gap that separates public- and private-sector economics and eventually produce a unified body of analytical and testable propositions. Some progress in that direction has no doubt been achieved in the last 40 years, but the gap is still very much a reality.

One of the central tenets of neoclassical economic methodology is that the forces that operate to determine any outcome can be classified into two separate, but interacting, sets usually labeled *demand* and *supply*. In this book, we focus solely on supply questions by concentrating on decision making and adjustments in governmental bureaucracies and business corporations. We are therefore assuming that the demand side in the private and public sectors can be modeled separately and that those demand models will be consistent with the suggested theory of supply. By the latter, we mean that it will be possible to formulate a theory of the interaction of the two, because the ultimate test of the validity of any theories of supply and demand is how they combine to generate desired outcomes.

The language used above implies that a single theory is sufficient to analyze bureaucratic supply, whether in public or private sectors. That is indeed our view, and we devote substantial space to its defense. If our reasoning is accepted, a significant part of the gap separating public- and private-sector economics will have been bridged.

Occupying center stage in the theory of bureaucratic supply is the problem of the relationship between superiors and subordinates, a problem that in the literature to date has taken many empirical forms, depending on whether the superiors are politicians, entrepreneurs, owners, managers, or employers and the subordinates are deputy ministers, directors, managers, or ordinary employees. As we will indicate again in subsequent chapters, in all hierarchical organizations bureaucrats are at once the superiors of someone and the subordinates of someone else. Only at the very top and very bottom of bureaucracies does this dual-role characteristic of bureaucrats break down. The superior–subordinate relationship is therefore as general as it is central to an understanding of bureaucratic conduct.

The superior–subordinate problem in the theory of supply has been, if not always acknowledged as central, then at least discussed many times in the literature. At one end of the spectrum are those who, like the classical political scientists, hold that bureaucrats – read, subordinates – have no significant influence on the supply of public policies by government, or who, like many modern neoclassical economists, believe that bureaucrats have no lasting effect on the production and supply of private goods and services (what, beginning with the next chapter, we will call *private policies*) in business corporations. These scholars in fact assume that bureaucrats always behave as true subordinates, single-mindedly pursuing the objectives and implementing the decisions of their superiors. This view, that bureaucrats (and bureaucracies) are neutral, must in turn be based on the assumption that bureaucrats have no interests of their own that are different from those of their superiors, or that if they do, they do not seek or are not able to realize them in their day-to-day activities.

Another way of formulating the assumption of subordinate neutrality is to say that bureaucrats always pursue with maximum efficiency the goals and objectives of their superiors. It then follows that in the analysis of supply decisions, one can concentrate on the behavior of superiors and neglect the existence of hierarchical structures, as is common practice in the classical political science theory of government and in the neoclassical theory of business enterprise.

At the other extreme, there are those who hold that bureaucrats never behave as subordinates are expected to, but instead pursue their own goals and objectives and effectively make all relevant decisions on the supply of public output in governments and, although with less consistency, of private output in business corporations. In this view, superiors do not count, because the subordinates do what they want all the time.

As we have stated it, there is a great difference between these two views of the role of subordinates. One must, however, recognize that in a way they both spring from the same basic conception of bureaucracy. According to one approach, subordinates are assumed to obey orders, to carry out instructions, and to follow commands from above, whereas according to the second, they disobey orders, do not carry out instructions, and disregard directives if these do not coincide with their own. In both, organizations and hierarchies are conceived as structures in which the interactions between individuals are governed by authority. In one important tradition of modern economics[1] dealing with types of economic organizations, the distinction between firm (bureaus) and market is based on the presence of authority in the first and voluntary exchange and transaction in the second.

In this and the following chapters, we suggest a different view of bureaucracy. We accept as central the dual superior–subordinate role of bureaucrats and focus on modeling the relationship of superiors and subordinates. But, even if we assign a role to authority (formal) structures in our model, we will assume that the relationships between superiors and subordinates in bureaus are generally governed by exchange and trade and not by the giving of orders and directives that can be "obeyed" or "disobeyed." In other words, we conceive the relations between superiors and subordinates in a bureau to be relations of exchange in which superiors pay their subordinates for their "obedience." We will also argue and seek to demonstrate that when the price is not right, subordinates will not "obey." It is clear, therefore, that the notions of obedience and disobedience are not appropriate in this context – hence the use of quotation marks – and consequently, we will not use them again.

The analytic tools used in our model of bureaucracy are those of neoclassical economics. Exchange is one of the main concepts of that approach, but perhaps equally important is the assumption of competition. That assumption is almost as foreign to traditional models of bureaucratic behavior as is exchange, even in those models of bureaucracy that have been developed by economists. Part of the reason for this is the historic identification of problems of bureaucracy with the relationship between superiors and subordinates, and the consequent neglect of relationships among subordinates. Another reason, we suspect, arises from the proposition in price theory that competition among the firms in an industry renders the firm an unimportant unit in the analysis of many problems, such as the determination of price and output. If the firm is unimportant, the behavior of the bureaucrats within it and other aspects of its internal structure cannot make much difference, either. So, another reason models of bureaucracy have also been models of monopoly is that apparently only under these circumstances does the behavior of bureaucrats have any significance.

In this book, we take the view that competition is the best general assumption to make about bureaucracy in both private firms and government bureaus. We also claim and try to demonstrate that this does not invalidate, but rather enhances, the importance of understanding bureaucratic behavior to explain or predict trends in price and output, as well as costs, productivity, and other variables of interest.

Refocusing the discussion of bureaucratic behavior away from authority, rules, control (policing), commands, and monopoly toward exchange and competition is not an easy task. Much groundwork will be required for our claim to be taken seriously, but if we are successful, the awesome gap, not only between public- and private-sector economics but also between the analysis of market and nonmarket phenomena and institutions, will, we hope, have been significantly reduced.

1.2   The structure of the model

Although the analytic structure of our model is that of neoclassical economic theory, we nevertheless integrate into the model a number of elements found in the vast literature on bureaucracy, elements that students of organizations believe important in the analysis of bureaucratic behavior. Three such notions are particularly salient.

1.2.1   Trust

The first of these is the notion of trust. To understand the role and importance of trust in exchange in bureaucracies, recall that one of the most basic assumptions of neoclassical economics – often, admittedly, only implicit or unstated – is that trade requires the existence of property rights. In the absence of such rights, the very notion of voluntary exchange ceases to have a clear meaning. But property rights have to be supported. The standard assumption – again, mostly implicit – is that law and law enforcement support property rights, although, as we document in Chapter 4, appeal has sometimes been made to social customs, norms of behavior, codes of honor, and other such phenomena.

Exchange, which we suggest characterizes the relationships of superiors and subordinates, also rests on property rights. However, except in special cases of no great importance for the bulk of bureaucratic behavior, these are not and cannot be supported by legal institutions. Instead, we suggest, they are supported by trust. We devote Chapter 4 to a discussion of how trust is produced and accumulated. In this first chapter, we rely on intuition and offer the following informal definition: An individual (A) trusts another individual (B) whenever A is confident in some degree that B will undertake to do what he (B) has promised to do. The existence of such a phenomenon, because it effectively supports property rights, makes it possible for A and B to trade with each other under circumstances in which the absence of legal institutions to enforce commitments would otherwise make this impossible.

The individuals who are linked with each other by more or less strong ties, such as that described between A and B, form a network. In our scheme, networks are the analog of markets, just as trust is the analog of law and law enforcement.

The structure of networks in an organization is the analog in our model of what organization theorists refer to as the *informal structure*. The distinction in the literature between formal and informal structures is so basic and so generally accepted that it is now common to observe scholars working with it without even mentioning it. This early and central contribution of sociologists and organization theorists plays a central role in our own model. We have followed the literature in calling the *formal structure* by that name, but depart from it in placing the label *network* on the informal structure. We do this to emphasize what the literature on organization theory does not: that the informal structure (network) is a variable and that its extent, complexity, and influence are all under the control of bureaucrats.

In the literature on organization theory, the informal structure is typically taken as a datum or, if it is seen as a variable, it is viewed as emerging from the affective rather than the cognitive motives of employees.[2] Informal structures are not discussed in the economic literature on organizations; the concept of trust, however, is often used in discussing behavior both in organizations and in markets. But trust is also treated as exogenous to economic behavior, and even as necessarily so.

In our approach, trust and networks are accumulated by rational individuals who wish to trade with one another over time. We suggest a model to explain how this asset is produced and to show when the amounts accumulated will be large or small. The informal structure or, more exactly, the distribution of trust and network links, is the outcome of these production decisions made by individuals acting in a competitive environment.

Although much of the book is devoted to modeling the informal structure in this sense, the model does give an important role to the formal structure. That structure is an instrument in the hands of superiors that can be used to influence the behavior of subordinates. This happens not because subordinates can be told what to do – they can, but they cannot be told to do things efficiently – but because the formal structure is an important determinant of the costs of accumulating or maintaining networks and hence of their distribution.

Trust, therefore, plays a central role in the functioning of networks and also, consequently, in shaping the relationship between superiors and subordinates in all hierarchical organizations. But in addition to trust – or, to put it differently, in addition to the costs of producing and accumulating trust – the relationship between superiors and subordinates is determined by the costs of policing and monitoring. There is a growing literature – mostly cast in the nominalist ethical framework of welfare economics – that focuses on the relationship between principal and agent and that assigns a central role to monitoring and monitoring costs.[3] Whatever value these models have in other contexts, they cannot shed much light on the real-world relationship of superior to subordinate in bureaucracies for at least two reasons. First, monitoring the behavior of subordinates, agents, employees, and others in a context of contractual, enforceable law is of necessity different from monitoring in a context in which relationships are based on trust. Second, in bureaucracies monitoring is typically carried out by bureaucrats, who themselves presumably have to be monitored. So, even if monitoring plays a role, it is ancillary to trust.

1.2.2   *Selective behavior*

The second concept employed in our analysis is that of selective behavior. We have already suggested that there are two classical views of the superior–subordinate problem. In one tradition – associated with Max Weber – there is the view that subordinates are neutral; they seek only to implement the wishes of their superiors, and they do so with maximum zeal and efficiency. In the other view – associated with von Mises and, at a more popular level, with C. Northcote Parkinson – bureaucrats are conceived as permanently bungling and inefficient individuals or, alternatively, as individuals who carry out only those decisions that serve their own interests, rather than those of their superiors. In the first view, bureaucrats, from the vantage point of their superiors, are always efficient; in the second view, whether through bungling or an ability to disregard the objectives of their superiors, they are always inefficient from that same vantage point. We associate ourselves with neither of these views, but we do make use of them. We believe that bureaucrats will sometimes behave in the way suggested by the first viewpoint and sometimes in the way suggested by the second. The essence of our theory, however, is that bureaucrats *choose* whether to be efficient or inefficient, that is, they behave selectively. The theory of selective behavior deals with the determinants of the capacity of bureaucrats to be either efficient or inefficient and the circumstances that will make them do one or the other.

The *capacity for selective behavior* is easily defined. It is the amount by which output costs are reduced when bureaucrats choose to be efficient and the amount by which they are increased when their behavior is inefficient. This, in turn, is determined by the price and quantity of informal labor services that bureaucrats can deliver through their networks. Informal services are not the services codified in the formal contracts and the formal description of tasks associated with positions in the formal structure. Instead, they are services that are commonly associated with bureaucratic phenomena such as slowdowns and speedups of operations, negative or positive entropy regarding information and command, and leakages and "plants" of information in the media or elsewhere.

A theory of selective behavior allows us to integrate such diverse elements as the notion of control loss, red tape, slowdowns, work-to-rule, distortions, information leakages, and others that sometimes play a central role, sometimes a more subsidiary one, in discussions and models of bureaucracy. In our view, however, although all of these phenomena are manifestations of selective behavior, none of them are necessarily either inefficient or efficient. To identify any of these instruments with efficient or inefficient behavior, one must know whether its use is intended to achieve the objectives of superiors or to frustrate them. To take a simple example, a subordinate can leak information to the press from a desire to prevent his superior from achieving his objective, but such leaks can also occur because his superior wants this done.

What determines whether subordinates will supply efficient or inefficient informal services may be stated as follows. Essentially, selective behavior is the outcome of a trading process – a set of explicit or implicit negotiations, conducted in bureaucratic networks, between superiors and subordinates on the one hand and among subordinates on the other. The outcome is determined by the price offered by superiors for efficient informal services relative to what subordinates can obtain or "take" by delivering inefficient informal services. These two factors, in turn, are determined by the cost of monitoring and by the distribution of trust in the network.

1.2.3   Bureaucratic competition

The third idea, which sometimes ebbs to the point of disappearance in the literature, is that of bureaucratic conflicts and bureaucratic power as the ability to win them. Stories abound of internal fights for control, of senior managers engaged in struggles with each other, and of fights among bureaus for "territory" or for more resources. The notion of conflicts is sometimes given recognition, but the role of conflicts in determining outcomes is seldom, if ever, modeled. We do not use the word "conflict," but stick to the economic term and the economic theory of "competition." We do not, however, restrict ourselves to price competition but make extensive use of the notions of competition associated with "Austrian" economists such as Hayek, von Mises, and Schumpeter.

We will suggest and try to show that competition is a dominant feature of bureaucracy. There are, however, many forms of competition – both within bureaus and between them. Within bureaus, there is competition for jobs, or *"managerial" competition,* as it is widely known. There is also a less well recognized form of competition and one that has not been previously modeled – *competition for network ties or for "membership" in networks.* Finally, and no less important, there is *competition between the bureaus* in a bureaucracy, sometimes informally discussed in the literature as competition for "territory," although never modeled. We distinguish sharply between bureaus – single units such as the department of the treasury in a government and the sales department or production division in a business corporation – and bureaucracies – aggregations of bureaus such as entire governments or corporations. We develop a simple general equilibrium model of competition among bureaus, which we view as competition for resources rather than for specific objectives such as territory.

Recognition that there are a number of ways in which bureaucrats can compete leads immediately to the question, how are the different forms of competition related? Broadly speaking, we suggest that the different forms of competition are substitutes for one another. This means that restrictions on or "imperfections" in one kind of competition will, in part, lead to more intense competition in other ways. We acknowledge and suggest reasons why each of these forms of bureaucratic competition tends to be inherently imperfect. But we emphasize that by looking at each one in isolation, we miss the point: Imperfections in one form of competition may be compensated for by competition in other ways. The world of bureaucracy is essentially a world of competition.

These three building blocks – trust, selective behavior, and competition – are the main ingredients of our model of bureaucracy. The object of the book is to develop each of these concepts more fully, and to use the tools of standard economic theory to construct a simple model that (i) is applicable to bureaucracy in both the private and public sectors; (ii) explains a number of aspects of bureaucratic behaviors that have puzzled us and other students of the subject; and (iii) is capable of empirical verification.

The plan of the book is as follows. Chapter 2 begins by discussing the nature of the decisions made in public and private organizations. In it, we contend that the production decisions made in private firms and formalized in standard economics textbooks – decisions on price and output – are second-order decisions. By far the more important decisions are what we call *policy decisions*. In the automobile industry, for example, policy decisions are decisions about what kinds of cars to produce and what design to adopt or reject. These decisions pertain to fuel efficiency, front- or rear-wheel drive, four, six, or eight cylinders, and so on, just as in a public department of welfare, decisions pertain to the kind of welfare program that should be implemented and to the design of alternative programs. In a way, in both public and private bureaucracies, decisions are policy decisions about the extent and type of product differentiation. They are decisions about which lines and designs to supply and which not to supply.

Policies are modeled as collections of *characteristics* in Lancaster's sense of that term.[4] Some of these characteristics appeal to citizens, others to politicians, and still others are perquisites that appeal to bureaucrats. This partly explains how bureaucrats are "paid" for their informal services – by having the characteristics they desire incorporated into policies. We suggest that the drafting of memoranda, the meetings, and the debates among bureaucrats are in part the locus of negotiation and exchange over the characteristics of policies. We point out, however, that bureaucrats are also paid in other forms, including cash, trips aboard yachts, generous expense accounts, large offices, and so on.

Chapter 3 presents the basic elements of the theory of selective behavior – the conditions that motivate bureaucrats to supply efficient or inefficient informal services. We describe a number of the instruments used in selective behavior and then show the circumstances that determine whether those instruments will be used by subordinates to help attain the objectives of superiors or to achieve their own objectives at their superiors' expense. A simple model of the supply and demand for informal services is introduced to determine the volume of inefficient or efficient services provided and the effects of either behavior on policy costs.

Chapter 4 then turns to the foundations of selective behavior and bureaucratic exchange: the theory of the accumulation of trust. The model of trust developed there is, however, broadly applicable to other circumstances (such as those found in primitive societies) in which trust plays an important part in exchange. It is emphasized that trust is a capital asset, variable in amount rather than all-or-nothing (zero or perfect) as it tends to be treated in the literature, and is jointly or collectively produced by rational individuals who wish to trade with one another. We show that the amount produced depends on the costs of production, the gains from trade, and other variables. In addition, we suggest that there are two margins along which decisions about the production of trust are made – an extensive margin (the number of individuals with whom to accumulate trust) and an intensive margin (the amount or extent of trust produced with each one). This provides us with a theory of networks – which is simply another term for the distribution of trust. We then discuss the factors that determine the distribution of trust or networks within organizations.

Chapters 5 and 6 are devoted to the analysis of competition in bureaucracy and the effects of competition on selective behavior. Chapter 5 discusses the impact of competition within bureaus – competition for jobs or formal positions and competition to enter networks. We show the impact of these forms of competition on bureaucratic rents, on the capacity of networks for selective behavior, and on the effects of selective behavior on costs of output. Broadly speaking, our conclusion is that competition in these forms does eliminate rents, but does not eliminate and in fact enhances, both the capacity for selective behavior and the impact of selective behavior on costs.

Chapter 6 considers the competition among bureaus for resources. We discard the fiction that organizations – firms or bureaus – produce a single product or service, and we model the struggle for resources among bureaus as a process of Schumpeterian (Austrian) competition or *entrepreneurship*. Unlike other models in that tradition, however, in our model of the allocation of resources among bureaus, Schumpeterian competition has a well-defined equilibrium, and systematic and testable implications may be derived from it. Again, the capacity for selective behavior plays a key role in the analysis: We show that the distribution of the capacity for selective behavior among bureaus – itself partly determined by the distribution of trust and network links – determines the ability of bureaus to compete for resources and hence the outcome of this struggle.

Chapter 7 considers some of the main implications of the model. An overview of these is presented in the next section.

1.3   Implications

Chapter 7 is devoted to developing a number of applications of the model. We have selected these with some care so as to illustrate the wide generality of our theory and its results. But, in addition, we present these applications as comparative static exercises designed to show the predictive capacity of the theory.

We first use the theory to explain productivity differences among firms. It is well known that such differences exist among firms providing similar services, even when differences in the quality and quantity of conventional (labor and capital) inputs are taken into account. We suggest that differences in productivity are ultimately related to differences among firms in the amount and distribution of trust.

Now, trust variables are not directly measurable, but we need not measure them in order to test the theory. The reason is that the amount and distribution of trust are not exogenous, but rather the outcome of a number of factors. In this application to productivity differences, we consider several of these factors, such as the frequency of promotion, the amount of turnover at different levels of an organization, and the number of perquisites that superiors make available to subordinates. All of these variables are readily measured. We then derive their effects on the amount and distribution of trust, and thence on productivity. The correlations between the independent variables and productivity are implications of the theory, which we suggest are fairly easily tested.

The same analysis of the causes of productivity differentials is also used to explain such diverse and mysterious phenomena as the procyclical behavior of productivity, why government bureaus appear to be less efficient than private bureaus when both provide similar services, and the extremely rapid growth in productivity experienced by Japanese firms since World War II.

Chapter 7 then uses our model of selective behavior to analyze a problem in the public sector – namely, the origin of the demand for wage and price controls. Why do governing politicians continually resort to the use of an instrument that, on the basis of considerable evidence, does not appear to deliver what it promises? We suggest that the use of this instrument can be understood as an example of selective inefficient behavior by the public bureaucracy.

Finally, our model is used to explain "Parkinson's Law" – perhaps the single most widely discussed (although not always seriously) example of bureaucratic behavior. We take Parkinson's Law very seriously, and we try to show that our model provides a consistent and plausible explanation of that phenomenon, and one that is capable of empirical verification.

We hope that the exercises in Chapter 7 will illustrate the value and power of the model. But that power is illustrated throughout the book when we discuss and suggest solutions, based on the theory, to problems that have plagued economic theory, sometimes for decades. For example, we discuss and suggest a solution to the old problem of the optimal size of the competitive firm. We also use our model of selective behavior to provide a neoclassical rationale for the phenomenon of X-(in)efficiency usually associated with Leibenstein.

The theory of selective behavior has many more applications than those mentioned and developed in this book. We are convinced that as the reader acquires familiarity with the main features of the theory, he or she will be able to explain many phenomena that have hitherto been considered puzzling or bizarre.

CHAPTER 2

Public and private policies

2.1   Introduction

Both public bureaucracies and corporate (private) bureaucracies are engaged in the production of goods and services. However, if we are to understand bureaucratic production, at the level of decision making it is necessary to distinguish between two types of production decisions: (i) policy decisions, which embody expedient courses of action to be pursued by the bureau or bureaus, and (ii) technical decisions, which relate to the choice of techniques and the combination of factors of production required to implement policy decisions. Because the first type of decision – the policy decision – is by far the more important, we focus on it in this chapter and in the book. Indeed, we assume that governmental bureaucracies produce[1] public policies, whereas corporate bureaucracies produce private policies. To put it differently, we assume that in governmental and corporate enterprises, what is properly bureaucratic pertains to decisions about what will be produced; the question of how it will be produced, although important, is secondary.

There is a long and respected tradition in the public finance literature that identifies the output of governments with public, collective, or social goods, sometimes defined as goods (and services) that are equally available to all[2] and sometimes, rather vacuously, as goods supplied by governments. There can be no useful quarrels about definitions. We would identify the output of governments with *public goods* if, first, this term were defined broadly enough to include not only such things as snow removal, police protection, street lighting, national defense, education, health, and lighthouses, but also policies such as price regulation, unemployment, interjurisdictional grants, nationalism, family allowances, inflation, diplomacy, war, censorship, tariffs, racism, concentration camps, language, and anti- or proabortion laws; and, second, if allowance were made for the distinction between policy and technical decisions.

However, because of the historical habit in economics of excluding from the concept of public goods a whole range of government outputs (such as those listed above) – in fact, possibly the bulk of public production – we prefer the term *public policies,* which may help avoid this bias.[3] There is, however, a second reason for preferring the notion of public policies to that of public goods in trying to analyze the production behavior of governments. If the term *policy* is used to describe the outcome of decisions related to courses of action that a bureau adopts and pursues, there can be little doubt that in studying production behavior, the proper focus of analysis must be on policies. For these reasons, we suppose that governmental bureaus produce public policies and corporate bureaus produce private policies.

There is, however, a third ground for our preference. We suspect that the identification of public policies with public goods such as lighthouses, battleships, fire stations, and public libraries is based on, or at least fostered by, the view that in practice these goods are made available and can be made available to populations or subpopulations only in more or less the same quantities and qualities determined by the preferences of a median voter, consumer, or citizen. Given this assumption, the quantities and qualities supplied to individuals whose preferences differ from those of that median person exceed or fall short of what they desire. For those whose preferences are not those of the median consumer, the supply of public goods almost always implies a welfare loss, coercion, or frustration.

In contrast, it is assumed that private goods are supplied in quantities and qualities that satisfy the preferences of all buyers, so that no welfare loss or coercion is present. Complications associated with economies of scale are recognized (especially in the literature on imperfect competition and product differentiation), but the contrast between public and private goods is usually associated with those suppositions.

However, when the focus of analysis is shifted from the degree of publicness of goods and services to the distinction between policy and technical decisions, it becomes clear that the output of both governmental and corporate bureaucracies is characterized by some degree of publicness in the sense given that term by Samuelson. The degree of publicness varies with types of output and classes of bureaus, not with whether that output originates in the public or the private sector.

It will be easier to develop our concept of policy decisions – public or private – if we first illustrate the term *policy decision.* Because public policies are somewhat familiar, we will choose our examples primarily from among private or corporate policies, although we will use public policies as points of reference.

As noted earlier, corporate policy decisions are decisions about specific courses of action, about what will be produced or not produced. As examples, we note the following: whether cars should have front-wheel or rear-wheel drive; whether warranties covering these cars should be for 15,000 or 50,000 kilometers; whether high-speed bicycles should have 3, 5, or 10 speeds, or some intermediate number; whether a radio station should specialize in rock-and-roll or country music; whether rubber overshoes should come in the same sizes as shoes or only in small, medium, and large categories;[4] whether department stores should carry all brand names of a certain product, a selected few, or only one; whether telephones and associated equipment should be rented or sold; whether paper napkins should be produced in three, five, or more colors; whether inventory of repair parts for lawn mowers should be carried for three or five years; whether refrigerators and freezers should defrost automatically or manually; whether the maximum size for window air conditioners should be 6,500 or 8,000 BTUs; whether soap should contain detergents or not; and so on. Readers who are not median participants in all markets will be able to add many items to the above list that they are unable to find in the marketplace.

The above examples refer to private or corporate policy decisions, at least if our frame of reference is North America. These policy decisions are no different from public or governmental policy decisions, for example, about whether there should be four or five postal classes in the mail service; whether or not licenses for radio stations specializing in news broadcasts should be issued; whether defensive or offensive armaments should be purchased; whether a three- or a four-lane expressway should be built; or whether police officers should carry handguns or not.

For all of the above cases and others like them, a decision to adopt a particular course of action implies that some other course of action will not be pursued and, consequently, that certain goods and services will not be made available to buyers. If warranties on cars are for 50,000 kilometers or six months, whichever is less, they will not be available for some other specifications. If the decision is made to produce cars with front-wheel drive, that is what consumers will have to buy. If the mail service is limited to four postal classes, all mail will have to be put in one of these classes and not in others. If police officers carry guns, that will determine much about the police protection available to citizens.

In a real sense, policy decisions deal with the extent of product differentiation. Because differentiation is costly, cost-minimizing decision makers will limit its extent, and consequently, some products desired by the public will not be available. As we have already noted, policy decisions by private and public bureaucracies pertaining to the degree of product differentiation – and therefore to the types of products that will or will not be produced – imply that all such decisions contain some element of publicness. When the U.S. automobile industry decided to remove the small, usually triangular-shaped ventilating windows from the front door of cars, or when the Ford Motor Company decided that heaters and fans in its cars would operate together, or when Breck Shampoo decided to add deodorant to its shampoos, they were all making public goods-type decisions. They were taking the same kinds of actions as a postmaster general who decides to reduce the number of postal classes from five to four or the City Clerk who decides to increase the number of regulations in a zoned area from 25 to 30, or as the Minister of Defense who decides to provide national defense with strategic system A instead of system B.

A second aspect of policy decisions, implied in the above illustrations, is that if bureaucrats – private or public – are rational, they will seek to provide the degree of differentiation that makes the value of the objective function they are maximizing as large as possible. Such rational behavior could, in some instances, lead to more differentiation in the output of some public bureaus than in that of private bureaus, for the same reason that the degree of differentiation is larger in soaps and shampoos than in food processors and filing cabinets. This point is important, because it is often implied that market competition will guarantee a supply of all the product lines needed to meet individual preferences. The problems of product differentiation and of policy decisions are rooted in economies of scale in production and not in the degree of market competition. In the absence of economies of scale, a profit-maximizing monopolist would produce all the differentiation desired by buyers.

Economies of scale imply both a limit on the extent of product differentiation, whether by governments or corporations, and the necessity of policy decisions. These decisions, in turn, must be based on an appreciation of the distribution of consumer preferences. If that distribution is single-peaked and satisfies other minimal requirements,[5] governmental and corporate bureaucrats will decide on the extent of differentiation by considering the median consumer. If the distribution of preferences is not single-peaked or symmetric, other considerations will influence the outcome. To reiterate, the factors determining decisions will be the same for both public and private bureaus.

To put it differently, whatever theory of product differentiation – that is, whatever theory of the extent and properties of product differentiation – is adopted, that theory will apply to behavior in both public and private bureaucracies. To analyze what constitutes the output of bureaucracies – public and private – our first task, undertaken in the next section, is to recognize that policies are collections of characteristics, and that in producing any one policy, some latitude[6] exists with respect to both the number and type of characteristics chosen. That discussion underlines the fact that policies with the same label often differ substantially from each other.

In the following two sections, we focus on public bureaucracies and discuss two problems whose resolution should establish that, in terms of their outputs, private (corporate) and public (governmental) bureaucracies are comparable. The first problem, discussed in Section 2.3, pertains to the class of public policies known as *regulatory policies* and to the problems that these pose for an analytically correct definition of public budgets. The application to private budgets is noted. The second problem, addressed in Section 2.4, is to define the word *production* for public policies. This term has a clear and generally accepted meaning for the goods and services produced by private corporations but is thought by some to be ambiguous when applied to the output of governments. We argue that such is not the case. In Section 2.5, we digress slightly to discuss the objective function of bureaucrats – public and private – that is, the analytical equivalent of the idea that bureaucrats pursue their own self-interest.

2.2 The characteristics of policies

Policies are collections of characteristics in much the same way that goods and services consumed by private households are sometimes assumed to be bundles of characteristics produced by these households.[7] To understand the meaning of this assumption, let us concentrate on one hypothetical policy. We choose an imaginary Family Allowance Act and look at its various clauses, sections, and subsections. That act will specify the sums paid to recipients; how these will vary over family size, region, income, and other such variables; to whom these sums will be paid – mother, father, or guardian – and the circumstances governing each alternative; whether the sums will be indexed for inflation and at what rate; whether the payments will be policed; if so, how that policing will be done; by whom, that is, by the department responsible for the act or by one or more others; whether research about the effect of the program will be conducted; and so on.

The above list is short and incomplete, as a perusal of practically any law will make clear, partly because we do not wish to impose on the reader but also because a family allowance program is, overall, a fairly simple policy to produce. The point to be stressed is that every item in that list is a characteristic – the clause specifying the sums to be paid, the one defining the recipients, the subsection pertaining to indexing, and similarly for every item listed.

Not all policy characteristics are required by logic, by necessity, or by nature. A characteristic requiring all mothers to collect family allowances at the post office, let us say, may appear no more necessary to a family allowance program than vinyl tops or headlight caps are logical requirements for automobiles. Consequently, although certain policies consist of widely differing characteristics, they may still be grouped by observers in a particular class and hence are given the same name. For example, both Canada and the United Kingdom have a public policy known as national health, although the characteristics of the Canadian policy are quite different from those of the British one in matters such as coverage, remuneration of doctors, and premiums of clients. The two policies carry the same name and are generally recognized to be of the same class, first, because they possess a common subset of characteristics and, second, because that subset is basic for the policies to be recognized as national health policies.

The existence of a basic subset of characteristics attached to policies with the same label is well known. What often escapes attention is the existence of an important additional subset that makes apparently identical policies vary considerably from one another. Examples include the national health policies of Canada and the United Kingdom just noted, the variety of cars in the small-car class and of deodorant soaps in the perfumed-soap class, and so on.

Another way of stating this idea is to conceive of all the possible characteristics of a policy as constituting a large, although finite, set such as

$$Z = (Z_1, Z_2, \ldots, Z_n) \tag{2.1}$$

These characteristics are assumed to be all objective and measurable. If we let S_1 stand for national health, we could say that policy S_1 would not exist unless characteristics $(_1Z_1, \ldots, _1Z_{10})$ (let us say) were part of the policy, in the same way that in the absence of wheels, motor, brakes, and other basic ingredients, one could not have an automobile.

Policy S_1 will require $(_1Z_1, \ldots, _1Z_{10})$, but it will still be identified as S_1 if one adds other characteristics to these basic 10. Thus, S_1 could take the form of

$$S'_1 = (_1Z_1, \ldots, _1Z_{10}; _1Z_k, \ldots, _1Z_m) \tag{2.2}$$

or

$$S''_1 = (_1Z_1, \ldots, _1Z_{10}; _1Z_v, \ldots, _1Z_n) \tag{2.3}$$

and so forth.

In effect, like Becker and Lancaster, but also like Chamberlin,[8] we are assuming policy differentiation in that policies of a class – Chamberlin would have said, of a group – differ from each other. This is because different characteristics, which for purposes of exposition we call *nonessential,* are attached to the policies in different numbers and/or proportions.

Two points need to be underlined. The first, already stated, is that policy differentiation is the outcome of policy decisions. In deciding, for example, that all rooms in a hotel under construction will or will not have TV sets and, given the first alternative, that these sets will show black and white or color pictures or that the rooms will or will not have small refrigerators, an entrepreneur chooses to differentiate his product in a particular way. Policy decisions necessarily imply policy differentiation, and this concerns the choice of policy characteristics.

The second point that is important for our hypothesis is that amenities, emoluments, or perquisites such as large offices, air conditioning, thick carpets, beautiful secretaries, expense accounts, research budgets, amiable work companions (through discrimination on the basis of race, sex, religion, and/or language), use of the company airplane, and, not least, the pursuit of personal goals deemed in the public interest[9] are also often the outcome of policy decisions and hence of policy differentiation brought about by the selection of policy characteristics. To put it bluntly, perquisites of office are often (although by no means always) policy characteristics. The existence of perquisites has often been recognized.[10] Here we note that they are often related to the decision about how policies are designed in the first place.

Before proceeding, we wish to address two additional issues bearing on this discussion. Both appear in the literature in relation to public policies but are related to private policies as well.

The first issue is raised by policies whose characteristics are not known a priori except in broad terms. This is because, in the words of Eric Hehner, the laws or acts of legislatures "leave the real operating provisions to be defined by persons other than the legislators who passed the statutes."[11] The real characteristic of these policies, it is argued, is the discretion they leave to bureaucrats. In discussing the Area Development Incentives Act of Canada's Twenty-Sixth Parliament, Hehner notes that "the capital costs in respect of which a development grant may be authorized are to be 'determined by the Minister.' The approved areas are to be 'designated after the commencement of this Act,'" and so on. Every statement such as this can be considered to embody a characteristic, but it is best, in such cases, to assume that characteristics are added as the policies are produced, so that the list of characteristics is open-ended.

The second issue is this: Bezeau has pointed out that an element of many policies is complexity.[12] That no doubt is the case, but complexity is probably only another way of achieving discretion over the set of characteristics, just as imprecision and lack of attribution do for the cases examined by Hehner. Complexity, like discretion, requires that characteristics be discovered in the process of policy implementation. Complexity, in effect, allows the introduction of characteristics that become integral parts of the policy.

2.3   Economic and accounting budgets

As noted earlier, this section and the next deal mainly with public policies. Consequently, we focus on this form of production, although we indicate and illustrate the nature of the problem as it applies to private bureaucracies.

Public policies constitute the output of governments. The value of the resources used in producing these policies, in turn, constitutes the budget of governments. Budgets can be defined as the sum of expenditures, either on policies or on the characteristics that make up the policies. In either case, it is imperative that all the policies or characteristics that respond to governmental decisions be included in the budget.

To emphasize this point, it is useful to distinguish between what we may call the *economic budget* and the *official accounting budget* of governments. The difference between the two is best illustrated by reference to purely regulatory policies - although, as is clear from the discussion in the last section, many characteristics of standard expenditure policies have the same property from a budgetary point of view.

Let us use the requirement that all cars be provided with seat belts as an example of government regulation and contrast this to a program of direct subsidies to industry in depressed areas.

Consider the seat belt regulation first. Suppose that out of 5 million car owners, only 1 million would have demanded seat belts, the others choosing to do without them in the absence of public regulation. The government now decides that all cars sold will have to be equipped with seat belts, which cost $25. The extra total cost to car buyers is therefore $100 million. That amount, although the result of a governmental decision, will not show up in the accounting budget of the government. However, it is, in effect, a governmental expenditure and should be reckoned as such in a true budget, which we call an *economic budget.*

On the other hand, if the government gives a 20 percent subsidy on every dollar invested in preselected depressed areas and if $100 million in investment is undertaken, the government's accounting budget will indicate $20 million spent on that particular program and so will the economic budget. If the subsidy program required investing entrepreneurs to purchase their capital from designated suppliers, the accounting budget would still be $20 million, assuming $100 million in investment still to be undertaken, but the true economic budget would be larger if the cost of capital goods from the designated supplier was higher than from alternative possible sources. If the cost of capital goods from designated suppliers was 5 percent higher, the true economic budget would be $25 million.

To summarize, although the accounting budget may in the case of certain policies and characteristics be small, limited to administration, implementation, and policing expenditures, the true economic budget – the one registering the flow of real resources responding to governmental decisions – may be much larger.[13]

One implication of this approach is that it is not easy to measure correctly the size and growth of the public sector. The usual index of size, namely, measured expenditures, although interesting and possibly enlightening if carefully interpreted, involves numerous problems. Growing measured public expenditures are consistent with a public sector, truly defined, that is growing, stagnant, or even shrinking. The proper measure of the size of any government is the real value of all the resources allocated by governmental decisions. These resources should include not only market goods and services but also the time lost by citizens, although not that of bureaucrats and politicians, which is already included in the accounts.

As this last point indicates, one cannot eliminate the problem that arises from the difference between accounting and economic budgets by counting the number of public employees instead of the volume of measured expenditures. It is the total value of the time allocated by governmental decisions that is relevant, not just the number of hours paid for by public treasurers.

For too long, economists and other social scientists have focused exclusively on the numbers provided in public accounts. This has not only biased their contribution to public debate,[14] it has impaired their ability to model the behavior of public bodies and, most importantly, has prevented the development of true measures of government size. Recent efforts to measure tax expenditures, namely, the costs to governments of waiving some tax payments by certain individuals and institutions, are very encouraging in furthering our empirical understanding of governmental behavior, but they are only a beginning.

The distinction between economic and accounting budgets has a counterpart in the private sector. For example, banks can do much of their bookkeeping after closing hours, as used to be standard practice in Canada before the advent of computers, or they can do that bookkeeping on the spot while customers are waiting in line, as is now general practice. The increased time spent in queues is a measure of the higher cost of banking services. It is the cost of private regulation and should be reckoned as such. Similarly, the true economic cost of a barbeque set, or of similar consumer durables, is not the cash or accounting cost alone but that cost plus the value of the time and effort needed to assemble the set.

2.4   The production of public policies

Much of the literature dealing with the production and supply of public policies seems to be exclusively associated, at least implicitly and somewhat thoughtlessly, with the notion of legislative debates and proceedings and with the administrative and bureaucratic activities surrounding these procedures. In particular, the political science and public choice literatures sometimes give the impression that policy making ends once the decision on a piece of legislation has been made. It is this view, we believe, that prevents many from understanding the nature of governmental policy making. We cannot overemphasize that this process, in addition to the decision making associated with bureaucratic and legislative procedures, involves the further continuous implementation of these decisions on a day-to-day basis.

To illustrate this point, consider tariffs on imports. The production of a public policy such as a tariff or a tariff schedule often entails introductory discussions of politicians and bureaucrats with business and labor, followed by the preparation of preliminary documents and memoranda, executive or cabinet decisions, drafting of bills, legislative deliberations, and signing into law. But production activity does not end there. As long as the tariff schedule remains in effect, governing politicians and bureaucrats are involved in its *daily* implementation. That is, they are involved in interpreting the law, deciding on the extent of its application, how to handle special cases not dealt with in the law, defining exceptions, and so on. It is this set of operations, together with those surrounding legislative activities and decisions, that are contained in the concept of production of public policies.

It follows that, as with private policies, public policy making must be thought of as a continuous process. We can, consequently, write a production function for public policies (S_i) in terms of the usual factors of production, plus those mentioned so far (others will be introduced in Chapter 4), as follows:

$$S_i = F(T_P, T_B, T_H, K_V) \qquad (2.4)$$

in which T_P, T_B, and T_H represent the services (time) of sponsors (politicians, because we are dealing with the public sector), bureaucrats, and the legislature (house), and K_V stands for the services of different capital goods. As with private policies, these various factors can be complementary, competitive, or independent, that is, politicians and bureaucrats can be substitutes for, independent of, or complementary with, each other.[15]

Given this fact, one must recognize that a useful distinction can be made between the *institutional processes* associated with new policies and those associated with old ones. We acknowledge this, recognizing that such a distinction is basic to the erroneous view of governmental production as a one-shot activity. We will try to use the distinction without accepting the fallacy that has so often accompanied it. Although what we say is expressed in terms of public policies – because that is the way the problem is presented in the literature – it should be clear that everything that follows applies equally well to private policies.

In presenting a stylized version of the production process associated with new policies – that is, with policies that have still not been approved by the legislature – one must recognize that the design of these policies is intricately interwoven with the hierarchical nature of bureaus and of bureaucracies. In trying to delineate that process, let us assume, temporarily, that it has already been decided which policy to design.

The initial stages usually consist of the preparation of studies by experts inside and/or outside the government that will define the alternative ways of making the policy operational. These studies are read and summarized. The summaries (and possibly even the studies) are discussed in committees of bureaucrats from the ministry or department (bureau) involved and by interdepartmental committees (a subset of bureaus). After discussion, it is decided that some alternatives are not acceptable and that only a few should be retained for further study. This process of refining the available alternatives continues with successive rounds of memoranda, committees of various sorts, and decisions. Once a final alternative is chosen, it will be further discussed until it is sufficiently operational to be translated into a bill that will be considered, clause by clause, by the legislature and its committees.

From our point of view, the drafting of memoranda and documents, as well as the surrounding committee debates, are the locus of negotiation and exchange pertaining to the characteristics that will ultimately constitute the policy. In other words, as a first approximation, we conceive of the bureaucratic process of preparing documents and memoranda, creating ad hoc committees, and holding meetings as a surrogate marketplace or exchange where single politicians or bureaucrats, but more often groups, seek to add particular characteristics to policies.

One can drop the above assumption about the choice of policy and imagine that this choice, the selection of alternatives for further consideration, and the form of the policy ultimately decided upon mirror a trading process. In this process, some individuals or groups can have the characteristics that they prefer incorporated into a policy, whereas others are unsuccessful.

In the foregoing discussion, we have tried not to prejudge the nature of the trading process, a distinctive feature of bureaus and bureaucracies, by not being specific about it. We must now deal with that problem. It is not clear what kind of model one should use to represent that process. Should the process be modeled as a logrolling mechanism, as a bargaining or game situation, or as a competitive supply-and-demand market? Logrolling theory is still devoid of any comparative static propositions and, except under fairly restrictive assumptions, even lacks stable equilibrium properties.[16] Given the even worse condition of bargaining theory and the excessive formalism of game theory, we have, for the development of our own theory of the supply of policies, chosen to model the bureaucratic trading process by using the theory of competitive[17] supply and demand.

Our choice appears justified because the stylized institutional process we have outlined necessarily entails rivalry, conflict, haggling, contestation, and disputes between bureaucrats. Indeed, it is difficult to conceive of the debates, discussions, negotiations, and transactions – what we have called the *trading process* – that are such dominant features of bureaucratic life as anything but the institutional embodiment of bidding and counterbidding between bureaucrats. However that may be, the adoption of a supply-and-demand framework will help remind us that competition is an integral aspect of bureaus and bureaucracies, one that has too often been neglected.[18]

Furthermore, as should become evident, the selection of a supply-and-demand framework is not as restrictive as it may appear for the theory suggested in this book, because most of the alternatives we can think of would affect only the quantitative, not the qualitative, nature of our conclusions. In any case, if the reader feels that the supply-and-demand analysis is too far removed from reality as he conceives it, he is advised to return, as we ourselves often did, to the simple stylized story of bureaucrats preparing documents and attending meetings in which endless debates take place about which characteristics should be retained or deleted from policies.

We now turn to old policies, that is, to policies that were put on the books in past years but are still operative. The administration required to implement these old policies constitutes the bulk of government output. It is important to understand that, although decisions to introduce these old policies were made in the past, choices about the level at which they should be implemented have to be made every period. First, funds have to be appropriated in every period's budget, and that leads to new decisions. Second, laws can never be precise and detailed enough; therefore, decisions about the mode of implementation have to be reviewed almost continuously. For this reason also, new decisions have to be made. The same point can be put in a different way. The legislative process and legislative decisions only partly define a public policy. Policy administration and implementation on a day-to-day basis by bureaucrats and governing politicians are also essential.

The necessity of new decisions related to the implementation of myriad old policies seems to justify, for this dimension of the production process, the choice of a surrogate competitive market model, because these ongoing decisions also imply debates, discussions, and arguments – that is, bids and counterbids.

Before moving on, we should note that competition describes the behavior of bureaucrats in every bureau – that is, bureaucrats in a given bureau compete with each other – but it also describes the behavior of bureaucrats across bureaus – that is, bureaucrats any-where in a bureaucracy compete with each other. The notion of com-petition inside a bureau plays a central role in the development of the next two chapters, whereas that of competition across the whole bureaucracy is crucial to the conclusions of Chapters 5 and 6. What should be remembered, however, is that even if we distinguish be-tween bureau and bureaucracy for purposes of exposition, competi-tion characterizes the whole of bureaucratic behavior and activity at all times.

2.5   The interests of bureaucrats

We have devoted a great deal of space to the definition of policies and their constituent characteristics because both, but especially the latter, play a central role in our theory of bureaucracy. We think of policy characteristics as one important constituent of the currency that circu-lates in bureaus and bureaucracies, through which exchanges are made and accounts cleared. In effect, we assume that what is traded in the surrogate competitive markets introduced above, and to which we return in great detail in the next chapter, are informal (labor) ser-vices[19] and some quid pro quo, which are sometimes policy charac-teristics.[20] To put it differently, we conceive of a world in which in-formal services are traded for characteristics, much as neoclassical economics conceives of a world in which labor services (leisure) are exchanged for goods and services (via money).

However, characteristics are not the only currency circulating in bureaucracies. Other objects also serve as quid pro quo. That may often be the case in trades with individuals outside the bureaucracy proper. But even within bureaucracies, money, access to villas and fishing lodges, free lunches, trips abroad, interest-free loans, gifts (vicuña coats, liquor, furniture, airline tickets, etc.), and other such objects can be used to pay for what is demanded.

In the next two chapters, we concentrate on surrogate markets for informal services. But we could, with sufficient care, just as easily analyze surrogate markets for characteristics and other forms of quid pro quo and obtain the same results. Indeed, if one were careful enough in dealing with currency components other than policy characteristics, it would make no difference, by Walras's Law, whether he focused on the market for characteristics or the market for infor-mal services. It would be merely a matter of convenience and prefer-ence.

The existence of supply-and-demand functions for informal services and for the characteristics and other objects that serve as currencies implies the existence of preference orders and utility functions defined over these variables, which bureaucrats individually maximize subject to constraints whose prices are determined in surrogate markets.[21] This approach, on which our theory of bureaucracy is based, raises the interesting, if somewhat marginal, question of the relationship between the interests (goals, objectives) that we impute to bureaucrats – whether superiors or subordinates – and those that have been assumed by other students of bureaucracy.

Whenever certainty is assumed, as we do throughout the book, we take it that bureaucrats (B) maximize well-behaved ordinal utility functions defined over informal services, policy characteristics, and the other objects that are traded in bureaucracies. Thus

$$U^{B} = U^{B}(Z_i, O_j, IS_k) \qquad\qquad (2.5)$$

where the Z_i's are the policy characteristics, the O_j's are the other objects exchanged and the IS_k's are the amounts of informal services demanded or supplied, depending on who equation (2.5) is supposed to represent – superiors or subordinates. If uncertainty has to be assumed, we postulate that bureaucrats maximize expected utility function of the von Neumann–Morgenstern variety.

Many current theories of bureaucracy make much more specific assumptions about the objective functions of bureaucrats. Some, following Niskanen,[22] assume that bureaucrats maximize the size of their budgets or the size of their bureaus, defined in various ways. Others, like Migué and Bélanger,[23] assume that managerial discretion is maximized. Others, like Chant and Acheson,[24] assume that bureaucrats seek the greatest possible prestige consistent with some preset degree of self-preservation. Others, although spurning the language of neoclassical economics, in effect assume that bureaucrats maximize power. Still others are not as easily characterized, mostly because their work is not as analytical, but also make specific assumptions about the goals of bureaucrats.

In addition to size, budgets, discretion, prestige, and self-preservation, it has been suggested that security, the avoidance of risk or responsibility, secrecy, complexity, career promotion, leisure, internal patronage, and a bureaucrat's personal conception of the common or company good are objectives of bureaucrats, either one at a time or in groups. To our knowledge, however, no one has ever suggested the whole list at once.

It is our view that one cannot build a generally applicable theory of bureaucracy on a specific objective function. We have the impression that many theories based on the assumption that bureaucrats maximize a specific goal were predicated on the observed behavior of a particular bureau. This seems to be true of the work of Chant and Acheson, whose target was to model the behavior of the central bank in Canada. Their work was constrained by that target, but also by a set of historical events. This led them to predict, among other things, that the Bank of Canada would never announce specific monetary targets because that would threaten its self-preservation. But the bank has, for a few years now, been announcing such targets.

The effect of concentrating on one kind of bureau also appears to be important in the work of Niskanen and Tullock.[25, 26] In Niskanen's theory, the aggressive search for larger budgets, which no doubt has characterized the behavior of the U.S. Department of Defense, seems to have played a crucial role in shaping perception. In Tullock's analysis, the passivity and the desire for security that one associates with bureaucrats in foreign affairs departments seem to have had a large influence.

It is concentration not only on a particular bureau, but also on a particular circumstance or historical period, that leads to the adoption of too specific goals. For example, one cannot help suspecting that the very rapid growth in measured governmental budgets and in the volume of regulatory policies during the years 1965–75 had a great influence in the formulation of "Leviathan models."[27]

Within the framework developed here, the idea of a specific target or objective for bureaucrats implies that one can unambiguously associate subsets of characteristics with certain goals. Because characteristics are arbitrarily numbered, it assumes that the characteristics from Z_1 to Z_q, for example, are associated with a goal such as security, in that if $(Z_1, \ldots, Z_q)$ are successfully incorporated in policies, that will give security to bureaucrats. To say that security is maximized, then, implies that $(Z_1, \ldots, Z_q)$ dominate all other characteristics and are the only ones sought. The same is true of other objectives.

It is not possible to object in principle to such propositions, because they are specific hypotheses about behavior and may, in the analysis of particular bureaus at certain times, be enlightening and instructive. We believe, however, that we will never have a good understanding of the workings of public and private bureaucracies if a representation of the behavior of bureaucrats requires as many models as there are bureaus.

We will discard all specific goals and assume that bureaucrats maximize utility functions in circumstances that allow an assumption of certainty and expected utility when uncertainty cannot be reasonably neglected. This generalization has served economists so well in other areas of analysis that it should also be a sure guide in the analysis of bureaucracy.[28]

2.6 Conclusion

We have argued that governments supply public policies and corporations supply private policies, and that these should be conceived as groups of characteristics. Some of these characteristics, in turn, are desired by subordinates in bureaucratic organizations. These individuals are able to acquire some of these characteristics by selling informal services to their superiors. This property of characteristics has led us to conceive of them and other objects as an internal currency of the public sector.

We have further argued that the bureaucratic mode of operation – preparing studies, documents, and memoranda, abstracting and summarizing them, and meeting in committees to argue about, discuss, and debate these documents and their summaries – is the institutional counterpart of a supply-and-demand model in a competitive institutional framework.

The stylized institutional process we have described concerning the design of policies and their characteristics is the framework in which we shall cast our theory of bureaucracy. We note that not all of the edifice presented would crumble if some of the assumptions we make had to be altered. Parts of its facade would probably have to be changed, but not in such a way as to make it unrecognizable.

CHAPTER 3

A theory of selective behavior

3.1   Introduction

As a label, the word *bureaucrat* is easily misleading, because a typical bureaucrat is at once a subordinate and a superior. This dual role of bureaucrats implies that it is not possible to formulate an adequate theory of bureaus unless at least three levels are distinguished in hierarchies. Let us call these levels $i, j,\ k$ and label the bureaucrats at each level B_i, B_j, and B_k. Typical bureaucrats B_j are at once the subordinates of B_i and the superiors of B_k. In a bureau with N levels, the bureaucrats at the $N - 2$ intermediate levels are all B_j – bureaucrats; hence the word *typical*. Moreover, if we recognize that the decision makers at the highest level in the hierarchy are not bureaucrats at all, but politicians in governments and managers in businesses, then our typical superior–subordinate, dual-role bureaucrat is to be found at $N - 1$ levels in hierarchical structures.

The dual role of bureaucrats plays virtually no part in the general literature on bureaucracy and is seldom recognized in the economic literature on that subject.[1] However, it is central to the discussion that follows and, we suggest, to a clear understanding of the workings of bureaucracies.

A theory of bureaucracy, as we emphasize in Chapters 5 to 7, must deal with the nature and outcome of competition between bureaucrats and between the bureaus that constitute the whole. A theory of the single bureau is an important, indeed essential, building block, but it is only one. In this chapter, we are concerned exclusively with this building block. The substantive implication of our focus on the single bureau here will be discussed later.

Our task in this chapter, then, is straightforward. It consists of developing, in the framework of a single bureau, a model of the relationship between subordinates and superiors in three-tier hierarchies.[2] We focus on bureaucrats at intermediate levels – those labeled B_j above – and assume that at the highest level in the bureau, one will find politicians or managers (entrepreneurs), who we will often call, following Niskanen,[3] the *sponsors* of the bureau. Therefore, we will seek to model the relationship of sponsors to bureaucrats, who, it must be reemphasized, are both subordinates and superiors. We label the outcome of that effort a *theory of selective behavior,* that is, a theory of the behavior of subordinates who choose to be sometimes efficient (cooperative, collaborative) and sometimes inefficient (uncooperative, uncollaborative) in dealing with their superiors. That theory is in effect a theory of the supply of labor services in hierarchical structures, but only that component of the total labor supply that we will call *informal services.*

To understand what informal services are, we can use the distinction originated by sociologists and organization theorists between the formal and informal structure of organizations. The first encompasses the codified assignment of tasks and hence the formal organizational division of labor, as well as the set of rules, rights, and obligations designed to regulate and govern the behavior of an organization's members. The formal structure is often portrayed on a chart depicting the official (i.e., formal) lines of command and the coded pattern of authority. If such a chart were complete, including official relationships with the outside world – not, of course, with the clientele of the bureau, but with those who influence its decision making – it would be a good approximation of what is meant by the formal structure.

An essential aspect of bureaucratic organizations is that rules, rights, and obligations that are formally set down are attached to positions and not to individuals, as Weber emphasized in his classic definition of bureaucracy.[4] These rules, rights, and obligations correspond to the formal demarcation of the salary structure, a structure that also pertains to positions and not individuals. In the standard economic literature, the term *formal structure* is not used, but the equivalent concept of *structured labor market* introduced by Doeringer and Piore[5] – basic to the new literature on internal organization[6] – refers to the formal organization of firms.

Focusing on that structure, we conceive of private (firms) and public bureaus, in a first approximation, as organizations that use capital equipment, (formal) labor services, and other factors of production to produce output (policies). With these organizations, we can associate formal cost curves depicting the behavior of unit and marginal costs as output varies with decisions made within the formal structure. To put it differently, we can conceive of cost curves for private and public bureaus that represent the outcome of the operations of the formal structure and that are, therefore, independent of the effect of the processes that we will later associate with informal structures.[7]

Bureaus may operate along these formal cost curves, but they need not do so; under certain circumstances, they may not even be able to do so. The presence of an informal structure, with its associated informal processes or mechanisms – to be described in Section 3.3 – may force a bureau to operate along informal or, as we may call them, *effective unit cost curves* that can be above or below the formal ones and at variable distances from them. The costs for all rates of a bureau's output can be higher than those resulting from the efficient operation of the formal structure. This may not be surprising, but the fact that they can also sometimes be lower may require more explanation.

To see this, it is sufficient to note that the official codes, rules, and procedures that typify formal structures often prevent individual initiative, forbid the deletion of unnecessary steps, inhibit the acceptance of risk and responsibility for terminating useless operations, and impose other more or less similar inhibitions.[8] All of these restrictions have the effect of preventing actions that could increase efficiency. Processes and mechanisms that permit some individual initiative, allow the deletion of unnecessary practices and operations, encourage the acceptance of risk and responsibility, and in general limit other such restrictions must increase efficiency and, therefore, give rise to unit cost curves that are below the formal ones.[9]

Bureaucrats – that is, subordinates – have the capacity to produce sometimes at rates that exceed those codified in the formal rules and procedures of organizations, and hence have the capacity to be more efficient than is implied by these rules. They also have the capacity, at other times, to produce at rates that fall short of those implied by the formal codes, and, therefore, to be inefficient. Up to now, this idea has not been used to characterize bureaucratic behavior. The tendency in the literature has been to adopt one view or the other, so that theories of bureaucracy are based on the notion that bureaucrats are either completely efficient or totally inefficient. To give relief and perspective to our theory of selective behavior, we devote the next section to a brief characterization of these two major strands of theory. Our idea is not to be exhaustive, but to provide an introduction to our own theory.

Then, in Section 3.3, as already noted, we examine and describe what subordinates do when they behave in a selective fashion. We do this by focusing on three instruments that can be used by bureaucrats who behave selectively. There is already a substantial literature on these instruments; for this reason, we have chosen them to illustrate our ideas. However, that literature, although it sometimes comes tantalizingly close, always misses the essential notion of selective behavior. We hope to show that many interesting ideas pertaining to bureaucratic organizations, which now appear to lead an isolated life, can be integrated into a coherent and complete theory of bureaucracy.

In Section 3.4, we describe and analyze those activities that constitute inefficient behavior. Then, in Section 3.5, we present our theory of selective behavior. In Section 3.6, we return to the distinction between formal and effective cost curves and show how selective behavior by subordinates affects the position of this second group of curves. Section 3.7 concludes the chapter.

3.2   Classical theories of bureaucracy

Our aim in this section is to indicate in a schematic way where our theory of selective behavior falls in the vast literature on bureaucracy.

One can argue that the study of bureaucracy is traditionally carried out in one of two broad traditions. One, which has long been dominant among sociologists and organization theorists and which, because of the great influence of Max Weber, may be called the *Weberian tradition,* views bureaucracy as the expression of rational and efficient administration.[10] Scholars who work in this tradition emphasize the technical competence and the monopoly of knowledge of bureaucrats. In the words of Weber, "bureaucratic administration means fundamentally the exercise of control on the basis of knowledge";[11] in those of Galbraith, bureaucracy "embraces all who bring specialized knowledge, talent or experience to group decision-making".[12]

Because of the belief that bureaucrats are competent and bureaus consequently efficient, Weberians emphasize the inevitability of bureaucracy and of further bureaucratization. For them, the chief social problem of bureaucracy is to prevent monolithically efficient bureaucracies from occupying a position of virtually absolute power in society.

It should be noted that bureaucratic efficiency in the Weberian tradition is largely definitional. For Weberians, efficiency is the natural consequence either of high-quality inputs in the bureaucratic process or of the large volume of output produced by modern organizations. More specifically, efficiency is assumed to follow either from the high qualifications, formal training, knowledge, skills, and technical competence of bureaucrats, and from the rational and systematic structuring of decision making that is assumed to exist in bureaucratic organizations; or, alternatively, efficiency is said to characterize bureaus, such as the modern business corporation, because these produce large volumes of output. Efficiency is seldom if ever measured, as it should be, by comparing outputs with inputs.[13]

We must also note that in this tradition, the monolithic efficiency of bureaus implies that bureaucrats never alter policies (public or private) according to their own preferences. Bureaucrats have, as it were, no effect on the policies produced by governments or private firms, but always act as neutral public or private servants carrying out the wishes of their superiors with unswerving efficiency. They therefore have no power and seek none in a situation in which it would be possible to acquire power by behaving differently.[14] It is noteworthy in this regard that Weber, when he undertook the analysis of the Prussian civil service of his day, discarded his own model and assumed that bureaucrats were interested in power.[15]

The other tradition is both older and newer than the Weberian one, and in it the word *bureaucracy* is always given a more or less pejorative meaning.[16] In that tradition, which we may call *Parkinsonian* to acknowledge its more recent popularization by Northcote Parkinson, bureaus are, in the words of Bendix, "complicated organizations" characterized by "blundering officials, slow operation and buck-passing, conflicting directives and duplication of effort, empire building, and concentration of power in the hands of a few."[17] That tradition is associated with many anecdotes and jokes; it is also the one that, to date, is becoming enshrined in the emerging theory of public choice. In its modern version, that tradition owes much to Parkinson,[18] Tullock,[19] Migué and Bélanger[20] and especially Niskanen,[21] but to many others as well.[22]

Although there are many differences among the above-named authors, the central idea in their tradition is that bureaucracy is always inefficient. The proofs of inefficiency vary from author to author, but all require the assumption that bureaucrats, either because they are pure discriminating monopolists, because there is no competition, or because of some other attribute or condition, are successful in obtaining what they seek, whether it be a larger budget, managerial discretion, security, secrecy, or some other target. Although Niskanen has accepted our earlier criticism[23] of this assumption, his recent attempts to abandon it have not, in our view, been altogether successful.[24]

In all these models, the proof of bureaucratic inefficiency, to put it differently, rests strongly on the assumption that bureaucrats can use instruments or engage in particular kinds of behavior that are socially inefficient – behaviors such as monopolistic pricing or price discrimination – and that allow them to extract a larger budget[25] from their superiors. It is easy to prove that this inefficiency relies on the use of

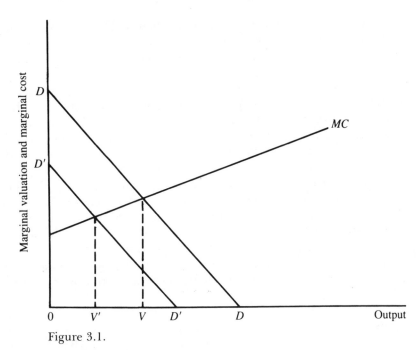

Figure 3.1.

these instruments or behaviors. For if bureaus could attract more of a society's resources only by being more efficient than competing organizations – including, in the case of public bureaus, competing private bureaus – they would never be too large, no matter how large they were or might become.

In addition, it must be noted that the incentive for replacing bureaucrats who are systematically inefficient must be the same in public and private bureaus. To hold to a different view – namely, that inefficient bureaucrats in government receive larger budgets and higher salaries than more efficient ones – it is also necessary to assume that the public sector is organized perversely. None of the current models of the public sector[26] can provide a rationale for such an assumption, yet no other assumption will do.

But although Parkinsonian models appear to rely on inefficiency to reach their conclusions, it can be easily shown that simple inefficiency does not pay in terms of getting a larger budget or more discretion, more secrecy, more survival, and so on. We can demonstrate this point by using Niskanen's model. In that model, portrayed in Figure 3.1, the demand for a bureau's services is depicted as DD and the true minimum marginal cost of these services as MC. As drawn, the bureau is in Niskanen's "demand constrained" region; that is, the only constraint on further expansion by the bureau beyond point D is that the public's marginal valuation of services beyond that point is negative.

Why is the equilibrium not at OV, but at OD? Is it because of monopoly or price-discriminating powers of the bureau? The best strategy to achieve output OD is not inefficiency but the bureau's use of production processes whose cost curves are *in fact* declining, so that the *actual* marginal cost curve on which the bureau operates is made to lie exactly above DD.[27]

How can bureaucrats achieve this? Not by being inefficient,[28] but by behaving in a selective manner, that is, by convincing their superiors or forcing them to accept the fact that the actual MC curve is *really* downward-sloping and identical to the DD curve. This is best achieved, we suggest, by choosing a production technology that displays high unit costs at low outputs and low unit costs at high outputs. If bureaucrats are successful in doing this, the output of the bureau will indeed be OD.

There are two implications of correctly specified Parkinsonian models that should be noted. First, bureaucratic survival and budget-maximization[29] are inconsistent under nontrivial circumstances. Second, a budget-maximizing bureau can expand – from a point such as D – only by a growth in demand for the bureau's services.

To understand the first point, consider a decline in the demand for the bureau's services from DD to $D'D'$. With cost given by DD and demand by $D'D'$, citizens, and hence politicians, desire none of the bureau's output, and the bureau will disappear. Bureaus do disappear,[30] but they would do so much more often if their managers employed the inflexible (i.e., nonselective) strategies implied by the budget-maximizing model. If the bureau's costs had not been distorted in the fashion indicated – or in any other fashion consistent with the model's logic – the bureau would still exist after the drop in demand; its output would have fallen from OV to OV'. Such a conclusion is easily overlooked by Parkinsonians because of the assumption that bureaucrats possess enough power to do what they want.

The second point is obvious. Once equilibrium is attained at D, nothing can change unless DD shifts outward. The shift would set a complicated process in motion, because it would have to be accompanied by maneuvers by bureaucrats to convince their sponsors that the hitherto efficient technology was no longer apposite. But if we assume that this can be done smoothly, the bureau would expand to a point along the output axis beyond D as demand expanded.

The reader should note that technological improvements in the bureau's ability to deliver its output would not alter its growth, because the bureau's costs are entirely determined by the demand curve. Apart from changes in demand, the only thing that could lead to expansion of output in Parkinsonian models is the change in the degree and extent of monopoly power in the hands of bureaus. Resort to that variable would have various implications for the properties of the static equilibrium such as that depicted at OD in Figure 3.1. We do not pursue that point here.

It may not be an accident that the more recent writings in the Parkinsonian tradition have attempted to formulate models in which bureaucrats have the capacity to control demand in a significant way:[31] Parkinsonian logic seems to require such models. But when suppliers control demand – as they do in these models, as well as in Galbraith's model of the business corporation – neoclassical economic methodology breaks down. One of the most difficult problems facing scholars working in the Parkinsonian tradition is to articulate models in which the suppliers who control demand are constrained in more than a tautological way. No one has yet answered the criticisms leveled at Galbraith on that issue;[32] these criticisms apply *mutatis mutandis* to recent Parkinsonian contributions.

In concluding, we note that both the Weberians and the Parkinsonians predict, albeit for opposite reasons, that bureaus and bureaucracies will grow continuously. In the first case, that growth represents the triumph of efficiency; in the second, the ability of bureaucrats to achieve unchecked what they want, and therefore the success of inefficiency.

3.3   Selective behavior illustrated

Selective behavior,[33] as already indicated, is the capacity of subordinates to be sometimes efficient and sometimes inefficient in pursuing the goals or objectives of their superiors. The theory of selective behavior is not a hypothesis about the preferences of bureaucrats, but about the means they can use to satisfy their preferences. Consequently, we begin by examining some of the instruments used. We focus on three instruments or strategies. Others certainly exist, but these three should suffice to illustrate what we have in mind. In general terms, they can be described as: (i) alterations in the flows of

Table 3.1. *Selective behavior*

Type of behavior	Instruments or strategies		
	Command and information entropy	Information leakages	Speeds of operation
Efficient behavior	Increase *or* reduce $(+, 0, -)$	True *or* false; large *or* small amounts $(+, 0, -)$	High *or* low $(+, 0, -)$
Inefficient behavior	Increase *or* reduce $(+, 0, -)$	True *or* false; large *or* small amounts $(+, 0, -)$	High *or* low $(+, 0, -)$

information or commands as these move through or across the hierarchical levels of the organization; (ii) variations in the quality or quantity of information leaked to the media, to other bureaus in the organization, to special-interest groups, and/or to opposition parties and rival suppliers; and (iii) changes in the speed of implementation of policies as these are put into effect.

We can associate the first instrument with information (and commands) entropy and note that its use entails increases or reductions in entropy. The second instrument can be related to information leakages; its use implies leaking true or false information, large or small amounts of it, or variations along other dimensions. The third instrument entails speeding up or slowing down the operation of a bureau or a whole bureaucracy.

Before examining how each instrument works, we must emphasize that all of them are associated with both efficient and inefficient behavior by subordinates. In other words, efficiency – that is, the cooperation of subordinates with their superiors to achieve the superiors' goals – may lead to increases or reductions in entropy, to leakages of true or of false information, and/or to speeding up or slowing down operations in a bureau. But inefficiency – that is, noncooperative behavior by subordinates in the pursuit of their superiors' objectives – can also lead to all of these: increases or reductions in entropy, leaks of true or false information, and/or high or low speed of operations.

The point is sufficiently important that we have summarized it in Table 3.1. Efficient and inefficient behavior both entail the capacity to put all three instruments or strategies to alternative uses. We have indicated this in words and by the signs +, 0, and −. We note that 0 stands for formal codified behavior, and that only + and − are associated with selective behavior: + with efficient and − with inefficient behavior.

An efficient bureaucrat can, for example, leak true or false information to the media. He will do whichever helps his superiors most. However, an inefficient bureaucrat may also leak true or false information to the media. That is what we mean when we say that a subordinate behaves selectively.

Let us now analyze each instrument. It has been argued convincingly that some distortion of information (entropy) as it flows through a hierarchy is inevitable, because vast amounts of information always flow through hierarchies. Information from the field flowing up to the decision makers at the apex of the bureau must be synthesized by lower-level bureaucrats so that only the most relevant information moves upward and in condensed form. Similarly, commands flowing down tend to be very general at first. It is the task of those at lower levels to interpret these commands, flesh them out, make them specific, and apply them to concrete problems. Accordingly, even in the absence of incentives to distort information selectively, some information will be distorted through natural entropy. The process of entropic distortion has been modeled by Tullock[34] and Williamson.[35] In its simplest form, if the fraction of information that is distorted is constant for each additional level through which it passes, the cumulative distortion of information – called *control loss* – increases more than proportionately with the number of levels through which it moves.

This is not selective distortion, because it is essentially a natural phenomenon. But what is important, even essential, for the theory of selective behavior is that the inevitability of some distortion in the natural workings of bureaucratic organizations makes it possible for bureaucrats, if they so choose, to increase or reduce entropy. That is, they can alter information and command flows in a self-serving fashion – namely, to be inefficient from their superiors' point of view – without being easily detected. The fact that some distortion is inevitable implies that the mere observance of distortion is no proof of deliberate inefficiency. Therefore, departures from formal behavior are much more difficult to police than they would otherwise be.

Inefficient behavior in this particular case, therefore, is the ability sometimes to increase and sometimes to reduce entropy against one's superiors. It is possible only because of the existence of natural entropy, which makes it difficult to ascertain whether any observed dis-

tortion or falsification of information is a random bureaucratic phenomenon or a deliberate act of inefficient behavior. In the absence of
natural entropy, only efficient behavior would be possible.[36]

We must stress that entropy is natural in the sense that it arises
automatically from the operations of the organization's *formal* structure. In other words, distortions occur when subordinates are at 0
(that is, behaving formally) as well as when they are at + (selectively
efficient) or at − (selectively inefficient). This helps us to understand
why the mere observance of distortion cannot serve as a proof of a +
or a − behavior.

The second instrument of selective behavior listed above is information leakages. Again, because some leaks are inevitable – namely,
because they are natural phenomena – inefficient leakages are possible. Bureaucrats, even fairly junior ones, must have contacts with
reporters, businessmen, politicians, consultants, and many others in
conducting the affairs of their bureaus and performing their social
duties. During these meetings and encounters, it is inevitable that
some information about what is being discussed and debated in the
bureau will be passed along. Indeed, unless the bureaucrat is exceed-
ingly careful, he may be revealing more than he believes about the
activities of his bureau and other bureaus with which he may be con-
nected, especially if those he is talking to are already well informed
about the affairs of the organization.

Consequently, if a bureaucrat, or a group of them, wish to increase
the demand for a policy to which they can easily attach characteristics
they desire, or if they wish to sabotage a policy they dislike, it may be
possible for them to leak information inefficiently – that is, against
their superiors – without being easily apprehended. The point is that,
although bureaucrats may sometimes leak whole documents to a
member of the press or to someone else, it is not necessary for them
always to take such large risks to achieve their ends. Most information
leakages comes in much smaller packages.

A third instrument that subordinates can use is changes in the
speed of policy making. In this case, also, there are natural forces
leading to variations in speed. This is a consequence of a more or less
diligent application of formal codes to decisions. Formal slowdowns
and work-to-rule are merely extreme cases of the more common and
more subtle practice whereby policies are held up through red tape,
because it is always possible to allege the need for formal clearance by
and coordination with other departments.

Again, in large organizations such delays are by no means rare.
Formal rules have to be respected in some degree, providing the

screen under which policies that are disliked by bureaucrats can be systematically sabotaged and those that are favored can be pushed forward. On the other hand, there are numerous ways of bypassing formal routines and thus increasing, sometimes to an amazing extent, the speed of operations. These methods can also be used to sabotage undesired policies or to force the adoption of desired ones.

Selective behavior, to repeat, is possible because of the presence, in the natural workings of formal organizations, of forces that permit distortions, leakages, and slowdowns with a low probability of apprehension. We must now note that, in addition to such natural phenomena, selective behavior requires the use of networks. In other words, whether they are used efficiently or inefficiently, the instruments of selective behavior require the collaboration and participation of individuals who trust each other. Why? Because selective behavior, whatever forms it may take, is the embodiment of trades or exchanges, and these take place in networks.

The next chapter is devoted to trust and to networks. Here, it is sufficient to note that networks are institutions, based on trust, in which informal services of subordinates are exchanged for the characteristics of policies and/or other objects. The informal services traded in bureaus are higher or lower entropy, true or false information leakages, and/or high or low speeds of operation. When behavior is efficient, these services are "sold" to superiors; for example, true or false information may be leaked to the media in an effort to achieve what superiors want. When behavior is inefficient, services are not sold to superiors but are "delivered" by subordinates; for example, true or false information may be leaked to the press to sabotage the superiors' goals and foster the subordinates' own objectives.

When the services are sold to superiors, the latter pay the subordinates in some form over a period of time; when the subordinates deliver their services, they themselves actually take the payment. Because this process involves a number of individuals in one or more networks, we portray it as network trading and model it as a form of surrogate market competition.

Before presenting the formal theory of selective behavior, we will examine a feature of bureaucratic behavior that often puzzles observers, sometimes destroys naive sponsors, and is usually not mentioned, still less discussed, in the literature. This examination will tell us much about both network trading and selective behavior. The behavioral feature is this: It is generally difficult, if not impossible, to give orders that are perceived as orders to bureaucrats. Usually when there is a change of government, politicians sometimes state that a particular policy is not negotiable, that the advice of senior bureaucrats on its design is not sought, and that its implementation will be a test of the bureaucrats' commitment to the new government. After such declarations, one usually observes that the policy is not implemented and that, even in totally unrelated domains and bureaus, bureaucrats do not cooperate.

This phenomenon is easily understood in our framework. Bureaucrats have to disobey such orders, because if they did not, their sponsors – in the example above, newly elected politicians – would think that they can obtain the services of their subordinates without paying for them. By disobeying, subordinates convey the message that cooperation – that is, efficient behavior – must be paid for. Otherwise, only inefficient behavior will occur.

Newly elected politicians cannot transact with their bureaucrats, because no trust has been accumulated with them and no networks therefore exist. The message conveyed by subordinates signals both that trust must be established and that the services demanded must be paid for. Without a quid pro quo, only formal or inefficient behavior should be expected.

3.4   Inefficient behavior

The notion of inefficient behavior, especially among economists, raises eyebrows. The difficult question is partly whether inefficient behavior can persist under long-run competitive conditions[37] but also whether this kind of behavior can exist at all and, if so, whether it is consistent with such intricate concepts as zero enforcement and zero information costs.

The following discussion will elaborate a central concept in our theory of bureaucratic conduct. Bureaucratic organizations are fairly tenebrous institutions, at least to academics who spend their lives in universities without thinking much about how these bureaucracies operate or about whether they themselves relate to their superiors efficiently or inefficiently. Economists, however, know a good deal more about markets and market behavior. For this reason, we supplement the foregoing discussion of inefficient behavior with illustrations taken from a market context. We then show how this market behavior relates to bureaucratic conduct.

Markets provide the most information about inefficient behavior; consequently, documenting the existence of such behavior and describing its properties are easier to do there than elsewhere. Next in order are public bureaus in democracies, where many are more or less open to public scrutiny, at least where a vigilant press exists. It is in the public bureaus of dictatorships and in private corporate bureaus that inefficient behavior is most difficult to establish. Except for occasional glimpses,[38] these institutions are essentially closed to the public.

Inefficient market behavior arises whenever the supplier of a product or a service generates a demand for his product or service in excess of true demand. Not all such attempts, however, are instances of inefficient market behavior. In analyzing the factors that distinguish true demand from demand associated with inefficient market behavior, it is useful to consider a few illustrations.

Perhaps the best-documented case of demand generation is that for medical services and surgery.[39] Considerable statistical evidence indicates that unwanted and unnecessary surgery is performed on and unneeded medical services sold to the public. There is less evidence that lawyers generate demand for their services, but casual observation of legal customs and court procedures reveals practices that are surely not inconsistent with their ability to do the same when it is profitable. It seems that many, if not all, professionals are in a similar position.

The capacity for demand generation is not restricted to professionals. This practice in the service and repair sector is legendary, as anyone who has a car, TV set, or other appliance knows. Stories abound of watered drinks in bars, of taxi drivers who take their fares for a long ride, of long-distance movers who delay delivery of furniture and other household effects, and so on. There are also the widespread practices of featherbedding, working-to-rule, and restriction of output practiced mostly, but not exclusively, by unionized labor. Finally, it has often been alleged and, some claim, documented that the manufacturers of certain products – for example, light bulbs and cars – have designed these products to become rapidly obsolete so as to generate a replacement demand. The analysis of fashions, although complex, also includes an element of demand generation.

The above list, which is short considering the innumerable cases that come to mind, is sufficiently illustrative. Demand generation is not, however, homogenous. To understand inefficient market behavior, we must distinguish between at least two types of inefficiencies, which we label *mystification* and *entrapment*. The essential characteristic of the first type is that the perpetrator can provide a convincing explanation of his actions and behavior. Consider the physician who performs an appendectomy. The appendix may or may not have required removal. That is not easy for the patient to establish, but even if he could later prove beyond doubt that no surgery was needed, he cannot be sure that the physician operated just to make money. To put it differently, genuine errors of diagnosis are possible. This implies that even if a patient knows that physicians generate demand for their own services by performing unnecessary operations, he cannot decide not to have an appendectomy based on this information alone.

The above illustration should help us to understand how difficult such concepts as zero information costs are. It is true that if information costs were really zero, errors of diagnosis would not exist – nor would diagnosis itself. But that is an absolute neverworld. For that reason, we chose to associate the inefficient behavior that we call *mystification* with the perpetrator's ability to provide a reasonable explanation for his behavior. Readers who have had to listen to physicians, lawyers, or automotive repairmen justify their actions will appreciate how difficult it is to distinguish necessity from fraud or error.

The case of physicians is instructive in another respect. It might be argued that the above dilemma could be reduced by appeal to other physicians. In some instances such recourse may help, but in the case of an already performed appendectomy or tonsillectomy, it is not likely to be very productive. But even if one could obtain other opinions as to whether surgery was necessary or not, one would soon encounter the code of medical deontology that prevents physicians from criticizing one another. Indeed, medical deontology is often a necessary element in mystification. And although the rules of medical deontology are more explicit, such codes of conduct in other professions are equivalent in practice.

The second type of inefficient behavior, or demand generation, is *entrapment*. People who have bought encyclopedias, vacuum cleaners, chinaware, and other products that they never wanted have been entrapped by salespersons; those who enter cabarets where no minimum or cover charges are advertised but are charged $10 for their first drink are entrapped; and those whose household effects are detained by movers beyond the agreed-upon date are entrapped. Entrapment is marked by the inability to stop a process after it is begun, either because the sales context has been rigged, because of the presence of bouncers, or because the household effects are in the hands of the movers and cannot be located by the owner.

In all these instances of inefficient market behavior and others like them, the standard apparatus of supply and demand can still be used. Demand, however, refers not to voluntary payments by consumers buying goods or services but to the money that suppliers are able to take from demanders for different quantities supplied. To put it differently, the demand curve represents the maximum average revenue that a supplier can extract from a consumer at different quantities under existing circumstances. In this context, it is best to think of the quid pro quos not as prices *paid* by consumers but as money *taken* by suppliers. We follow this practice throughout.

In bureaucracies, inefficient behavior of both types exists. In the first case, mystification, the logic is not very different from that governing inefficient market behavior. Should a superior discover that a policy is against his interest, he may not be able to blame it on anyone, either because its design was collective or because he cannot know whether the damages were willfully inflicted, given a good rationale for the policy decision.

In a bureaucratic context, as in a market context, the possibility of genuine mistakes by subordinates makes it difficult, if not impossible, to remove inefficient behavior. For example, if a superior's instruction is not carried out as expected, the superior could infer inefficient behavior with certainty only if it could be shown without doubt that the instruction given was completely clear. Any ambiguity makes blame impossible and creates the possibility of inefficient behavior.

One is tempted to relate bureaucratic entrapment to the preparation of agendas that are structured so as to lead away from one's desired goal.[40] But the phenomenon is more pervasive than that. Entrapment exists whenever one knowingly makes decisions that are bad but for which no feasible alternatives exist. Elements of entrapment are certainly needed to explain such events as the Vietnam War.

A good illustration of entrapment is the co-called Coyne affair, in which the governor of the Bank of Canada, James Coyne, was pitted against the government. The facts are straightforward.[41] Beginning in 1958, the governor of the bank, a senior civil servant, chose to pursue a tight monetary policy with the explicit purpose of increasing the volume of savings to reduce Canada's dependence on U.S. capital. In addition, in a number of speeches, the governor castigated the government for its fiscal policies, which he found too lax. The government disapproved of both tactics and asked the governor to alter his stand; he refused. He was asked to resign, and again refused. Then, to quote Bothwell, Drummond, and English,

on June 14 [1960] Fleming [the Minister of Finance] told the House [of Commons] that he [the governor] would be fired; on June 20 he [the Minister] announced that there would be a royal commission on banking and finance; on June 23 Diefenbaker [the Prime Minister] introduced a bill by which the office of the governor of the Bank of Canada would be deemed to have been vacant; on July 13, following stormy scenes in the Commons and distressing ones in the Senate, where the governor shed tears before the legislators, Coyne at last resigned.[42]

The effects of the Coyne affair on the economic life of the country were negligible. But what was not, according to virtually all commentators, was the effect on the government. Three years later, a government elected with the largest majority in the history of Canada was out of office after a steady erosion of popular support. Coyne did not bring about the demise of the government single-handedly, but his behavior certainly contributed significantly to the image of incompetent politicians.

The Coyne affair is a good example of entrapment, not in the sense that Coyne set out to destroy the government but because the government came to be ruled by a logic of events that was essentially controlled by a subordinate – the governor of the bank. Entrapment is easy to identify; it has provided the plot for virtually all the great classical Greek tragedies, for Shakespearian drama, and for innumerable modern novels. As it applies to bureaucratic conduct, the case of wage and price controls analyzed in Chapter 7 provides another illustration.

3.5   The theory

We have defined and illustrated selective behavior, introduced networks as surrogate competitive markets, identified the currencies and the (informal) services traded in these networks, and assigned objective functions to superiors (sponsors) and subordinates.[43] We can now formulate our theory of selective behavior, which deals with the forces that cause subordinates to be sometimes efficient and sometimes inefficient in pursuing their superiors' (sponsors') objectives.

The theory rests on the notion that the supply of informal services by subordinates can be divided into two separate decisions. The first pertains to whether behavior should be efficient, inefficient, or formal; the second concerns the volume of efficient or inefficient informal services supplied. That notion of separation is similar to the one underlying the theory of finance.

We analyze both decisions by postulating a supply curve of informal services provided by subordinates. We also assume a demand curve for these services by superiors (sponsors). When that demand curve reflects a desire for efficient services by sponsors, it is easy to understand its meaning. However, the demand curve can also reflect a desire by sponsors for inefficient services, in which case it must be interpreted as follows. Consider, as an illustration, persons who decide not to purchase the alarm and lock systems that are technically the best protection against burglary because the cost of these systems is too high. These persons can be said to reveal a demand for crime against their property whose size is reflected in the shortfall in protective quality provided by the systems they purchase versus that given by the best systems. Because that difference varies with the protective quality of systems, these persons' demand for crime varies with the cost of the systems. Similarly, persons who carry a wallet conspicuously reveal a demand to be robbed whose size varies with the degree of conspicuousness displayed. In the same way, sponsors in bureaus who put themselves in a position that motivates subordinates to behave inefficiently toward them reveal a demand for inefficient informal services whose size varies with the inducement to be inefficient.

Based on these two interpretations of the demand curve, we asserted earlier that when efficient services are desired, demanders *pay* suppliers for them; in contrast, when inefficient services are desired, suppliers *take* the quid pro quo from demanders.

The position of the demand curve is determined by the competitive interactions between bureaus and will here be taken as a given.[44] We have already noted that the meeting place of supply and demand is the network, and the network is a structure of relationships based on trust. We return to this question in the next chapter.

For simplicity, we begin the analysis of the first decision – the one pertaining to the type of services to be supplied – by assuming that the amount of trust is fixed at exogenously determined levels and, therefore, that the system of networks is given. In the easiest case, we assume that trust between sponsors and subordinates does not exist, whereas trust between subordinates does.[45] This assumption, in effect, means that sponsors are not part of bureaucratic networks – these being made up exclusively of bureaucrats. In such circumstances, bureaucrats calculating the net value to themselves of supplying efficient or inefficient informal services will discover that in all instances the latter have the highest yield. They will supply only that kind of informal service, at least as long as the risks and penalties are fixed and small enough.

In trying to determine why this is so, it is well to recall that bureaucrats do not supply inefficient services because these would harm their sponsors. In a competitive context, a bureaucrat is totally indifferent to his sponsor's welfare; it is only his own self-interested, utility-maximizing point of view that counts.[46] We must look elsewhere for an explanation of the asymmetric supply of informal services.

The point is easily stated once it is recognized that the absence of trust between sponsors and bureaucrats is a simple case of network failure.[47] Sponsors seeking efficient informal services would presumably be willing to pay the going equilibrium network price for them. However, in the absence of trust the price cannot be paid, unless all the aspects of a transaction can be wrapped up on the spot. This point needs to be emphasized. If a sponsor (or a superior such as B_1) has to promise a certain characteristic of policy, a promotion, attendance at an international conference, a solid recommendation for a private-sector job, or something of that kind to obtain efficient informal services from a bureaucrat (or a subordinate such as B_2), there must be trust between them; otherwise the present value of the promise is nil, and no trade can be effected.

Because bureaucratic trades are trades over time, trust is needed; without it, bureaucracy would be characterized by a "war of all against all." In the same way that property rights permit harmonious, gainful trade in private markets, trust allows gainful trade in bureaucratic networks. In the absence of trust and therefore of networks and of trade, subordinates would never supply efficient informal services, because they could not be paid for them. They would supply only inefficient services because, in that case, they take payment for them.

We have asserted that network failure leads to the exclusive supply of inefficient informal services if the risks and penalties necessarily associated with that kind of behavior are fixed and low enough. We must now recognize that inefficient behavior can be monitored or policed – at a cost – and that what bureaucrats can take for delivering inefficient services can be reduced by increased policing. If the supply of inefficient services could be reduced to zero, bureaucrats would then supply only formal services to their sponsors.

Trust may also exist between sponsors and bureaucrats. Does this imply that all services supplied by subordinates will be efficient? Or can inefficient services still be supplied? To answer these questions, we must emphasize that trust is not an all-or-nothing phenomenon; it can vary widely in quantity. Given this fact, we can examine the choice between supplying efficient or inefficient services within the framework of our surrogate competitive market. We proceed with the help of the following diagram. To simplify, we assume that the level of monitoring is fixed and low enough. We drop this assumption below.

In Figure 3.2, S is the supply of informal services. We assume that the volume of these services supplied, whether efficient (I_e) or inefficient (I_i), will be an increasing function of their supply price, based on the postulate that the marginal rate of substitution between these

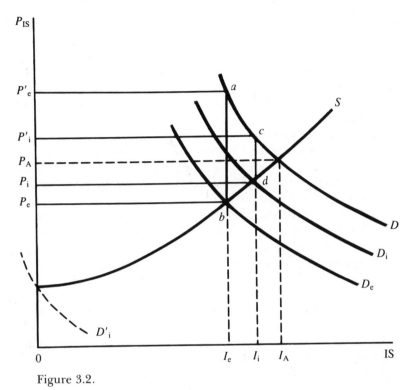

Figure 3.2.

services and the alternative uses of a bureaucrat's time is diminishing. The aggregate or network supply curve will be more elastic than the individual curves if bureaucrats differ in their ability to supply informal services and therefore enter as suppliers at different prices. At the same time, the larger these differences, the less elastic the supply curve.

The curve labeled D is the demand curve for informal services by sponsors. Its position, as explained earlier, is determined by bureaucratic competition – a phenomenon we examine in Chapter 6. The curve D_e represents the demand for efficient services or, more exactly, the price received by subordinates at different levels of informal efficient services. If trust between sponsors and bureaucrats and among bureaucrats were absolute, D_e would coincide with D and the return to efficient informal labor would, in surrogate market equilibrium, be P_A. But, because trust is not perfect, there are "transactions" costs to trading, which are like a tax or transportation cost.[48] In other words, given D_e, the price paid for efficient informal services is P'_e, whereas that received by bureaucrats is P_e. It is legitimate to think of the area $P'_e abP_e$ as representing the total cost of transacting because the volume of trust between sponsors and bureaucrats and among the latter falls short of the maximum by an amount proportional to ab. Consequently, as trust between sponsors and bureaucrats increases – that among bureaucrats being held constant – distance ab decreases; the opposite occurs when trust is reduced.

The curve D_i represents the demand for inefficient informal services, that is, the amount, net of transaction costs, taken by subordinates at different volumes of informal inefficient services. Its position is determined by the volume of trust *among* bureaucrats, that between sponsors and bureaucrats being held constant. As with $P'_e abP_e$, the area $P'_i cdP_i$ measures the expenditure on transacting resulting from the shortfall from perfect trust. If, in other words, trust among subordinates was greater, that between sponsors and subordinates remaining unchanged, subordinates could take more from sponsors; the price for informal services would be higher than P_i.

But curve D_i is not strictly comparable with curve D_e. Efficient and inefficient behaviors are both risky, but the nature of the risk varies. The risk associated with efficient behavior is that the sponsor may not pay the subordinate. That risk rises as the difference between actual and perfect trust increases. It is therefore already incorporated in Figure 3.2.

In the case of inefficient behavior, there are risks due to the existence of transaction costs among subordinates, which are incorporated in Figure 3.2, but there is also an additional source of risk: the possibility that inefficient behavior is discovered and penalized by sponsors. This second risk is not incorporated in Figure 3.2. To do so, we can convert the value of inefficient services into certainty equivalents or riskless sums. This can be done as follows. Assume that P_{i0} is taken by subordinates for the supply of a given volume of inefficient services. If the subordinates are apprehended, a penalty of f is imposed. If p is the probability of detection and Y the salary from supplying formal services (the formal salary) the expected utility derived from supplying the given volume of inefficient services is

$$(1 - p)\, U(Y + P_{i0}) + pU(Y - f) \tag{3.1}$$

and the certainty equivalent of equation (3.1) is the certain sum that yields the same utility.[49] H is then the certainty equivalent of equation (3.1) if

$$U(H) = (1 - p)\, U\,(Y + P_{i0}) + pU\,(Y - f) \tag{3.2}$$

The certainty-equivalent curve D_i is then constructed by plotting the marginal increments to H corresponding to different values of informal services (P_{i0}).

Once we recognize the possibility of policing and detection, we must also acknowledge that the position of D_i depends on the extent of monitoring and therefore on the cost of these activities,[50] as well as on the volume of trust among bureaucrats. This means that as the extent of policing increases – trust held constant – the D_i curve shifts to the left. Consequently, the area $P_i'cdP_i$ measures transaction costs among subordinates only in the special case where the risk of being discovered and penalized by the sponsor is nonexistent. In all other cases, this area must be interpreted as including the costs due to this risk as well as transaction costs among subordinates.

In Figure 3.2, the volumes of trust between sponsors and bureaucrats and among the latter, as well as the level of policing assumed, induce a supply of inefficient services. Given these assumptions and the positive slope of the S curve, $P_i > P_e$, indicating that the rewards of inefficiency are larger than those of efficiency. An increase in policing would shift the D_i curve to the left and could eventually induce a supply of efficient services.

Let us return to the case of network failure discussed earlier and examine it with the help of Figure 3.2. That case, based on the assumption that trust between sponsors and bureaucrats is zero, implies that D_e does not exist. Only inefficient services are then supplied. However, if policing should shift D_i to D_i', the supply of inefficient services would also dry up. Only formal services would be supplied.[51]

Whether efficient or inefficient informal services will be supplied, therefore, depends on the following: (a) the volume of trust between sponsors and bureaucrats; (b) the amount of trust among bureaucrats; and (c) the riskiness of an inefficient supply of services, which in turn depends on the extent and therefore the cost of monitoring.

The reader should note that an exogenous comparative static change in the position of the D curve would not alter the relative positions of the D_e and D_i curves and consequently would not affect the decision about whether efficient or inefficient services will be supplied. Anticipating the result of the second decision, it is easy to see that the volume of either type of service supplied would be altered.

The analysis based on Figure 3.2 can be summarized as follows: (i) subordinates are either efficient or inefficient in producing a policy, never both; (ii) efficient and inefficient behaviors are both risky, the first because trust is generally less than perfect and the second because of policing; (iii) when subordinates are efficient, sponsors pay them for informal services. When they are inefficient, subordinates take payment for the services supplied. The analysis is obviously predicated on the possibility of inefficient behavior. We have associated this behavior with mystification (the ability of subordinates to provide credible explanations, due to certain features of the formal structure, for counterproductive behaviors), entrapment (the fact that all choices open to a superior have been reduced to second-best or worse choices), and the difficulty of measuring output. In Chapter 6, we will discuss whether inefficient behavior can persist in a competitive environment over the long run.

It is easy to go from here to the second decision. Once the decision has been made to be either efficient, inefficient, or formal, only the D_e or D_i curve remains with the S curve to determine the volume of informal services – either efficient or inefficient – supplied and the price received or taken for them. To determine the price paid (and the volume of resources absorbed in the transaction because trust is less than complete), the D curve is also required.

Whether efficient or inefficient services are supplied, the volume of either produces *one particular* policy. For example, the volume of efficient services supplied at a certain point is for the production of one policy, S_k. If the same bureau produces two policies at the same time – S_k and S_j – it is possible that subordinates will be efficient producing S_k and inefficient in producing S_j. Such a possibility may be caused by either or both of the following factors: (i) behavior is more easily monitored in the production of S_k; (ii) trust among subordinates varies because the subordinates engaged in producing S_k and S_j are not all the same.

This second factor needs some emphasis. Whether efficient or inefficient informal services are supplied by subordinates to superiors (at the top of the organization, sponsors) depends on the ratio of the amount of trust between superiors and subordinates to the amount existing between the subordinates. Consequently, if policy making in a given bureau requires the contributions of different groups of subordinates, both the numerator and denominator can be expected to vary between policies, so that the ratio itself will vary. Consequently, it is possible that efficient services will be supplied for the production of one policy and inefficient services for another policy by the same bureau.

This point is important, because it is easy to fall into the trap of believing that superiors and subordinates who worked well together on one project will do so on every project. Sometimes the discovery that such is not the case causes surprise. A good understanding of how informal services are supplied would protect us from such surprises.

Before analyzing how selective behavior affects the cost of public policies, we must ask, what is the desired level of policing or monitoring by superiors and sponsors?[52]

The probability that inefficient behavior will be discovered by sponsors is represented by variable p in equations (3.1) and (3.2). Here, p is the joint outcome of two factors – the amount of resources used in, and the difficulty or cost of, monitoring. *Ceteris paribus,* the greater the difficulty of monitoring – because the activities are complex, secretive, and nonroutine – the smaller is p for any quantity of resources allocated to that endeavor. Conversely, given a particular monitoring cost function, p will rise as the resources allocated to monitoring the activities of a particular bureau increase. Of course, p is not under the direct control of superiors; only the volume of resources devoted to that task is. However, if the difficulty of monitoring is fixed and does not change as resources allocated to this task are increased or decreased, sponsors may be thought of as selecting the level of p.

The benefits of monitoring are clear. An increase in p reduces the gains and hence the incidence of inefficient behavior. In equation (3.2) above, H decreases as p rises. Alternatively, as we have already noted, as p rises, D_i (in Figure 3.2) shifts downward, so that the equilibrium volume of inefficient informal services falls, reducing the damages inflicted on superiors.

If we bring together the benefits and cost of monitoring, we can derive an equilibrium volume of monitoring services desired by sponsors, at least as long as the benefits decline and the costs increase with the level of monitoring. We do this in Figure 3.3, where the volume of monitoring services is depicted on the horizontal axis and the marginal costs and benefits on the vertical.

MC is the marginal cost function. The costs of monitoring include the salaries of personnel and the price of resources absorbed in creating and operating overlapping bureaus, duplicating services, and purchasing and acquiring information from alternative sources, including sources at lower levels in the bureau itself. MB_a and MB_b are marginal benefit curves for two bureaus, a and b. Marginal benefit curves represent the losses not incurred from inefficient behavior as a result of monitoring.

MB_b depicts the benefits in monitoring bureau b, whose activities are more complex, more secretive, and/or more nonroutine than those of bureau a. *Ceteris paribus,* if the same volume of monitoring

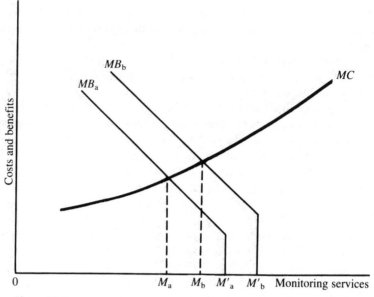

Figure 3.3.

services were used in both bureaus, p – the probability of detection – would be higher for subordinates in bureau a, whose activities are relatively simple to monitor. Hence the marginal benefits in monitoring bureau b are greater, and in equilibrium more monitoring services will be used in b than in a, as shown by M_b and M_a, respectively, in Figure 3.3.

For either curve, there is a point at which marginal benefits to monitoring fall to zero – the point at which p is raised sufficiently high that D_i falls below D_e in Figure 3.2. This point is reached in Figure 3.3, with M'_a of monitoring services in bureau a and with M'_b in bureau b. If the MC curve is sufficiently low so that it intersects the MB curves beyond these points, inefficient services would never be supplied.

3.6   The cost of public policies

Earlier in this chapter, we associated a formal cost curve depicting the behavior of formal unit costs as the volume or quality of a particular public policy varies with the formal structure of a bureau. We also noted that the informal structure would make effective costs either

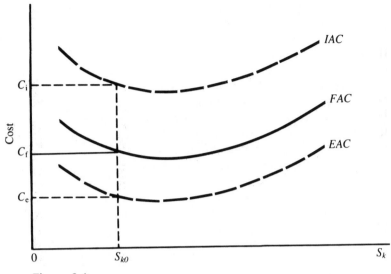

Figure 3.4.

higher or lower than these formal costs. Let us now return to these assertions and examine them with greater care.

Let us assume that the formal unit costs – those associated with decision making by the formal structure in the absence of influences from the informal structure – for supplying a particular policy (S_k) by a given bureau have the standard U shape. In Figure 3.4, we label such a curve *FAC* (formal average cost).

Efficient informal services supplied to sponsors (or to any superiors) will lower unit costs, that is, will shift the average cost curve downward for every time rate of output S_k. This curve is labeled *EAC* in Figure 3.4. Why this downward movement? Because in network equilibrium – that is, when superiors buy exactly the amount of efficient informal services it is worthwhile buying, given the surrogate market (network) price for these services – the business of the bureau will be conducted more expeditiously and more efficiently – that is, in a way that makes the outcome conform more exactly with the superiors' goals and objectives.

Conversely, when inefficient informal services are supplied, the average cost curve will lie above the *FAC* curve and, therefore, above the *EAC* curve, as does the *IAC* curve in Figure 3.4. The reason, again, is that in equilibrium the competitive volume of inefficient informal services produced, by impeding the achievement of a superior's objectives, renders the production of policies more costly than it would be if the bureau operated according to the rules and codes of its formal structure.

It must be emphasized that the EAC and IAC curves, like the FAC curve, are based on the assumptions of rational (that is, maximizing) behavior by all agents and stable equilibria in the surrogate markets (networks) for informal services. Consequently, all these curves and the corresponding marginal ones reflect minimum production costs for S_k, given the prevailing conditions for each.

Given these cost curves and their derivation, we can examine two questions that relate to the neoclassical economic theory of private business firms (bureaus) but that could just as easily be applied to public bureaus (firms). The first, not chronologically, was asked by Harvey Leibenstein;[53] it relates to the existence of observed inefficiencies that are not allocative. These were called *X-(in)efficiencies* by Leibenstein. The second pertains to the classical issue of the optimal size of competitive firms. We address these questions in turn.

Leibenstein has always denied the assumption of maximizing behavior and has attempted to base his theory of X-(in)efficiency on some alternative assumption.[54] Consequently, if we decided to measure X-efficiency or X-inefficiency by the vertical distance between the FAC and EAC or the FAC and IAC curves in Figure 3.4, we would be measuring something different from what Leibenstein is measuring, because our assumptions about behavior are different.

We must note, however, that Leibenstein has introduced the notion of X-inefficiency as a direct measure of the excess of actual cost over minimum cost or as "the difference between maximal effectiveness of utilization and actual utilization."[55] In terms of Figure 3.4, it is not clear whether Leibenstein, disregarding momentarily our assumption of rationality, would define X-inefficiency as $(C_i - C_f)$ or as $(C_i - C_e)$ when S_{ko} of S_k is produced. The formal definition, given above, seems to point toward the second. The definition of minimum costs as the costs associated with inputs "combined in such a way as to lead to maximum output,"[56] as derived in the standard neoclassical economic theory of the firm, seem to point toward the first, because as we emphasize below, conventional maximum output must be associated with the formal structure.

However that may be, and disregarding Leibenstein's strictures against maximization and his concepts of *selective rationality, inert areas,*[57] *constraint concern,* and so on, we suggest that the theory of selective behavior developed in this chapter provides the foundation for a neoclassical theory of X-efficiency that is more complete than Leibenstein's. It accounts for X-inefficiency – the distance $(C_i - C_f)$ – and X-efficiency – the distance $(C_f - C_e)$. It also indicates that the extent of X-efficiency or inefficiency varies according to what is produced within the same firm; it will not be the same for S_k and S_j.

We feel confident in making these claims because the various factors that Leibenstein associates with X-inefficiency – except non-maximizing behavior – are factors that sociologists, social psychologists, organization theorists, and an increasing number of economists use to describe the informal structure of organizations.[58] Therefore, many ingredients in Leibenstein's theory play a role in ours. They are, however, packaged differently.

The empirical evidence[59] on X-(in)efficiency is difficult to interpret, because very little of it is direct or pertains to the phenomenon itself in isolation. The paper that more nearly isolates it from other phenomena is Sheldon's.[60] Sheldon examines the change in profits consequent on a change in management from company manager supervision (CM) to franchisee ownership (FO) and vice versa. The evidence, he notes, points to a better profit picture when there is a change from CM to FO, and also that the profit/sales ratio is higher with FO than with CM. We do not deny this fact, but point to the no less significant observation that of the 31 changes in the relationship of superiors and subordinates – measured by the total of changes in CM to FO *and* of FO to CM indistinctly, as reported in Sheldon's Table I – 20 are associated with a *fall* in the profit/sales ratio and only 9 with an increase (the other 2 having no change). This appears consistent with our theory of selective behavior if the changes in superior-subordinate relationships just noted are used as proxies of a reduction in trust between superiors and subordinates – on the necessarily untested but not unreasonable assumption that trust between subordinates remains unchanged. Changes from CM to FO or from the latter to the former induce inefficient behavior and reduce the profit/sales ratio.[61]

The second question we address concerns the optimal size of competitive firms. The modern literature on this subject assumes the existence of a simple hierarchical structure in which the top manager or *peak coordinator*, as he is sometimes called, makes the decisions and issues instructions to his subordinates, who then carry them out. Within that structure, and assuming a size of firm sufficiently large that all production economies of scale are exhausted, there are three factors that affect average costs as size is further increased. First, there is the *administrative overload* factor discussed by Williamson:[62] As size increases, the absolute number of issues that arise and must be communicated to the manager for decision increases proportionately, placing an ever larger burden on him. So long as there are no perfect substitutes for the top manager in resolving issues or making decisions, this factor alone results in increasing average costs.

A second factor that also results in increasing average costs is *control loss*,[63] or distortion of information on which the manager's decisions are based and of the content of the command passed down to lower levels in the hierarchy. If information becomes distorted each time it is reproduced or transmitted, and if it must be reproduced each time it passes through a layer of a hierarchy, then the cumulative distortion of information in an organization will be related to the number of hierarchical levels, and hence to its size. Control loss, like administrative overload, therefore leads to diminishing returns to scale and forms the basis of the model elaborated by Williamson in his well-known paper on optimum firm size.[64]

However, Williamson implicitly ignored a third factor, namely, the possibility of economies of scale in information collection – a point emphasized by Robert Wilson.[65] It is possible that these economies are sufficiently important within the firm that they will overwhelm the first two factors mentioned. Consequently, it is now accepted that the standard account of ultimately increasing average costs does not necessarily hold.

We shall now show that the theory of costs for the single bureau that is associated with the theory of selective behavior does imply ultimately diminishing returns to scale and therefore an optimal size for the competitive firm. To see this, note that the three factors traditionally considered in the standard theory of the firm and briefly reviewed above pertain only to the shape of the formal cost curve or to an organization conceived exclusively in terms of the operation of its formal structure. To establish that proposition, it is sufficient to note that, in this theory, labor services are obtained from subordinates exclusively by command or authority. There are no exchanges between superiors and subordinates other than those that define the subordinates' contract, namely, the specification of formal salary in exchange for a set of formal responsibilities. Once the firm has been defined in terms of its formal structure, the only remaining issues concern the quality of the decisions of superiors and the fraction of the intentions of superiors that is effectively carried out by subordinates. These issues, under various guises – the problem of coordination, the problem of control, and so on – form the subject matter of the literature on the size of the firm.

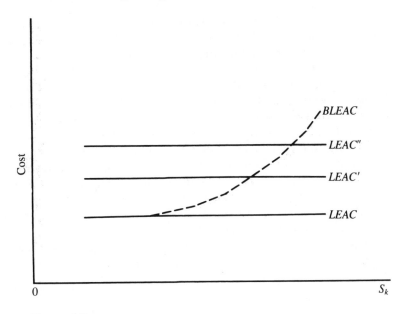

Figure 3.5.

In contrast, the basic assumption of our theory of selective behavior is that private and public bureaus need not operate exclusively in terms of their formal structure. Furthermore, their actual costs tend to reflect the characteristics and the efficiency of the market for informal services in the firm. In particular, costs are affected by the extent to which superiors can establish trust with subordinates – and therefore by the supply of efficient or inefficient informal services by subordinates and by the price at which informal services are traded. We will discuss the first variable only after presenting our theory of trust in the next chapter. However, the effect of bureau size on the price of informal services, and the effect of this variable, in turn, on the firm's cost curve, can be elucidated with the model at hand. To do so, assume for simplicity that all subordinates are efficient, and that the long-run average cost curve that reflects efficient behavior is strictly horizontal,[66] as is the *LEAC* curve in Figure 3.5. That curve is derived on the assumption that any or all superiors in the bureau can enter any or all networks and purchase informal services *at a given network price*. These networks, as we have repeatedly emphasized, are surrogate competitive (informal) labor markets. Therefore, as the demand for informal labor services increases with expansion in S_k and in the size of the bureau, the price of these services must rise.

Consequently, the long-run average cost curve must shift upward parallel to itself to *LEAC'* and to *LEAC''*, thus tracing a long-run curve, such as *BLEAC*, for bureauwide adjustments.[67]

The *BLEAC* (or *BLIAC* curve, if inefficient services were supplied) is in all respects like an industrywide curve. It is internal to the bureau (firm), reflecting the fact that the bureau's internal workings are importantly characterized by trade and exchange and not exclusively by authority and command. As just indicated, as long as the bureau is considered the exclusive embodiment of a system of authority relationships, one must look for an optimal bureau size in dealing with problems associated with management, coordination, control, and so on. However, once it is recognized that the problem of management is largely one of trade between superiors and subordinates, and that trades are effected at certain prices, the optimal size of firms and of bureaus is easily determined. We will return to those questions in Chapter 6.

3.7   Conclusion

The theory of selective behavior – that is, the theory of the positive or negative use of certain instruments to help or hinder one's superiors – is at the heart of our theory of bureaucracy. Selective behavior, in turn, requires networks, namely, institutions in which informal services of subordinates can be traded for objects that these subordinates desire.

But networks must be built on trust if the property rights supporting the contracts, loans, and other network transactions are to be enforced. Consequently, selective behavior rests on trust, and therefore, so does bureaucratic behavior. Further elaborations of the theory of selective behavior now require us to examine the properties and workings of networks and trust. It is to that task that we turn in the next chapter.

CHAPTER 4

The accumulation of trust

4.1   Introduction

As we have stated in previous chapters, informal labor services in bureaucracies are bought and sold in networks; in other words, selective behavior originates, takes form, and unfolds in networks. We have also argued that the activities taking place in these networks are best modeled as mimicking market supply and demand situations,[1] hence our references to surrogate markets.

However, markets – whether competitive or not – presuppose the existence of property rights[2] that are generally supported by laws and law enforcement. Although we treat networks as surrogate markets, we must insist that they differ from markets in the fundamental sense that the property rights that they presuppose are not supported by legal arrangements. Instead, they are supported by trust. In other words, whereas market exchange requires law-based property rights, network exchange necessitates trust-based property rights.

The analogy between law and trust should, however, not be pushed too far for at least two reasons. First, as we shall note in Section 4.6, the nature and properties of such market phenomena as externalities, moral hazard, and contingent contracts are different under the two arrangements. Second, many real-world property rights – in both markets and networks – are supported by both law and trust, albeit in sometimes dramatically different proportions. These arguments notwithstanding, it is enlightening to suppose that the distinguishing trait of markets is legally enforceable property rights and that of networks property rights based on trust. In the remainder of this chapter, we will assume that markets are supported only by legally enforceable property rights, whereas networks are supported only by trust.

The theory of legally supported property rights, although still in its infancy, is the more developed of the two views of property rights, even if it still lacks a hypothesis of how laws that support property rights are produced.[3] Many discussions seem to rest on the supposition that law-supported property rights are costlessly produced. The literature on externalities, for example, often imputes market failure to undefined or improperly defined property rights and often leaves the reader with the impression that if only governments were a bit more willing, these property rights could be easily defined. The difficulties posed by real-world copyright, patent, and free-speech laws – to name only a few – indicate how hard it sometimes is to define law-based property rights, even in principle.

But that is not our problem in this chapter, except indirectly. Our preoccupation is with trust-supported property rights. We must ask and seek to answer the following questions:

  (i)   Why are some property rights supported by trust and not by laws?
  (ii) How is trust produced and accumulated by individuals?
  (iii) What is the equilibrium amount of trust that individuals will accumulate under different circumstances?
  (iv) How will truncation in networks affect the production costs of a bureau's output?
  (v)   What is the effect of trust on such phenomena as externalities, moral hazard, and contingent contracts?

In the next two sections, we address the first two questions. Then in Section 4.4, we digress briefly to look at some literature that is relevant to the discussion of Section 4.3. In Section 4.5, we seek to answer questions (iii) and (iv), and in the last sections, we address the issues raised in question (v).

4.2   Why trust?

Instead of asking "why trust," we could just as easily have asked, "why not laws or legally enforceable contracts?"[4] The short but uninformative answer is that, relative to trust, laws are inefficient in certain contexts and situations.

Before examining these situations, we must make explicit an underlying assumption, namely, that individuals want to exchange because they expect to be better off as a result of such exchanges, but that unless property rights can be established for the objects to be traded, exchange – especially intertemporal exchange – cannot take place. If the legal system (in general, the state and the courts) is able to establish property rights and if these laws are enforced, exchange will take place if there are gains to be reaped. More precisely, the more effective the legal system in establishing property rights and the more effective the enforcement of these laws, the larger *ceteris paribus* the value of gainful exchanges.

The *ceteris paribus* in the foregoing refers to the possibility that a real alternative to laws may be used to support property rights. In this section, we concentrate on the reasons why laws and legally enforceable contracts are sometimes inefficient. In the next section, we examine the conditions under which trust is accumulated to permit exchange. In part, these two questions are mirror images of each other, but by dealing with them separately, although possibly repetitively in certain respects, we will help clarify the issues and underline the central role of trust in bureaucracies.

Imagine that two individuals, A and B, believe they would both gain by repeated exchanges with each other, and that as a result, a demand exists for legally enforceable property rights or for some other arrangement that would allow them to trade. Under what circumstances would the first arrangement – legally enforceable contracts – be difficult or impossible to establish? A first circumstance arises whenever the value and/or quality of the goods or services traded are difficult to measure.[5] A second set of circumstances is more complex. To appreciate it, suppose the existence of a barter economy in which trade is intertemporal, in the sense that goods and services are delivered and paid for at different times. Suppose further that although A, the demander, knows the general class of goods and services he wants from B, the supplier, he cannot specify exactly what subset he will want at any given future time. Or alternatively, suppose that A knows what goods and services he will want at every point in time but is unable to say what he will be able to give in exchange when the time comes to pay, although he may be able to ascertain the set of all possible objects at his command. Or finally, imagine that A knows exactly what goods and services he wants as well as what he is willing to pay in exchange, but cannot specify when he will be able to repay his supplier for the goods delivered or for the services rendered.

Under any of these circumstances, a legally enforceable contract could not be drawn; if drawn, it could not be enforced; and if enforceable, breach of contract could not be successfully litigated. In particular, our second set of circumstances describes a true *barter economy* – not in the sense in which Marshall, Walras, or Edgeworth use that term but in the sense in which real-world primitive barter economies tend to look like.[6] Such an economy is characterized by the importance of credit, that is, by the presence of numerous outstanding loans and debts rather than by a search for a "double coincidence of wants" so often stressed in discussions of barter economies.

But how can these loans exist if they cannot be legally enforced? Before answering this question, we note that the network trading in bureaucracies described in the last chapter is identical to the barter exchanges just described. Bureaucrats are placed in contexts in which they interact with each other over long periods of time. Therefore, it would be unreasonable to assume that they do not eventually perceive opportunities for gainful exchange. The objects traded in bureaucratic networks are informal labor services, both efficient and inefficient, as well as policy characteristics and other valued objects. In these exchanges the quid pro quos cannot be defined in advance, not because of ill will but because those who demand informal services do not know, at the time the services are required, what they will be able to give in exchange. And finally, demanders do not know when they will be able to repay suppliers. Bureaucracies, like the barter economies they resemble, are characterized by numerous outstanding loans (favors owed).

We asserted earlier that these loans are supported by trust. Because B, the supplier, trusts A, the demander, he delivers informal labor services without immediate payment and thus creates a debt on the part of A. B not only delivers informal services to A but also is able, because of trust, to induce other subordinates in his network to cooperate with him in producing the services he delivers. In the absence of trust, he could not produce these services, because he could not enter into an exchange relationship with these other subordinates.

Trust is not a given of nature; it is produced and accumulated by individuals. In the next section, we seek to model this process of trust accumulation. The model requires that we view trust, not as something that either exists or does not exist but as something whose volume can be increased or reduced continuously. Further, we must recognize that the benefits of trust accrue over time; trust is, in effect, a capital asset that can be augmented by investment or reduced through disinvestment. If these two points are granted, the theory of trust accumulation we suggest below is fairly straightforward, as the reader can easily verify.

4.3   The production of trust

In *The Limits of Organization*, Arrow writes: "Unfortunately [trust] is not a commodity which can be bought very easily. If you have to buy it, you already have some doubts about what you've bought" (p. 23). Not only do we concur, we would underscore that statement by adding that if one tried to buy trust by offering money for it, one would destroy it if it already existed or, if it did not, would make its development more difficult or even impossible. But the fact that trust cannot be bought in the marketplace or in private exchanges between two or more individuals does not mean that it cannot be produced and accumulated. Laws cannot be bought in the marketplace either, but they are produced – daily.

To proceed, we suggest a formal definition of trust that is restricted to a particular context or type of exchange.[7] Assume, therefore, that all transactions take the form of $1 loans. Then, if A has a belief $_at_b$ or is confident in the same degree that B will honor a promise to repay $1 (plus interest) at some specified time in the future, we say that A has an amount $_at_b$ of trust in B.

There are a number of things to note about this definition. First, $_at_b$ is a variable that can be normalized to vary between 0 and 1 or between any other reasonable limits. It is not a constant. Second, the amount of trust is defined for a given sum ($1) that is expressed in monetary units but that could be denominated in other units, such as utility. Consequently, if the sum is raised from $1 to $2, we expect changes in the amount of trust (in $_at_b$). Third, the size of A's trust in B tells us nothing about the amount of B's trust in A. It is logically possible, as we indicate below, that A may trust B by a certain positive amount, whereas B does not trust A.

The definition implies, as it should, that trust is not an all-or-none phenomenon. An individual may declare that he has absolute trust in someone else, that is, that he believes he will never be cheated or taken advantage of by the one he trusts. Implicitly, however, in such a statement the size of the transaction ($1 in the above definition) and hence the opportunity to cheat is fixed. If someone says that he trusts his grocer to always give him the correct change, he is not saying that he is certain his grocer would not cheat him if the possible gain was much larger than it is in transactions of the size they usually engage in.

Recognizing that $_at_b$, which measures A's confidence that B will repay a $1 loan, does not tell us how confident A is that B will repay larger or smaller loans, we introduce a vector $_aT_b = (_at_b^1, _at_b^2, \ldots, _at_b^x)$ – in which the superscripts index the size (from smaller to larger) of the transactions – to describe A's trust in B for loan transactions of any size. We make two assumptions: First, we suppose that even if the coefficients (the $_at_b^i$'s) are all different from each other, they all move together; that is, all coefficients will rise together for an increase in any one $_at_b^i$ and decline together for a fall in any $_at_b^i$. This assumption implies not only that $_aT_b$ rises when one $_at_b^i$ rises, but that all $_at_b^j$'s (for $j \neq i$) also rise. This seems to be the meaning implicit in such propositions as "I trust him more than before," which is sometimes heard after the successful conclusion of an exchange (of a given size). The second assumption is that the coefficients $_at_b^i$ are inversely related to the size of the transactions. One implication of the two assumptions is that as $_at_b^i$ increases, all right-hand coefficients rise, but by declining amounts. We hold to these two assumptions throughout.

How, then, is trust produced? In other words, what is the process of interaction between individuals that leads to trust formation? To answer this question, consider again the case of $1 loan by A to B. Once that case is understood, it will be easy to add complicating features to the analysis and to extend it to bureaucratic networks in which informal labor services are traded.

Let us begin by assuming that A offers to lend $1 to B. That offer must be understood as a signal by A that he would like to trade with B, and because, by construction, legally enforceable contracts are not possible, it is a signal that A would like to trust B. The exact magnitude of the signal, it seems reasonable to suppose, will depend on the prospective costs and benefits of the signal to A. Consequently, we assume that A offers to lend $1 for a year at a pure interest rate of i_B. However, because B could default on the loan or fail to satisfy exactly all the conditions stipulated by A, we must also assume that A notionally "places" B in a "default class," which we label d^1, and charges a risk premium r_1 associated with that class. The rate on this $1 loan is therefore $(i_B + r_1)$. The cost to A of extending it, or, alternatively, the measure of the extent to which A wants to trust B in $1 transactions, is established by considering what opportunity A foregoes by lending to B. The simplest assumption to make is that in the same default class A could lend at a maximum of $i(>i_B)$, so that the cost to A of lending $1 is

$$C_A = (1 + i + r_1) - (1 + i_B + r_1) \qquad (4.1)$$

which is positive as long as $i > i_B$.

We must also assume that B responds to A's signal by promising to repay the loan plus interest (and risk premium) and to meet the other conditions that may be attached to the loan, including the one-year date of repayment. B's decision to repay the loan and to meet the other stipulated conditions must be interpreted as a decision to forego cheating A and indicates that B wants A to trust him. We must recognize that B invests in trust on each occasion that he demonstrates to A the value he derives from a relationship with him by not exploiting an opportunity that would be to his own advantage but would harm A. The amount invested by B is the net value of the foregone opportunity.

To determine a priori the cost to B of not exploiting such an opportunity requires that all cheating (or breaching) opportunities be known. At worst, B could default on the loan altogether; in that case, the foregone opportunity is equal to $(1 + i_B + r_1)$. But breaching need not be that extreme. It could take the form of a delay in repaying, or of partial default, or of any other breach in the agreed-upon conditions. If we let X be the foregone dollar value of the opportunity to cheat and let these opportunities vary continuously, the cost to B of not breaching and hence of responding positively to A's signal is

$$C_B = X(0) - E[C(S_A)] \tag{4.2}$$

in which $X(0)$ is the money value of cheating opportunities (0) foregone and $E[C(S_A)]$ measures the expected cost of sanctions that A can impose on B.

We must recognize that the cost to B of responding to A's signal will be affected by losses that could be inflicted on him by sanctions imposed by A. The question of sanctions is a complicated one that is closely related to the question of communication between A and B, which we still have to introduce. Consequently, we delay its discussion briefly to pursue further the process of how the asset "A trusts B" is produced. In so doing, the communication factor to which sanctions are related will be introduced; it will then be time to analyze the role and place of sanctions in the theory of trust.

The first point to emphasize is that if B responds positively to A's signal by repaying the loan and meeting the other conditions agreed upon, A will be able to trust B in the sense that A will consider the probability of B's defaulting or cheating in a second transaction to be $d^2(< d^1)$. For \$1 loans, $_at_b$ will have increased from $_at_b^0$ to $_at_b'$; consequently, A will place B in a better default class, charge a risk premium $r_2(< r_1)$, and be able to obtain for his money a pure rate i_B' better than i_B, which, for this second transaction, is still larger than the next best alternative. The cost to A would therefore be

$$C_A' = (1 + i' + r_2) - (1 + i_B' + r_2) \tag{4.3}$$

in which $i' > i_B' > i_B$ and for which $r_2 < r_1$. Consequently, $C_A' < C_A$.

Similarly, and disregarding altogether the possibility of *changes* in the expected losses from sanctions, the cost of B's response by foregoing cheating will be

$$C_B' = X(0)' - E[C(S_A)] \tag{4.4}$$

such that $C_B' < C_B$.

We must insist that in principle the cheating opportunities open to B vary. His response can differ from his promise when the loan was extended by a larger or smaller magnitude. Therefore, we can assume that $X(0)'$, like $X(0)$, is continuous.

As the number of \$1 transactions between A and B increases, the

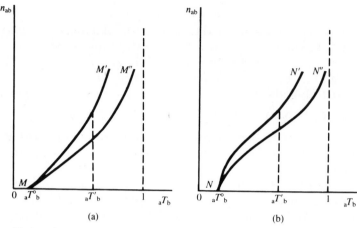

Figure 4.1.

cost to each of them falls. After a certain point, they can trade with each other and both can be better off than in the absence of the asset "A trusts B." What this trust does is to allow them to lend and borrow at lower transaction costs. The relationship between the amount of trust ($_aT_b$) and the number of trades between A and B (n_{ab}), in which the net yield to trust is embedded, can be portrayed by curves such as MM' and NN' in panels (a) and (b) of Figure 4.1.

Both of these curves incorporate the notion of diminishing returns: MM' throughout and NN' after a region of increasing returns. We make the assumption of (eventual) diminishing returns on the ground that it seems reasonable to suppose that after a certain point, the net benefits accruing from reductions in transaction costs for $1 transactions will increase at a slower rate.

Curves MM'' and NN'' indicate that larger amounts of trust will be accumulated from larger trades (trades of $100 rather than $1), which also seems plausible, because both A's cost of signaling and B's cost of responding – the foregone opportunity to breach – are larger. It also seems reasonable to assume diminishing returns to increases in the size of trades on the ground that rapid, instantaneous, and large increments in trust are not generally observable in interpersonal relations.

It is important to emphasize that after a number of trades have taken place and an equilibrium volume of trust has been created, both A and B benefit from the asset "A trusts B." The amount of the benefits accruing to each represents a division of the gains from trade between them, a division determined by the usual conditions of supply and demand. Appeal to these conditions implies that A's signals and B's responses are governed for each by the prospective benefits of signaling and responding with other individuals in their environment.

We must emphasize that the asset created is "A trusts B" and that it is *jointly produced* by A's signals and B's responses, whose costs were analyzed above. But in addition to being jointly produced, "A trusts B" has the property of a quasi-public good. It is an asset available to both A and B in that it allows A to earn interest on his money and B to borrow from A. We are, therefore, in agreement with Arrow that "trust and similar values, loyalty or truth-telling are examples of what the economist would call 'externalities',"[8] although in our analysis neither A nor B is the passive beneficiary of the externality, as one would have to assume if trust were a standard externality. Finally, even if it is jointly produced and like a quasi-public good, trust need not be mutual, that is, the fact that A trusts B does not necessarily imply that B trusts A. We return to this issue below and examine the precise sense in which trust need not be mutual.

We have so far left two closely interrelated questions unasked and unanswered. The first pertains to A's decision to signal that he wants to trust B. Why send such a signal? The second relates to the choice of B. Why not signal to C or to some other person? In answer to the first question, we must assume that A signals to B because he perceives prospective gains from trade that could be realized over time in repeated exchanges with B. This is the reason A offers to lend a sum to B even if the risk of loss is positive. In his desire to produce the asset "A trusts B," A is similar to entrepreneurs in a law-supported property-rights market system, who risk sums in the expectation of receiving a stream of legally appropriable future benefits from such investments. Similarly, B foregoes cheating A because of the prospects of repeated gainful exchanges with A that he foresees.

But that is only part of the answer. How does A know that repeated exchanges are possible with B? How does he know that B will respond to his signals? We suggest that decisions on these questions will be based on the meaning attached to indicators or traits possessed by individuals and used by A to establish the likelihood of repeated trades with different individuals and the likelihood of their positive responses to his signals. We are assuming that A must resolve a communication problem and that he does so by using indicators. There is a large and growing literature on indicators in economics[9] and other disciplines, but it tends to be a trifle restrictive.[10]

We conceive of indicators as signals, signs, guides, or beacons. An individual – in the foregoing discussion, A – uses these indicators to ascertain whether certain other individuals are likely to interact and thus have the opportunity to exchange repeatedly with him over time, to respond positively to his signals, and thus to indicate whether they can be initially trusted.

Indicators are of two basic types: (i) those that are, for all relevant purposes, given, such as race, sex, ethnicity, and family background; and (ii) those that can be altered by the use of resources, such as reputation, education, club memberships, connections, language, religion, dress, politeness, speech, deportment, consumption patterns, and others. The exact meaning and significance of these indicators will vary with persons[11] and places, but one expects that this significance will vary – for those in the second group – inversely with the cost of their acquisition.

What we are saying is that A forms an opinion of the profitability of repeated exchanges with B by using indicators that have acquired significance for him, presumably because in the past they were positively correlated in other individuals with behaviors that A is seeking or seeking to avoid. In other words, we must assume that A has learned through experience that when an individual displays certain indicators, he can be expected to respond positively to A's signals and to engage in repeated beneficial interactions over time.

A's communication problem is complicated by the fact that (i) past correlations between indicators and behavior are not perfect; (ii) past correlations, even if virtually perfect, are an imprecise measure of future correlations involving different populations or samples; and (iii) individuals can invest in indicators and thus sometimes blur their meaning.[12] But whatever the difficulties, A must use indicators if he is going to initiate the production of the prospectively gainful asset "A trusts B."

The effects of indicators on A's behavior are not symmetrical. If indicators foster the development of trust between A and B, their role will be transitory, because after a few trades, it is B's response in previous trades that will govern A's behavior thereafter. However, if indicators serve as barriers to the development of trust between two individuals, because (let us say) A thinks all persons possessing a particular trait are unreliable, the role of indicators may be much more permanent. We will have more to say on this question in Section 4.5, and also in Chapters 5 and 6, when we study the effect of competition on trust formation.

We now turn to sanctions. These impose a cost on malfeasance – in our example, on cheating by B. We assume that sanctions can either be inflicted by A or are exogenously determined because of something internal to persons[13] or to cultures. In this study, we shall be concerned only with *endogenous sanctions* – those under the control of individual A. If one chooses to assume that A himself can sanction B, that is, impose damages on him, one must also assume that doing so will be costly to A; otherwise exchange would be supported by sanctions and not by trust. To put it differently, if A can sanction B at no cost to himself, he would not want to allocate scarce resources to accumulate trust, but would instead use sanctions.

Endogenous sanctions can be either private or public. The size of the loss in either case is not necessarily limited to the trust accumulated between the individual sanctioned and those with whom trust had been built in the past. It can also affect the possibility of building trust in the future with other, quite different, individuals as well. In the first case, however, only a few individuals are made aware of the untrustworthiness of the identified individual, B, so that the loss tends to be smaller than when sanctions are public and the demonstration of untrustworthiness is broadcast.

The interesting thing about endogenous sanctions is not that they exist and help to determine the cost to B of reneging on his promise, but that they dramatically complicate A's problem: When sanctions exist, A cannot be certain that when B repays his loan, he is not doing so out of fear of being sanctioned by him instead of a desire to build trust. The presence of sanctions, in other words, compounds A's communication problem with B in that B now has two motives for repaying his loan: the fear of sanctions and the possible desire to produce trust jointly with A.

We noted earlier that if sanctions were under A's control, one would have to assume a cost to A of sanctioning B; otherwise, trust would not be needed. One dimension[14] of that cost is now clear: that of making the meaning of B's action more difficult to interpret. Consequently, we must assume that A will sometimes not sanction B, even if he could, so as to be able to ascertain more easily the meaning of B's actions. More precisely, by not sanctioning B and by communicating to him that sanctions will not be imposed in the event of malfeasance, A can present B with larger opportunities to cheat, and thus to build trust with A by foregoing these opportunities. It is true that if A always possesses sufficient sanctions to deter B from cheating, and if the discovery of cheating is costless, then the yield on trust would be zero and it would not be produced; malfeasance would be prevented solely by sanctions. But if A's sanctions are limited and B's malfeasance is sometimes difficult to discover, then the ability to trust B is a valuable asset to A. This is why A cannot rely on sanctions alone.

The advantage of sanctions to A is therefore as follows: If A cannot impose sanctions, he cannot withdraw the threat of sanctions in his dealings with others. Consequently, his signal that he would like to trust B is not as clear-cut as it would be if he could use sanctions and chose to withdraw the threat of using them. To conclude, A's *possession* of sanctions enhances his capacity to build trust with B, provided the sanctions are not used. If they are used, or their use is threatened, the cost to A is that less trust in B will be accumulated.

We have, so far, assumed that A has signaled his desire to produce trust jointly with B by offering to make a loan and that B has signaled a similar desire by repaying his loan. The asset so produced was "A trusts B." Suppose now that B wishes to produce another asset, namely, "B trusts A." He will make an offer, valued at $1, to A. But assume that A defaults, that is, chooses to cheat by not repaying the loan; would such an action on A's part affect the value of the "A trusts B" asset and the prospects for its growth? To put it differently, we noted earlier that trust need not be mutual, that is, that the asset "A trusts B" could exist in the absence of the asset "B trusts A." We are now asking, can the asset "A trusts B" exist even if the behavior of A toward B makes it impossible to produce the asset "B trusts A"?

If we think of the lack of trust as we think of tariffs – both are obstacles to trade – we would have to conclude that the impossibility of B trusting A would not impede the production of the asset "A trusts B." This is because, as with tariffs, except for the "optimum tariff" case, a country is better off by reducing its tariff barriers even if other countries do not lower, or even raise, their own.

However, as Harry Johnson and others[15] have shown, in a world in which the production of tariffs is endogenous, orthodox propositions about unilateral tariff reductions no longer hold. Similarly, in the production of trust, cheating by A might affect communication between A and B so adversely that in practice, trust will be mutual, although generally not equal. However, if *bargaining* (to use Johnson's term) between A and B is easy, that is, if communication is clear, trust may not be mutual unless both parties find trust profitable in both directions.

In the preceding discussion, trust exists between two individuals; we could say that it is two-sided. The production process we have described implies that trust is always two-sided and never multisided. We hasten to add that this does not imply that only two individuals need be involved. We could, for example, assume that A is one person and B a group of two or more persons. We could also assume that because A trusts B and B trusts C, it will be easier (less costly) for trust to develop between A and C, because communication would be easier. However, we must emphasize that trust is not and cannot be transitive.

Even if the process of trust accumulation is a fairly simple one, it may help to fix ideas and to focus the remainder of the chapter if we provide a list of the main propositions of this section. These can be stated as follows:

1. Trust is a capital asset whose volume can be increased continuously by investment, that is, by foregoing the immediate use of resources; it can also be reduced by disinvestment.
2. Trust is a jointly produced and jointly consumed asset for the two parties involved.
3. A's decision to produce trust with B instead of with C is determined by the prospective value of repeated trading with B compared to C estimated by the use of indicators. To the extent that the initial transactions are successful, the value of these indicators declines, to be eventually replaced by the transactions themselves.
4. If A could impose sanctions on B without costs to himself, exchange would be based not on trust but on sanctions, because it would be irrational to produce costly trust when free sanctions are available.
5. In practice, however, the cost of using sanctions is positive because the costs of ascertaining malfeasance are positive and because sanctions make it more difficult to establish whether a loan repayment is motivated by a fear of sanctions or a desire to build trust.
6. The ability to use sanctions, however, makes it possible to withhold them. If the significance of such withholding can be communicated, the content of A's signal to B that he wishes to trust him will be enhanced.
7. Finally, in the world of everyday experience, trust is most likely to be mutual, although unequal, even if mutuality is not logically necessary.

4.4 A digression inspired by the literature on trust and related phenomena

We are not the first to believe that in the absence of legally supported property rights, an alternative arrangement is needed and will normally develop at least if the present value of the expected net[16] gains from trade is high.

Something of this was recognized by Kenneth Arrow, who

suggested that trust (or moral codes, internalization of rules, or honor) could "compensate for market failure."[17] Vernon Smith postulated the existence of social customs as guarantees of property rights.[18] Williamson, Wachter, and Harris, after a lengthy demonstration that in some contexts legally enforceable contracts are not possible, appealed to "private collective action" à la John R. Commons and to "norms of socialization" to deal with what they call the *opportunistic behavior,* the *bounded rationality,* and the *information impactedness* that prevent the full exploitation of gains from trade.[19] Roland McKean described some of the circumstances under which trust and moral codes can be expected to be effective in making life more pleasant.[20] And, finally, Mordecai Kurz presented a model of an economy with no legally enforceable contracts, but in which social norms or social sanctions support trade.[21]

There is, however, an important difference between our view of alternatives to contract law and that of the writers just mentioned. Our view, as stated in the last section, is based on the notion that in the same way laws and law enforcement that support property rights are collective[22] capital assets, so are norms, codes, internalized rules, and trust. Consequently, like all capital assets – private or collective – they can be increased through investment or reduced through disinvestment.[23] This is not a trivial point, because norms, social conventions, social customs, internalized precepts of behavior, codes of honor, fidelity, reliability,[24] and trust – concepts that are found in various places in the literature – are all not only exogenously given but, more importantly, not allowed to vary. They take values of 1 or 0 only.[25] This implies that the problem of cheating in exchange relationships or other interpersonal interactions is either solved or does not exist and therefore, strictly speaking, is left unresolved. Only by allowing the amount of trust to vary continuously can one see the central role it plays in exchange relationships.

In addition to the foregoing approaches, one finds in the literature at least two other solutions to the problems of exchange and cooperation in a world in which legal arrangements are absent. We consider them in turn and conclude with a few words on the relationship between trust and utility interdependence, altruism or caring.

Let us begin by looking at the standard representation of the problem of cooperation[26] – the well-known prisoner's dilemma game. In that game, two parties or "players" each stand to gain from mutual cooperation or trade, but each can gain even more if one cooperates while the other cheats. If the game is played only once, cheating is the dominant strategy for either player, despite the mutual benefits of cooperation. However, in a "supergame" – where the game is repeated a large number of times – it seems reasonable to assume that each player has an incentive to cooperate, knowing that, if he or she cheats, the other player can retaliate on the next round. The supergame, then, seems to offer a way out of the prisoner's dilemma. The argument of "repeat business" is often used to explain why cheating[27] is not a more prevalent feature of economic life than it actually is.[28]

There is, however, a well-known paradox that appears to destroy this argument. Suppose that the end of the supergame (the last play) is the nth play. On that play, cheating is the dominant strategy for both players, for at that point the supergame reverts to the single-play situation. But if each player expects the other to cheat on the nth play, then cheating is also the dominant strategy on the $(n - 1)$th round, and therefore on the $(n - 2)$th round, and so on. Consequently, the structure of the supergame unravels and cheating remains the dominant strategy throughout.

Theoretically, the paradox disappears only if there is no last play, that is, if the game is repeated an infinite number of times, or if there is a constant probability of the game continuing at each play. Yet, this is not seen as a complete solution. Why should uncertainty about how long the game lasts make it *easier* for the parties to cooperate?

The paradox is a genuine one. Everyday observation suggests that in situations of repetitive or continued interaction, people typically cooperate with each other. This observation is confirmed by experimental studies of repetitive games in which cooperation turns out to be the dominant pattern.[29]

The heart of the problem, we submit, is that the concept of trust is used implicitly in the analysis, but used incorrectly as a variable that is either absolute or nonexistent. The proposition that repeat business leads to trade implies absolute trust, whereas the proposition that on the last play cheating is inevitable implies that trust drops from absolute to nonexistent at that point. Indeed, a 1 or 0 treatment of trust is implicit in the representation of strategies as *either* cooperation *or* cheating.

According to our model of trust, players in a supergame want to invest in trust if they expect or want to continue to trade. The larger their investments in trust, the smaller will be the costs of transacting in the future. So, repeat business or repetitive play does not *by itself* resolve the prisoner's dilemma problem. What the possibility of repeat business does is to increase the future returns to investments in trust.

Moreover, trust is never absolute. For example, if the number of players is not restricted to two, then no matter how large the possibility of repeat business between any two players – even if the game is repeated an infinite number of times – there is always the chance that a third party will come along and offer one of the players even greater gains. Consequently, there is always a positive probability of cheating or of the game continuing or not continuing, not as a deus ex machina but in the nature of trust as a capital asset. To sum up, if the present value of investment in trust is large relative to its costs, players will accumulate some of it. If the last play is sufficiently far in the future, it has no relevance, the present value of gains on that play being approximately 0. If it is closer to the present, investments in trust will be smaller. The prospect of a last play reduces the gains from investing in trust, but in this respect it is no different from that of other variables – cost of investment, size of the gains from trade on each play, the discount rate, the possibility of other, more advantageous relationships appearing – all of which affect the costs and payoffs from investing in trust. What the paradox really shows is that treating trust as either absolute or nonexistent leads to nonsensical results.

Another important line of inquiry into the underpinnings of trade and exchange when legal contracts are not possible is the work of Geertz[30] and that of Posner[31] – which relies on Geertz to a degree – on primitive and bazaar economies.

Both Geertz and Posner[32] assume that the dominant feature of these economies is ignorance of sellers by buyers and vice versa, ignorance of product characteristics, prices, and so on. They then hypothesize that many of the institutions peculiar to these economies exist to solve this information problem.[33] Such, for example, is the role of *clientization* – the matching of particular sellers and buyers – focused bargaining instead of shopping around, "insurance" that includes gift giving, loans without interest, and so on.

We suggest that all the institutions described and analyzed by Geertz and Posner can be explained as the result of efforts to develop trust, and, because production is costly, to economize on it. They did not develop, as those writers suggest, solely as a means of solving information problems. Because space is limited, we cannot review all the institutions described in these two fascinating papers, but we will look at a few and indicate that the authors were really searching for an alternative model to the one they use.

To rationalize clientization, Geertz writes: "Once you have found a particular bazaari in whom you have *faith* and who has *faith* in you, he is going to be there for awhile." Then he adds, "search is made accumulative."[34] Obviously, it is not search that is accumulative, but what search yields; we suggest that in this cont?xt it is faith in each other – what we call *trust*. In a way, Section V of Geertz's paper is an excellent introduction to the process of trust formation in bazaars and also, incidentally, in bureaucratic networks.

We now turn to Posner. Early in his paper, he writes that the high cost of information in primitive societies also applies to "information concerning the probability that the party to a contract will perform (there are no courts to coerce his performance) or that the quantity delivered in a sale is the quantity bargained for (there are no scales in primitive markets)."[35] In a way, this is a true information problem,[36] but it pertains to the extent to which the trading partner can be trusted to perform, deliver, and so on, and therefore is related directly to the volume of trust between two people.

Later, in discussing the *insurance principle,* Posner notes that "in these circumstances a transaction whereby A, who happens to produce a harvest that exceeds his consumption needs, gives part of his surplus to B in exchange for B's commitment to reciprocate should their role some day be reversed, will be attractive to both parties."[37] We cannot deny that this form of insurance seems attractive, but we fail to see how its attractiveness alone would, in the absence of legal enforcement assumed by Posner, lead to its being carried out. If A is to give part of his surplus to B, he must be able to believe that B's commitment will be honored; one of the ways this can happen is if A trusts B.

A final quotation from Posner will further underline our point and indicate the nature of trust. Posner writes: "Even without formal sanctions for breach of promise, most promises will still be honored simply because the promisor wants the promisee to deal with him in the future.[38] The possibility of repeated exchanges certainly enhances the present value of the gains from trade, but the mere prospect of large gains does not tell us that they can be realized. Even in markets based on law-supported property rights, large gains from repeated trade will not necessarily be realized if these laws are not strictly enforceable.

Geertz's and Posner's approach does not tell us under what conditions clientization, focused bargaining, insurance, and the other practices they analyze fail. Yet there do seem to be cases in which gains from trade in primitive societies remain unexploited. Colin Turnbull devotes a book to describing how members of the Ik tribe avoid the simplest forms of cooperation and exchange.[39] The lack of cooperation among the Ik is general, extending to intrafamilial, kinship, and other relationships. Clearly, this lack of cooperation cannot be ex-

plained by appeals to informational problems, because every Ik seems
to know everything about every other Ik. We suggest that the patterns
of behavior documented by Turnbull can be explained by the
virtually total absence of trust among the Ik, a situation that rests on
the low expected yield from trust. This low yield, in turn, results from
the material inability of the Ik to promise repayment of any loan. The
reason for this, alluded to only briefly by Turnbull, seems to be the
restrictions imposed on Ik mobility by the governments of the three
countries in which the territory of the Ik lies.

   Let us look briefly at the relationship of trust to altruism, caring, or
utility interdependence. These two phenomena should not be confused, as is sometimes done.[40] The confusion originates in the fact
that C may forego personal consumption to benefit D, either because
C cares about D or because C wants D to trust him. In the first case,
caring, C's motivation is the fact that his welfare or utility depends
directly on the consumption level of D. C reduces his own consumption because his marginal utility loss from the reduction in D's consumption level is greater to him than the marginal utility gain from
the increase in his own consumption. In the second case, trust, there
need be no utility interdependence. C may forego an opportunity to
benefit himself by harming D and yet be perfectly selfish. He would
do so if he expected the damages to his own long-run trade gains with
D to be greater than the shorter-term gains from the harmful action.
Trust is therefore not the same thing as caring, and trust can easily
exist between parties who do not like each other.

4.5   Networks and the equilibrium volume of trust

In Section 4.3, we suggested a model of trust formation. However, the
equilibrium amount that will be produced by two or more individuals
has not been determined. Let us turn to that problem. However, we
should note beforehand that trust relationships or trust ties between
individuals define what we mean by a network. These relationships or
ties can be weaker or stronger, depending on whether the volume of
trust is smaller or larger; symmetric or asymmetric, depending on
whether trust is mutual or not; and so on. Consequently, if someone is
provided with an exact description of a network, including the degree
of weakness or strength of the ties between members, the extent to
which these are symmetric or asymmetric, and so on, he would also
have an exact measure of the volume of trust in a given network.

   Given this fact, the capital value of trust between individuals is
exactly equal to the capital value of a network. Consequently, in de-

termining the equilibrium value of trust between these individuals, we will also be determining the optimal size, density, symmetry, and so on of the network. From this equivalence between the equilibrium value of trust between individuals and the equilibrium value of networks between them, it follows that much can be learned about the volume of trust in bureaucratic organizations by a careful study of networks.

For that reason, we note certain characteristics of bureaucratic networks. Importantly, they may be internal or external to an organization. The first attribute refers to the informal trust ties between bureaucrats (public or private) in either one bureau or a number of bureaus in the organization. The second refers to the informal trust ties between bureaucrats in an organization and outside people, such as media representatives, governing or opposition politicians, other private or public bureaucrats, professionals, labor union officials, businessmen, and bankers.

To illustrate, in a recent paper[41] we have argued that to understand the use of moral suasion by central banks and the response of commercial banks to that instrument of monetary policy, it is essential to suppose that moral suasion is a process whereby the cooperation of commercial banks in the pursuit of certain objectives of central banks is exchanged for information from the latter. The ties between central and commercial bankers engaged in moral suasion constitutes an external network for the bureaucrats of both the central and commercial banks.

Bureaucrats may often derive personal satisfaction from the contacts received from media people, business firms, public enterprises, labor unions, law firms, politicians, or management consultants. We do not believe that it is useful, however, to conceive of networks as instruments used for that purpose. Networks, to put it differently, are not consumption but production instruments. Bureaucrats use them to achieve production objectives, even though the contacts received in network trades may bring them satisfaction. The higher the satisfaction derived per unit of payment, the less money (or its equivalent) paid by those who trade with bureaucrats. Networks, in other words, are capital instruments (factors of production) used by bureaucrats to affect the output of policies.

If this is granted, we can rewrite the production function (2.4) as

$$S_i = f(T_P, T_B, T_H, N_P, N_B, K_V) \tag{4.5}$$

in which, as before, S_i represents policy i, which can be either public or private; T_P, T_B, and T_H stand for the formal services of sponsors, bureaucrats, and organizations associated with the formal structure;

K_V is a measure of the services of such capital goods as buildings, airplanes, trains, pens, pencils, and paper; and N_p and N_B measure the informal services of sponsors and bureaucrats associated with networks (or trust).

We can now determine the equilibrium volume of trust. We must recognize that there are two margins along which trust can be accumulated. The first relates to the amount invested in a single relationship (the intensity of trust), and the second pertains to the number of relationships invested in (the extent of trust or the size of networks). Changes in the environment will alter an individual's desired pattern of investment by altering the returns along these two margins. In an open, mobile, and relatively impersonal society, large investments in trust in a small number of relationships – investments in intensive trust – are seldom observed, whereas the profitability of many contacts and relationships – investments in extensive trust – are usually the rule. It has been alleged, for example, that because the British civil service is relatively small and closed – the contacts and relationships of these public bureaucrats are mainly with other public bureaucrats – the members trust each other far more than do public bureaucrats in the U.S. federal civil service, which is much larger and includes relationships that extend beyond the boundaries of the bureaucracy.[42]

We consider first the intensive margin and then turn to the extensive margin and the problems posed by the existence of barriers. We begin with a world consisting of only three bureaucrats B_i, B_j, and B_k. Because the number of bureaucrats is fixed, we are focusing on the amount of trust accumulated with each, holding network size constant.

Consider Figure 4.2 and assume that B_i and B_j wish to trade with each other, as do B_j and B_k. (Recall from Chapter 3 that B_j is our typical superior–subordinate bureaucrat.) Each pair will seek to produce trust for itself. The question is, how much? Let the volume of trust produced jointly by B_i and B_j be denoted as $_iT_j$ and that produced by B_j and B_k be $_jT_k$. Then we can establish that if the yield on trust for B_j is equal to r_j', B_i and B_j will jointly produce an amount $_iT_j'$, whereas B_j and B_k will build $_jT_k'$ if some mechanism exists that allows B_j to produce with B_i, and separately with B_k, amounts of trust (or networks) that would equalize the yield r_j' accruing to himself.

Does such a mechanism exist? Recall our earlier statement (in Section 4.3) that trust cannot be bought; consequently, it is not through a market mechanism that the yields on $_iT_j$ and $_jT_k$ can be equalized. We will argue later that there are many circumstances that will pre-

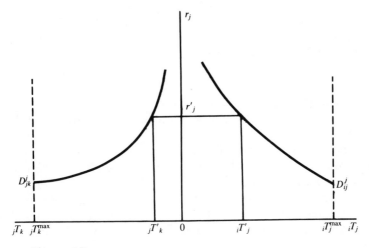

Figure 4.2.

vent equalization. But if we rule out all these factors temporarily, the only force that would produce equality is the desire of B_j, who is in a network with B_i and also with B_k (although the last two are not members of a network of their own), to maximize his total wealth. Recall that B_i pays for a share of the trust produced with B_j, so that the curve labeled D^j_{ij} in Figure 4.2 can be understood to belong to B_j (hence the j superscript). That curve reflects B_j's demand as the volume of trust jointly accumulated with B_i is varied, on the assumption that the cost shares of B_i and B_j are fixed. D^j_{jk} is derived in a similar fashion, although the shares are not necessarily the same as those of D^j_{ij}.

The position of D^j_{jk} is determined by the forces analyzed previously in our discussion of the production and accumulation of trust: the anticipated frequency and size of future opportunities for gainful exchange between B_j and B_k, the costs of communicating, and the cost to B_j and B_k – assumed fixed for the sake of simplicity in Figure 4.2 – of producing trust. A similar set of variables determines the position of D^j_{ij}. Given these positions and B_j's subjective rate of discount, $_iT'_j$ and $_jT'_k$ are the amounts that maximize his wealth and therefore the amounts he will seek.

The cost shares of producing trust to B_i and B_j have been assumed fixed, as have the shares to B_j and B_k. In other words, we have assumed that B_j's shares of the cost of trust accumulation with B_i and B_k are constant at all volumes of trust. Such an assumption simplifies the drawing of Figure 4.2, but it is not essential. As long as the ratio of cost shares is monotone over variations in the volume of trust, curves such as D^j_{ij} and D^j_{jk} exist, although they will have different slopes than those portrayed in Figure 4.2.

If $_iT^{max}_j$ and $_jT^{max}_k$ in Figure 4.2 represent the maximum (absolute) level of trust possible between B_i and B_j on the one hand, and B_j and B_k on the other, then the distance $(_iT^{max}_j - _iT'_j)$ measures the level of transaction costs in exchanges between B_i (the superior) and B_j (the subordinate), whereas the distance $(_jT^{max}_k - _jT'_k)$ measures the same thing among subordinates of B_i. These transaction costs or shortfalls from absolute trust are the same as those pictured in Figure 3.2. Consequently, Figure 4.2 can be used to determine whether efficient or inefficient behavior will prevail, because that decision is determined by the volume of trust between superiors and subordinates relative to the volume among subordinates, a ratio easily measured in Figure 4.2.

To analyze how equilibrium along the extensive margin is determined, we will make an assumption that simplifies the exposition and allows us to deal directly with the various barriers that produce network truncation, that is, discontinuities or jumps in the rate of return accruing to networks (or to trust). The assumption is this: The size of a network is proportional to the flow of informal services produced and supplied by that network. Given that assumption, a natural strategy is to examine the equilibrium size of a network (the equilibrium flow of informal services) in the presence of barriers that lead to network truncation. The equilibrium when truncation is absent is a special case of the more general analysis. Therefore, we will now analyze network truncation.

The accumulation of trust ties with a number of individuals and therefore the extension of networks, like the process of trust accumulation, is based on indicators. As noted in Section 4.3, some of these facilitate the formation of trust, whereas others impede it. For example, it has been argued that in tightly knit subgroups or subsocieties whose boundaries within the larger group or society are delineated by race, religion, language, ethnicity, color, kinship, or other factors, intragroup networks are more frequent than intergroup networks.

In reading the literature, one often gets the impression that racial, ethnic, or kinship status is at the base of trust and hence provides the basis for networks. At best, that view is incomplete. It certainly cannot explain why some individuals, who share a particular trait, are not members of networks in that status group, and why other individuals sometimes play an important role in networks outside their own status group.

In view of our discussion in Section 4.3, the reader knows that social groups may provide the basis for network formation, because by supplying the basis for repeated gainful interactions between members of the group, they give members virtually constant opportunities to signal to and communicate with each other and therefore to forego cheating each other. Similarly, the trust that exists between members of a family is often greater than that between casual acquaintances. However, the extent of involvement in a relationship is not a measure of the amount of trust in that relationship, as noted in Section 4.4. But a close relationship does make *possible* the accumulation of a large amount of trust by providing many opportunities for interaction.

If the members of a society abide by the Judeo-Christian Golden Rule, by Kant's Categorical Imperative,[43] by the Confucian code of ethics,[44] or by any other rule of that kind, networks will form more easily among them irrespective of the status groups to which they belong. There are many historical examples of networks across status-group lines, based on such rules, that have been effective instruments of individual exchange. The reason for this is easy to appreciate. The canons of behavior summarized by the above rules make both signals and responses more precise, thus reducing the cost of communication and, therefore, of trust formation.

But traits or indicators that unite may at the same time separate. If language, color, dress, sex, or any other indicators make the attribution of some initial trust by a lender to a borrower easier, and if they make communication between them simpler and therefore less costly, these same indicators make trust and communication more costly between those who do not have them.

To illustrate, if A finds it easier to signal (by lending at a lower interest rate, say) to B; if B is white, male, English-speaking (or speaks with a proper accent); was schooled at Upper Canada College and Queen's University; chose engineering instead of liberal arts; through family connections has held relatively high-level summer jobs in Toronto's Bay and King Streets firms; been successfully sponsored for membership in the Empire Club by a respectable and reputable elder; declared genuine interest in the Progressive Conservative Party, although not been rash enough to become a member; and has at least formal membership in the Episcopal Church, then A will find it more costly to signal and communicate with C if C does not possess all or most of these traits.

When indicators operate in their second role, we say that they lead to network truncation. To put it differently, when behavior is based on indicators, we observe the existence of a phenomenon that, vary-

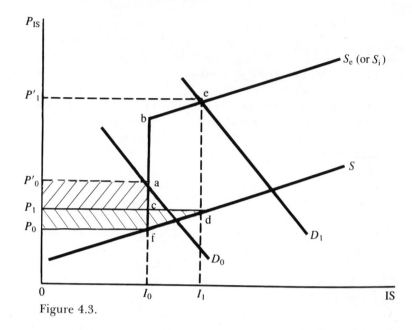

Figure 4.3.

ing with the context, has been called *social segmentation, social bound-aries, social cleavages,*[45] or *statistical discrimination.*[46] The important point for the theory of trust formation is that these cleavages, fron-tiers, barriers, or social lines of demarcation, which produce network truncation, are real barriers in that it requires the use of real re-sources to overcome them. If communication between Hokkien and non-Hokkien or between francophone and anglophone Canadians is difficult, because a social distance[47] – varying with the strength of such variables as language, ethnicity, color, dress, or accent – must be traversed, or because new attitudes must be developed or new lan-guages invented, old symbolic meanings destroyed, and so on, then resources will be required for that voyage.

We have argued that networks are used for the purchase and sale of informal bureaucratic labor services. Using the supply-and-demand diagrams introduced in the last chapter, we can now portray network truncation and in the process determine equilibrium network size. This is done in Figure 4.3.

The S curve represents the volume of informal services supplied at alternative prices if transaction costs are zero, whereas S_e (or S_i; whichever obtains does not affect the present argument) is the supply curve incorporating these costs. Therefore, the vertical distance be-tween the two is a measure of transaction costs occasioned by the fact that trust is not perfect. Segment ab is a measure of the distance that must be traversed due to the social cleavages or barriers. It is a measure of the costs that must be incurred if a network is to expand to include individuals who possess "inappropriate" traits.

To understand the meaning of network truncation, consider a shift in the demand for informal services (IS) from D_0 to D_1. That shift elicits an increment in the supply of informal services of $(I_1 - I_0)$ and therefore an increase in the size of the network proportional to $(I_1 - I_0)$. The price paid by demanders for this new supply rises from P_0' to P_1', whereas that received by suppliers goes up by a much smaller amount, from P_0 to P_1. The value of extra resources expended to increase IS from I_0 to I_1 is $[(P_1deP_1') - (P_1caP_0')]$; because the second term in that expression is a sum already foregone in transaction costs when demand is at D_0 and I_0 of informal services are supplied, it cannot be counted again when demand goes to D_1. A fraction of the extra resources – proportional to the vertical distance ab – represents the resource cost of overcoming social barriers or bridging social cleavages.

The increase in demand from D_0 to D_1 also increases payments to suppliers of informal services by an amount equal to P_0fdP_1. To decide how to interpret this sum, two cases should be distinguished according to the network's mode of operation. Suppose that all trading in networks is bilateral in the sense that interaction between any two individuals is independent of network size. In other words, trade is bilateral when A and B trade with each other and only with each other whether individuals with inappropriate traits are brought into the network or not. In this case, growing demand does not increase transaction costs between A and B. Consequently, area P_0fdP_1 in Figure 4.3 is a measure of the increase in rents accruing to inframarginal traders due to the increase in the supply price of informal services.

In the second case, characterized by multilateral trade, all members always transact with each other, so that new entry in the network makes life more difficult. In this case, area P_0fdP_1 is best interpreted as an increase in the cost of supplying an extra volume of informal services. It is, in other words, a measure of the extra compensation required to attract these additional informal labor services from alternative uses.

Interestingly, a policy of quotas aimed at mixing people who fall on different sides of social demarcation lines will be supported by network members in bilateral trade patterns and opposed in multilateral patterns. It follows that if network trade patterns are related to the structure of bureaus – between, let us say, the functional and the multidivisional[48] – then one could favor mixing whereas the other opposed it. In other words, if a company decided to promote mixing, it would be inclined toward the multidivisional form of organization, in which network exchanges are more likely to be bilateral.

Another point can be emphasized with the help of Figure 4.3. A policy of mixing, which would induce or increase truncation, could make the situation of network exchanges worse if it was not accompanied by an increased demand for informal services. That is not all. Such a policy would raise the cost of informal services to demanders and therefore raise the unit cost curves of the bureaus affected (see below). If the mixing policy is not applied with the same vigor everywhere, or if some bureaus can adjust easily, the bureaus whose costs had increased most sharply might have to fold.

One obvious point follows from the above discussion: The extent of network truncation can be *reduced* by the existence of schools from which all or most senior bureaucrats are recruited. In some countries, such as France, schools exist for the express purpose of preparing the "*grands commis de l'Etat*," whereas in other countries, such as England, recruitment to the higher civil service is restricted de facto to a small number of schools. Similarly, certain measures, such as public service laws, which restrict entry into the bureaucracy by the introduction of a merit system, can also reduce truncation.[49]

Truncation can, as we have just seen, be increased by mixing policies or by the introduction of quotas, even though such truncation may be only transitory. If the degree of truncation becomes large and appears to be somewhat permanent, "middlemen" or "brokers" may appear to reduce it.[50] These middlemen will form a network that may mediate exchange between nontrusting individuals or groups. The effect of such arbitrage would be a reduction in social barriers or social distance.

We conclude this analysis by repeating that if the size of networks is proportional to the flow of informal services supplied and demanded, then when the demand for these services is D_0, the equilibrium network size is proportional to I_0; when the demand is D_1, it is proportional to I_1.

Truncation obviously reduces the equilibrium volume of informal services exchanged relative to the volume that would be traded in its absence. Consequently, if the net-of-transaction-cost supply of informal services is of inefficient services, truncation will *improve* the cost performance of bureaus, that is, it will make the unit cost curve lower than it would be in the absence of truncation. If, as before, the *FAC*

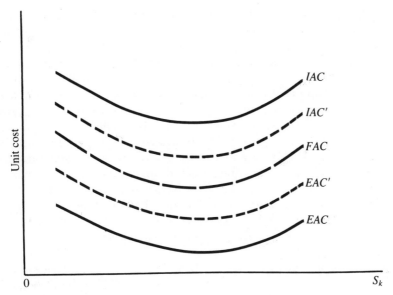

Figure 4.4.

curve represents the unit cost curve of decisions made by the formal structure, and *IAC* is the unit cost curve for inefficient services, then in Figure 4.4, curve *IAC'* represents unit costs with truncation, whereas *IAC* stands for inefficient behavior without truncation.

The same argument holds *mutatis mutandis* for efficient behavior, except that in this case the unit cost curve will increase with truncation, from *EAC* (when there is no truncation) to *EAC'*.

The argument need not be emphasized. Because truncation is effectively a barrier to trust formation, its presence must reduce selective behavior and bring a bureau's performance closer to that produced by its formal structure.

4.6   Notes on sundry topics suggested by the theory of trust

In this concluding section, we note four issues that pose particular problems in legally supported property-rights market systems but seem to vanish in a trust-supported property-rights network system: competition in the presence of small numbers, market failure in the presence of externalities, moral hazard and other similar phenomena, and incentives in bureaucratic hierarchies. We briefly look at each of these in turn.

In Chapters 2 and 3, we assumed that the prices of the informal services traded in networks were competitive. That is, we represented networks as surrogate competitive markets.

That assumption contradicts a reality that has often been noted: the fact that in networks the number of traders is often small. Much of the literature on internal labor markets is concerned with this problem. The reason is that in a small market, there is a serious trading problem because "there [is] only one buyer and one seller and no competitive forces to drive the two of them into competitive equilibrium."[51]

We suggest that in exchanges based on trust-supported property rights, prices tend to gravitate toward what in a market would be competitive prices. The process involved is not the same as that in a competitive market. However, the kind of interaction that trust requires and upon which it is based seems to preclude systematic departures from "network clearing" to the advantage of either party in the exchange.

In his paper, Geertz states, "clientship [in bazaar economies] is symmetrical, equalitarian and oppositional."[52] This generally characterizes exchange in networks as well. Consequently, we suggest that surrogate market competition in networks can be defended by reference to the nature of trust and constitutes a good working assumption.

Third, some problems in the workings of competitive markets, such as (i) externalities; (ii) opportunism, or the exploitation of all profitable opportunities as they arise;[53] (iii) moral hazard, and (iv) the high costs of writing contingent contracts, are greatly reduced or even eliminated in networks. The reason can be found in the nature of trust. Because trust accumulates partly as a result of the response of an individual who foregoes cheating, opportunism, moral hazard, and the incompleteness of contracts for all contingent states of the world will have less significance the higher the amount of trust.

Finally, we note that for the same reason, the problem of incentives is reduced in networks, as long as we take the amount of trust as a given. This is an important point, because it is often asserted that a characteristic of large organizations is the lack of incentives for members to do what is expected of them. We argue that to the extent that every member is able to accumulate an optimum amount of trust, the problem of incentives does not exist. In that case, increasing incentives would require the investment of further scarce resources and would be wasteful. It is, therefore, in the obstacles to trust building that we must seek to understand the problem of incentives.

CHAPTER 5

The compensation of bureaucrats

5.1　Introduction

The existence and extent of competition within organizations – whether public or private (corporate) bureaucracies – is clearly of fundamental importance. In the literature on corporations, there appear to be two classes of models. In one class are those models that postulate competition; in the other are those that (implicitly or explicitly) ignore it completely. Models that ignore competition among bureaucrats (called "managers" in that literature) explain corporate behavior as based solely on the interests of these bureaucrats or managers and lead to fears of excessive growth and power in the corporate sector of the economy. One well-known writer in this tradition visualizes the entire economy as if it were a single giant corporation.[1] On the other hand, models that postulate competition among managers lead to the easy dismissal of these fears and to an understanding of the growth of the corporate sector as prima facie evidence of its efficiency[2] rather than just a lurid reflection of managers' interest in that growth.

Turning to the literature on governmental bureaucracy, we find a conspicuous absence of the counter-accusations characteristic of the debates over corporate power. Instead, we find models based single-mindedly on the monopoly assumption. All the theories of public bureaucracy put forward to date assume that bureaucrats are monopolists. Sometimes the monopoly assumption is explicitly made, as in Niskanen's work[3] or in that of Migué and Bélanger.[4] Sometimes it is implicit, as in the model of Chant and Acheson,[5] where the monopoly assumption is embodied in the supposition that bureaucracy may be modeled as a single bureau, and that decision makers within that bureau have a single objective or set of objectives, so that the bureau itself behaves as a monolithic unit.

This chapter and the following one develop and justify our thesis that competition is the most general assumption to make about bureaucracy – no less in government bureaus than in private corporations. Impediments to competition do arise in bureaucracies. But we believe that these impediments are best understood as restrictions imposed within a general framework of competition.

Most importantly, we suggest that competition in bureaucracy is much more complex and subtle than is usually supposed. Previous writers have not taken into account the existence of bureaucratic networks but have simply analyzed the competition for jobs among individual bureaucrats or managers. When networks are considered, it is immediately apparent that there are many different forms of competition in bureaucracy. Bureaucrats compete for jobs or formal positions, as in the Alchian model, but they also compete for "positions" or "membership" in bureaucratic networks. These are the two forms of bureaucratic competition discussed in this chapter. Chapter 6 analyzes a third form of competition – the competition for resources between networks and bureaus.

Our main purpose in both chapters is to integrate the theory of selective behavior with a model of bureaucratic competition. This complete model of competition and selective behavior is, we believe, more general and more plausible than the models of simple competition or simple monopoly mentioned above (and discussed below). In Chapter 7 we suggest that this model also possesses a richer set of testable implications, (that is, it explains more bureaucratic behavior) than do either of these alternative models.

In this chapter, our first task is to outline the arguments that have been put forward to support monopoly models of bureaucracy: (i) bureaucrats must be monopolists because each bureau is the sole producer of particular services; (ii) bureaus are monopolies because governing politicians have a monopoly over public office; and (iii) bureaucrats must be monopolists because they are inefficient and do not work very hard, and these are the classical symptoms of monopoly. These arguments are discussed in Section 5.2.

Section 5.3 shows that there is a family relationship between these models and models of managerial monopoly in the corporate sector. We then contrast the latter to the model of managerial competition originated by Alchian[6] and others and discuss the relevance of that line of reasoning to models of bureaucracy in the public sector.

Section 5.4 integrates the model of managerial competition and our theory of selective behavior. We demonstrate there that competition does not eliminate, but rather enhances, the capacity of bureaus for selective behavior. We also explain why an understanding of the nature of trust and networks, which make that kind of behavior possible, leads to a rather different view of managerial competition.

Section 5.5 looks at the limitations on managerial competition. We show that competition can never be perfect and that consequently, even in equilibrium, managers will benefit from rents over which they have some degree of control. The chapter ends by asking whether other forms of competition can compensate for this and eliminate managerial rents.

5.2   Monopoly models of bureaucracy in the public sector

Many arguments or assumptions have been advanced to justify the analysis of public bureaus – or of bureaucracy itself – as monopolies. This section lists the main ones and then considers the evidence sometimes used to support the monopoly hypothesis.

One popular argument[7] is that bureaucrats are monopolists because the public sector is a monopoly under the control of politicians. Second, monopoly is assumed because most bureaus tend to be the sole producers of their services. It has been said that in the United States, for example, no government bureau or agency other than the Post Office delivers mail, only the Department of Defense is mainly responsible for directly producing defense services, and so on. This is not always true. Downs[8] has pointed out that in many cases bureaus overlap in their functions, or are redundant, as are the National Security Council and the State Department. Moreover, central agencies, such as the Treasury in the United States, the United Kingdom, and Canada, often duplicate studies made by other bureaus. But the argument is broadly true. The analogy is therefore drawn between a monopoly firm and its customers and a monopoly bureau and the citizenry. Such an analogy is, however, misplaced. Public bureaus are not dependent on citizens for resources or revenue in the way that private firms are dependent on their customers. Public bureaus do not sell their services to citizens, nor do they raise taxes directly from citizens to pay for their programs. Governing politicians, not bureaucrats, are responsible to and raise taxes from citizens, and bureaucrats serve politicians, not citizens. If there were a thousand Departments of Defense in Canada or elsewhere, instead of one, these would still not compete for citizens, because citizens are not their customers; politicians are.

A third argument grants that politicians, not citizens, are the customers of the bureau and suggests that monopoly bureaus exploit their customers, the politicians. Niskanen, in his 1968 paper, was the first to systematize the idea that monopoly bureaus can use their position to extract monopoly rents from politicians. Although the relationship between bureaus and governing politicians is, he suggested, nominally one of bilateral monopoly, politicians do not have and cannot acquire the information – information pertaining to the true costs of bureaucratic services – necessary to control the bureaucracy. In contrast, it is comparatively easy for bureaucrats to exploit politicians by acquiring information about the true value to politicians of their services. Because bureau heads are budget maximizers in Niskanen's model, they choose to take their monopoly rents in the form of larger budgets. On these assumptions, Niskanen demonstrated, bureaus will grow up to twice as large as politicians (and citizens) would like them to be.

Finally, the monopoly model is often supported by the observation that government bureaucrats are inefficient and appear to lead a life of leisure compared to their counterparts in the private sector. Because "the quiet life" is often thought to be a characteristic, if not *the* characteristic, of monopoly behavior,[9] the inference is drawn that bureaucrats must be monopolists.

Evidence that bureaucrats live the quiet life has two sources: One is the casual observation, amounting to folklore, that bureaucrats do not work very hard. The daily life of the civil servant in Ottawa, for example, is sometimes caricatured as follows. He arrives at work at about 10 A.M.; from 10:00 to 10:45 he peruses the morning newspaper; it's then time for coffee; after a half-hour coffee break, he makes two or three phone calls, one of which is to arrange lunch with a fellow bureaucrat. Lunch is a long, elaborate, and carefully conducted affair, invariably accompanied by several martinis. At around 2:30 P.M., the civil servant arrives back at work, unsteady but refreshed, in time for his afternoon meeting. Accounts differ on the typical nature of these meetings: In one version, the meeting is brief, nothing of importance is discussed, and half of the participants are asleep in any case. In another, the meeting is conducted with some alacrity, as new and ingenious schemes are hatched either to filch more money from the taxpayers or to squander what has already been taken from them on useless public sector projects. Both versions agree, however, that the meeting must end in time for the bureaucrat to drive home well in advance of the evening rush hour.

These folkloric accounts are, however, only part of the basis for the picture of bureaucratic lethargy. The other part is the host of empirical studies that document the inefficiency of public as compared to private production. These studies are too numerous to mention here, but they have been ably surveyed by Borcherding.[10] Almost universally, they show that when similar services are provided by the private and public sectors, the costs of the latter are higher.

Our purpose here is not to criticize either the folklore or the studies but to point out that an identical folklore exists concerning the activities of management in large private corporations, activities attributed to the "separation of ownership from control";[11] and although that folklore is surely equal in its ability to capture the popular mind,[12] it has not been treated with the same reverence in mainstream economic circles.[13] With respect to the empirical studies, even an observer as astute and sympathetic as Borcherding finds their results hard to accept at face value. He points out that the usual interpretation of these studies – that they indicate greater waste in public than private institutions – runs contrary to neoclassical economic theory:

Waste in a practical sense . . . cannot exist, unless there is persistent and remedial error in the choice of social institutions. The latter possibility cannot readily be accepted, however, without seriously compromising the economists' paradigmatic commitment to rational choice modeling. If rational choice is to be retained, the answer to the hypothesis that "waste" is present is to suggest the accuser look instead for other explanations.[14]

What must be stressed in the present context, however, is that the truth of neither the folklore nor the studies can be considered evidence in favor of the monopoly model of bureaucracy. The theory of the relationship between monopoly and efficiency was developed by Alchian and Kessel.[15] They pointed out (with respect to the behavior of monopolists versus that of competitors in private markets) that the costs of inefficiency – the pursuit of nonpecuniary gains such as leisure – are no lower to a monopolist than they are to a perfect competitor; in each case, there is the same sacrifice of profits.

What does create an incentive for the pursuit of nonpecuniary gains in the private sector are restrictions on or impediments to the receipt of pecuniary rewards (profits). So, Alchian and Kessel tried to rationalize Hicks's proposition by suggesting that if monopolies tend to live under the threat of regulation, or of antitrust action, and the likelihood of state intervention increases with their profitability, they would have less of an incentive to maximize profits and more of an incentive to pursue nonpecuniary gains. In short, their argument is that monopoly per se does not lead to the pursuit of the quiet life; the attenuation of the right to profits does. So, we would expect monopolists to pursue the quiet life only if ceilings are more likely to be imposed on monopoly profits than on the profits of competitive firms.

Now, because the output of public bureaus is not sold, and no pecuniary profits are earned from the production of goods and services in government bureaus, it is difficult to see how monopoly in the public sector could ever be associated with an attenuation of the right to profits there.[16] There is, however, a related property-rights approach that is sometimes used to explain government inefficiency. The argument is that public employees have less incentive to be efficient, or greater incentive to pursue nonpecuniary rewards, not because they are monopolists but because they cannot take home the profits or benefits of greater efficiency. Alternatively, it is suggested that in the absence of profits there is no good index of their efficiency.[17] In either version of the argument, government bureaucrats, although not monopolists, are nevertheless restricted in the sense that that they themselves cannot reap the rewards of greater efficiency. For example, if they were paid the same formal salary no matter what their level of performance, they would have little incentive to be efficient and every incentive to maximize leisure or other forms of nonpecuniary consumption.

But there is an obvious flaw in this line of reasoning. Employees in the private sector do not take home the profits of their activity either, but are paid on the basis of their superiors' assessment of their performance, just like employees in the public sector. In both the private and public sectors, there is an adequate measure of the overall performance of the organization – profits in private firms and popularity in the government. In neither case is this measure a useful guide to or reward for the performance of any one subordinate, for the obvious reason that individual contributions to the firm's profits or the government's popularity are negligible.

So, the property-rights approach does not, in fact, predict greater inefficiency or greater pursuit of nonpecuniary consumption in the public sector. Indeed, a casual glance at the typical offices of senior management in public bureaus compared with those in private corporations – the quality of the carpets, the drapes, the chairs, the desk, and the secretary – suggests that it is the private rather than the public sector that offers greater possibilities for at least these kinds of nonpecuniary consumption.[18]

5.3   Competition

To appreciate the basic flaw in monopoly models of public bureaucracy, it is useful first to note the strikingly similar arguments concerning the separation of ownership from control in the modern corporation. First, ever since the work of Berle and Means,[19] it has been widely suggested that where stockholdings are widely dispersed, corporation managers tend to neglect the owners' interests in favor of their own. Second, the main interest of corporate managers, it is often suggested, is growth, for reasons similar to those that prompted Niskanen to suggest that the main interest of bureaucrats is size.[20] The operation of the large corporation, like that of public bureaucracy, is thus explained in terms of managerial motives, and the growth of corporations, like that of bureaucracy, is explained in terms of managerial rents. Finally, corporate managers, like public bureaucrats, are also held to be interested in nonpecuniary forms of consumption, such as excess staff, leisure, or the quiet life (sometimes called *organizational slack*), and their monopolistic position is said to allow them to pursue these forms of managerial discretion[21] at the expense of stockholders. So the literatures on the role of modern corporate managers and that on public managers have developed very similar themes.

The literature on corporate management contains a substantial counterattack to theories based on the motives of managers and their presumed monopoly power. The essential argument can be found as far back as Alchian's 1969 paper.[22] Important recent contributions include Jensen and Meckling and Fama.[23] The basic point made in these papers is this: The separation of ownership from management presents no difficulty because there is a market for managerial jobs, and this market is competitive. Managers face competition for their jobs both from lower-level managers and from managers in other firms. So, managers need not be owners in order to be motivated to be efficient. All that is necessary is that managers' rewards depend on their performance, so that efficient managers tend, over the longer run, to earn more than inefficient managers – what Fama calls *ex post settling up*[24] – and that there is effective competition for managerial jobs. Evidence for the latter proposition is found in the substantial managerial mobility among corporations.

Proponents of the model of managerial competition do not deny that there are substantial opportunities for managers to pursue growth, sales, the quiet life, or other forms of nonpecuniary consumption. However, they point out that this must be imputed to the cost to owners (stockholders) of policing the management, not to monopoly power. If the costs to owners of supervising managerial efficiency are high, these writers admit, managers will no doubt have discretion to pursue their own interests. What they do argue, and in this they are surely correct, is that the existence of such opportunities should not be confused with monopoly power. If competition for managerial jobs is perfect, managers earn no rents no matter how large their discretionary opportunities may be. To the extent that managerial jobs intrinsically offer opportunities for discretion – because of the high costs of policing for owners – managerial wages will be bid down by competition among managers for jobs. In short, opportunities for managerial discretion are identical to other nonpecuniary advantages sometimes attached to jobs, such as prestige or pleasant working conditions. As in the analysis of other forms of nonpecuniary advantage, the greater the opportunities, the lower the salaries of managers will be in competitive equilibrium.

To be sure, there are real effects of managerial discretion. Corporations are less efficient than they would be if managers could be policed without cost (the output of corporations from given inputs will be smaller), and the corporate sector itself is smaller. But stockholders will not bear the costs of managerial discretion; managers pay for it themselves in the form of lower wages.

Some proponents of the managerial discretion model are aware of this logic. Its most distinguished adherents in recent years have disputed not the logic but the effectiveness and efficiency of the market for managers.[25]

The efficiency of the market for managers can be evaluated on at least three a priori criteria: (i) the ease of manager mobility among firms; (ii) the efficiency of techniques and the adequacy of information for evaluating the performance of managers; and (iii) the strength of the incentives to replace inefficient managers. Proponents of the managerial discretion model argue, first, that the mobility of corporate executives is not very high; second, that the use of profits or stock market performance as a guide to the efficiency of chief executives does not adequately isolate that executive's contribution to profits, and therefore does not prove or disprove the competence of either the chief executive or that of junior executives who are his or her possible replacement; and third, that the incentives to boards of directors to replace inefficient managers are not as strong as one might wish.

Whether the managerial market is efficient enough to eliminate managerial rents is largely an empirical issue, and one that cannot be settled solely on the basis of a priori criteria.[26] The striking point is that, based on these criteria, the market for managers in the *public* sector appears at least as competitive and efficient, if not more so, than the market for corporate managers. Consider each of the criteria in turn. The first is managerial mobility. It is surely easier to go from one government bureau to another than it is to go from one private corporation to another.[27] On the second criterion (difficulty of evaluating the performance of managers), we have already argued[28] that this poses equal problems in both the public and private sectors. On the third criterion (the strength of the incentive to replace inefficient management), governing politicians in democracies must call elections at preset intervals, whereas business managers are not periodically submitted to takeover bids. The incentives provided by takeover bids in the private sector depend on the efficiency of the market for corporate control, which is difficult to assess.[29] But it seems unconvincing to argue that the incentive to replace inefficient bureaucrats is smaller in the public sector, where political control is legally and formally up for grabs at set intervals, than it is in the private sector, where no such contests occur. For this reason, one expects governing politicians to monitor the performance of both senior and junior bureaucrats rather better than boards of directors monitor business managers.[30]

A government bureaucracy, from this point of view, appears to be a competitive labor market, a market in which there is competition among subordinates for jobs and competition among bureaucratic superiors for subordinates. Public managers who do not perform satisfactorily will be replaced; those who do perform well are still under pressure to do better from ambitious underlings, from bureaucrats in other agencies, and from outsiders. In short, although public bureaus may be monopoly producers of their services, public *bureaucrats* are clearly not monopolists. If this point is accepted, it follows that the analysis of resource allocation in the public sector in terms of the alleged preference of bureau chiefs for larger budgets or nonpecuniary rewards, and of public sector growth in terms of bureaucratic monopoly, is entirely misplaced.

To see this, let us reconsider the monopoly models of the public sector outlined earlier. Consider first the argument that bureaucrats are monopolists because politicians are monopolists. At any point in time, politicians may have a temporary monopoly on public office.[31] The competitiveness of the political process is an important question that has received some attention in the literature.[32] But this has nothing to do with the issue of competition in the bureaucracy. Even if politicians did possess monopoly power over public office, there is no reason why they would cede this to the bureaucracy. Suppose, to consider an analogous case, that the owner of a private monopoly hires a manager to run the firm for him. Suppose the market for managers is perfectly competitive. Does the manager exercise any monopoly power – does he earn more than a competitive wage – because he is managing a monopoly? The answer must be no.

Consider next the impact of competition among bureaucrats on the results of the Niskanen model. As we have pointed out elsewhere,[33] mobility of bureaucrats among bureaus means that bureau heads are unlikely to behave as budget-maximizers, as Niskanen assumes they do, because the most efficient way to obtain a bigger budget may be to move to a larger bureau rather than to attempt to expand the budget of one's current bureau.[34] But let us suppose that bureaucrats did behave as budget-maximizers. Suppose, moreover, that the costs to governing politicians of policing bureaucratic distortions of information or, more generally, inefficient behavior are high. In this case, politicians cannot effectively police the bureaucracy and reduce the budgets of bureaus in that way. As we have shown elsewhere,[35] this is also implicitly assumed by Niskanen. Granting these two assumptions but assuming also that competition exists among bureaucrats for jobs implies the reverse of Niskanen's conclusions. Each bureau – and hence the bureaucracy – would be too small rather than too large.

To see this, suppose that initially no competition for positions in a particular bureau exists. Therefore, as in Niskanen's extreme case, the bureau will grow to be twice as large as politicians would prefer it to be. Now, suppose that perfect competition for positions in that bureau is introduced. Bureaucrats throughout the bureaucracy – including those at lower levels in the bureau itself – will bid for positions in that bureau, and salaries will fall. If this competition eliminated the bureaucratic distortions of information or inefficiency responsible for the bureau's excess budget, then in equilibrium, salaries would fall until the bureau's budget was optimal from the politicians' point of view. But, on Niskanen's assumptions, opportunities to distort information are built into the position of bureaucrats versus politicians. So, despite competition, whoever is the bureau head will find himself exposed to the same temptation. Apparently a larger budget can be obtained by distorting information rather than giving true information to politicians. Consequently, bureaucratic production is less efficient than it otherwise would be. Although politicians cannot obtain the information necessary to counteract the distortions of the bureau and so discover its true costs of production, they do know that the information is distorted and incorrect, and that any resources they give to the bureau will be used less efficiently than if this were not the case. So, they will allocate fewer resources to the bureau than they would if its distortions could be policed without cost, and the budget of the bureau will be smaller than it would be if bureaucrats there did not attempt to maximize it by distorting information.

5.4 Selective behavior and managerial competition

Up to this point, we have shown that none of the monopoly models of bureaucracy can stand up to close scrutiny. In particular, competition among bureaucrats for positions has a devastating impact on the Niskanen model – showing that budget-maximization would lead to a public sector that is too small rather than too large.

Nonetheless, we believe that the model of competition among managers developed by Alchian and others is not adequate to describe competition within organizations in either the private or the public sector. The reason is that it does not take into account the existence of networks and trust. Once these are recognized, it must also be clear that there are two kinds of competition in bureaucracies: competition for formal positions and competition for positions in networks. In this section, we shall introduce the second kind of competition and analyze the effects of both kinds on selective behavior.

Recall the model of selective behavior in Chapter 3. Figure 5.1, a reproduction of Figures 3.2 and 3.4, contains the essence of that model. Figure 5.1a depicts inefficient behavior. D_i is above D_e, so bureaucrats choose to supply inefficient informal services and the associated cost curve for policy S_k is IAC. The total "earnings" received by subordinates are their formal salaries plus the value of the characteristics or other emoluments taken, as represented by the area $OP_i dI_i$. Average costs of output are IAC rather than FAC because the productivity of subordinates is less with inefficient than with formal behavior. Figure 5.1b depicts efficient behavior. Because D_e in this case is above D_i, the total earnings received by subordinates are equal to their formal salaries plus the value of the characteristics or other emoluments received from their superiors, or the area $OP_e bI_e$. The associated cost curve for policy S_j is EAC, because bureaucrats who behave efficiently are more productive than when they behave formally. This increase in productivity is sufficiently large to more than outweigh the cost of the emoluments paid to subordinates.

Now, suppose that the market for bureaucrats is perfect. There is perfect competition among subordinates for positions and perfect competition among superiors for the services of subordinates. Consider first the impact of competition on the inefficient behavior of bureaucrats portrayed in Figure 5.1a, who are assumed to belong to

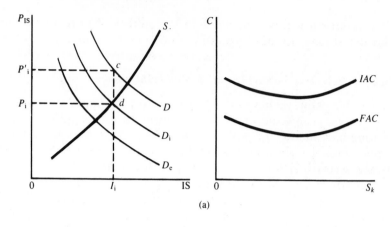

(a)

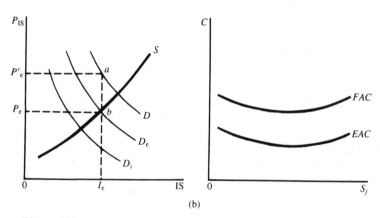

(b)

Figure 5.1.

bureau A. Inefficient behavior implies that the total emoluments received by subordinates in bureau A are greater than the opportunity
costs. Bureaucrats in other bureaus, such as bureau C (not depicted),
are, let us suppose, earning only their salaries. In an Alchian-like
world, all bureaucrats in C would want to move to bureau A, whereas
no subordinate in A would want to move to C. The situation depicted
in Figure 5.1a then appears to be one of disequilibrium. If competition exists, should we not expect that bureaucrats elsewhere will bid
down the formal salary in bureau A until the opportunities there are
no greater than those elsewhere in the system?

Similarly, would not the efficient behavior of subordinates in
bureau B (depicted in Figure 5.1b) mean that superiors in other

bureaus or other branches of the same bureau will want to bid for their services? If this were to happen, and competition among superiors for subordinates were perfect, the formal salaries of subordinates in B would be bid up until costs in B were exactly equal to FAC. Again, the impact of selective behavior on the bureau's cost curve would be dissipated by competition.

The matter, however, is far more complex than this. The basic reason is that participation in selective strategies is restricted not to members of the same *bureau* but to members of the same *network*. So, if the situation depicted in Figure 5.1a were a disequilibrium, it would create attempts to join not the bureau, but rather the network.

Now, there are costs to joining a network. The first implication of this distinction is that the situation depicted in Figure 5.1a may not be one of disequilibrium at all. Joining a network implies incurring the cost of investing in trust with members of the network in bureau A, and the benefits of joining the network may not compensate for this cost. To put it differently, the excess earnings of subordinates in A over their formal salary are not necessarily rents, but may simply be the return on their investment in network capital. As such, they will not attract entry and will persist in full equilibrium.

So, our first conclusion is that competition is consistent with selective behavior so long as the price received for such behavior is the competitive price – namely, the return that, if it were to persist, is just sufficient to induce bureaucrats to maintain their investment in networks. In competitive equilibrium, therefore, selective behavior – efficient or inefficient – will, to at least this extent, have real and permanent effects on the position of cost curves that are not dissipated by competition among bureaucrats.

Second, even when the price is higher than the competitive price, so that entry is induced, the effects of entry do *not* eliminate, and indeed sometimes magnify, the effects of selective behavior on costs. To see why, suppose that the return to selective behavior becomes greater than the competitive return, so that "insiders" – those in the network – are earning rents, and "outsiders" wish to join. The analysis of entry is complicated because although some individuals are in both the bureau and the network, others are only in the bureau and still others are only in the network. Further, sometimes[36] it may be easier to enter the network – that is, to build trust with one or more of its members – by entering the bureau because contacts and communication are essential to building trust, and these tend to be more frequent among members of the same bureau than among members of different bureaus. For our analysis to be complete, we must therefore consider

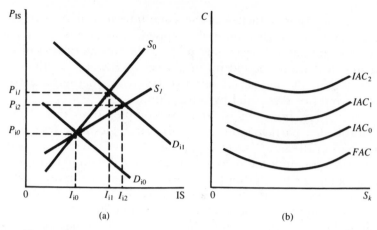

Figure 5.2.

three cases: (i) competition to enter the network among subordinates who are already employed in the bureau; (ii) competition to enter the bureau by subordinates who are already members of its network; and (iii) competition to enter both the bureau and the network.

Let us first look at the effects of entry into a network in bureau A by individuals already employed there. Figure 5.2 illustrates this situation. The initial position is the same as that in Figure 5.1a. Suppose that when the costs of accumulating trust are taken into account, that position is a true long-run equilibrium, that is, P_{i0} – the price received for inefficient services, given the positions of D_{i0} and S_0 – represents a return on network capital that is just sufficient to compensate network members for the costs of accumulating trust. The marginal subordinate, not in the network, would have to incur a higher cost of accumulating trust than those in it, and if P_{i0} is expected to persist, he will not wish to invest. Now, assume a comparative static change in either the costs or the returns from network participation. This could result from a change in the position of either the D (and hence the D_i) curve or the S curve, due to a change in the costs of accumulating trust, its rate of depreciation, or the rate at which subordinates discount future returns.

Suppose, for purposes of illustration, that the demand for informal services increases.[37] In Figure 5.2a, D_i shifts from D_{i0} to D_{i1} (the D curve is omitted for simplicity), the price received for inefficient services rises from P_{i0} to P_{i1}, and the quantity of inefficient services supplied by those in the network rises from I_{i0} to I_{i1}. Because more inefficient services are supplied, and because they are supplied at a higher price, the cost curve in Figure 5.2b rises from IAC_0 to IAC_1. If an efficient rather than an inefficient strategy were being pursued, the change in demand would have similar effects on the price and quantity of informal services,[38] and the EAC curve would fall.

Subordinates in the bureau but outside the network will therefore be motivated to build trust with those in the network so that they can participate in the efficient or inefficient strategy. In the long run, some of them will be successful. The long-run supply curve of services is, therefore, more elastic than the short-run curve due to this possibility of entry into or exit from the network, in the same way that the long-run supply curve for a competitive industry is more elastic than the short-run curve. The long-run equilibrium (in the case of inefficiency) is therefore at the intersection of D_{i1} and S_1, the long-run supply curve; the equilibrium price received is P_{i2}; and the equilibrium quantity of informal services forthcoming is I_{i2}. Because the quantity of inefficient services supplied increases, IAC rises further in the long run to IAC_2.

To sum up case (i), the effect of competition for network membership among subordinates in the same bureau does reduce the rents earned by members of networks, but this *increases* rather than reduces the capacity of bureaucrats to be selectively efficient. It has, in other words, precisely the opposite effect of Alchian-like competition for jobs or formal positions.

To isolate the pure effect of Alchian-like competition for positions in bureaus, consider case (ii): the effects of competition *among members of the same network* for formal positions in *different* bureaus. We suspect that a large fraction of observed mobility within the bureaucracy is mobility of this kind, because the costs of this form of mobility are relatively low. Not only does a new bureau member who is not in the network have to incur costs of accumulating trust with fellow bureaucrats; the other members of the network must also incur costs of establishing trust with him, because such costs are always jointly shared, as was shown in Chapter 4. Both of these costs are barriers to outsiders who are not in the network, but not to network members.

The effects of interbureau mobility among members of the same network are straightforward. Because employees of bureau C who are in the network of bureau A are already participating in the efficient or inefficient strategies of bureau A even though they are not employed by that bureau, they will want to move from C to A only if formal salaries are larger in A. So, this form of mobility, if perfect or costless, will not result in a compensating differential between the formal salaries earned in A and C, but rather in the equalization of formal salaries between those bureaus. Neither the rents due to selective behavior nor the effects of selective behavior on costs are affected.

We can now consider case (iii): the effects of simultaneous mobility among both bureaus and networks. Suppose that all networks are bureau-specific, and that all members of a bureau are also members of its network. Subordinates in C will then want to move to A if the formal salaries in A, plus the earnings received from the supply of informal services there, are sufficiently large compared to the formal salaries in C, plus the gains from participation in C's network, to compensate for the costs of moving to and building trust in A. The combined movement – to bureau A and to A's network – will bid down both the price of informal services and the formal salaries paid in A until rents in A are eliminated, that is, until total emoluments in A are no larger than formal salaries elsewhere, plus the competitive return on the investment of network capital in A. The effect on the cost curve, however, is uncertain. On the one hand, the amount of informal services provided by the network in A will increase, causing IAC to shift upward. On the other hand, the fall in formal salaries will tend to shift IAC downward (as well as FAC); so the net effect on IAC is indeterminate. Clearly, however, there is no tendency for IAC to return to its initial long-run equilibrium position. In the equilibrium condition, total emoluments are no greater than those obtainable elsewhere. This condition is consistent with various combinations of formal salaries and prices of informal services.

The effects of competition on the impact of selective behavior on costs may therefore be summed up as follows. Competition for positions in networks does eliminate the rents due to selective behavior, because the price received for informal services tends to fall to the competitive level. The effects of selective behavior on costs – the capacity of bureaucrats to make real changes in the cost curves of services – are, however, increased rather than diminished by this competition. Competition for positions in bureaus tends to decrease these effects only when membership in the bureau is required for participation in that bureau's network. Even in that case, there is no presumption that the diminishing effect of competition for positions will outweigh the amplifying effect of competition to join the network.

In short, the capacity of bureaucrats to behave selectively and the influence of the bureaucracy on the costs of output are forms of bureaucratic power that, unlike power in the other models of bureaucracy reviewed earlier, are not necessarily reduced by competition. Competition does reduce the power and the rents of individual bureaucrats, but it does not necessarily reduce, and in general magnifies, the influence of bureaucratic behavior on the costs of output.

In the last section, we argued that if we recognize the existence of trust and networks in bureaucracies, we must modify the standard Alchian view of competition among bureaucrats or managers. Bureaucrats will compete for network membership as well as for formal positions. We showed that selective behavior and the associated capacity of bureaucrats to affect the costs of output is consistent with both forms of competition. However, bureaucratic or managerial rents would be eliminated if competition for network membership were perfect.

In this concluding section, we qualify this last conclusion. We recognize that although competition for network membership undoubtedly exists within bureaucracies – public and private – in principle, *it can never be perfect.* Hence, this competition alone can never eliminate managerial rents when these rents arise from network membership.

To see why, recall that an important effect of competition among bureaucrats or managers is to bid down any rents accruing to investors in network capital. More specifically, if rents are being earned in a network, competition means that outsiders – those not in the network – will seek to enter by accumulating trust with one or more network members. But the costs of entry into the network cannot be borne partly by insiders and partly by outsiders, because trust is always produced and financed jointly.[39] Consequently, insiders can forestall competition and prevent a reduction in their rents by refusing to share in these costs, that is, by refusing to admit new members into the network.

The insiders' calculus must take into account that outsiders may then be tempted to join, or even to form a competing network or networks or to invest more heavily in them. That is, forestalling competition from one direction will, in part, result in more competition from other directions. But even taking the dangers of increased network competition into account, the best strategy for a profitable network is obviously not to admit and to share in the cost of building trust with whoever wishes to join. So, there are always barriers to entry into networks. It is inherent in the concept of a network that barriers exist, that is, that it is closed to some extent. It follows that competition among bureaucrats or managers for network membership can never be perfect, and that some rents to that membership will persist even in the long run.

This point implies that monopoly models of public bureaus and private corporations, discussed earlier, are not entirely misplaced, as we suggested they would be based on Alchian's model of competition among managers. But the source of monopoly power lies in the nature of networks, rather than in monopolistic elements in the public sector, the separation of ownership from control, or any of the other sources suggested in that literature. Moreover, this monopoly power would disappear if competition between networks were perfect. This leads to two questions. Can internetwork and interbureau competition substitute for imperfections in managerial competition and eliminate managerial rents? Would it also eliminate selective behavior? These questions are taken up in the next chapter.

CHAPTER 6

The size distribution of bureaus

6.1   Introduction

In this chapter, we develop a theory of the allocation of resources among bureaus. We explain why some bureaus grow and others decline, or to put it differently, how some bureaus can obtain more resources from sponsors over a given period of time, whereas others cannot. We shall not be concerned with the growth or decline of the bureaucracy as a whole; that subject is not addressed in this book.[1] We deal with the relative growth or decline of bureaus in a context in which the size of the bureaucracy as a whole may be constant, increasing, or decreasing.

The starting point for our theory of resource allocation among bureaus is the theory of selective behavior. Viewing selective behavior in terms of supply and demand for informal services, that theory up to this point has been based on the assumption of a fixed or predetermined demand curve. We shall therefore begin by developing a theory of the demand for informal services.

Coupling this theory with that of the supply of informal services – developed in the last chapters and elaborated further in the present one – gives us a complete theory of the quantities of informal services traded in different bureaus and, therefore, a theory of the size distribution of networks. To go from there to a theory of the size distribution of bureaus requires one additional assumption. That assumption, discussed in more detail below, is that in the absence of informal services, the costs of producing policies in different bureaus (the *FAC* curves) are identical. It follows that the only factor that makes some bureaus more efficient than others is the market for informal services in them. With that assumption, a theory of the size distribution of networks is a theory of the size distribution of bureaus.

The size distribution of networks and bureaus may be thought of as the end result of competition among bureaus for resources. This competition is obviously different from the competition for positions in bureaus and networks considered in the last chapter. There is, however, a straightforward relationship between the two forms of competition. To the extent that there are barriers to competition via mobility, bureaucrats tend to compete more fiercely by attempting to obtain more resources for their own bureaus. Similarly, restrictions on competition among bureaus for more resources, tend to increase competition among bureaucrats for positions in bureaus and networks.

We shall model the competition for resources among bureaus as a process of "Austrian" or Schumpeterian competition. This is done in three stages. The first stage is presented in Sections 6.2 and 6.3. Section 6.2 outlines the fundamental properties of Schumpeter's model of competition, whereas Section 6.3 illustrates the application of these ideas to the bureaucracy in a broad and informal way. Section 6.4 describes the equilibrium positions of the demand curves for informal services in different bureaus – and therefore of the allocation of resources among bureaus – on the assumption of fixed supply curves for informal services. In Section 6.5, the factors that determine supply conditions in bureaus – the capacities of bureaucrats to accumulate trust and networks, first discussed in Chapter 4 – are reexamined, and the Schumpeterian notion of competition through entrepreneurship or entrepreneurial capacity is analyzed in that context. The notion of entrepreneurial capacity turns out to have a precise meaning in our model: It is the capacity to accumulate trust and networks. We shall show that this capacity, combined with other determinants of the supply of informal services, determines the capacity of bureaus to obtain resources over the long run.

The analysis of Sections 6.4 and 6.5 is based on the assumption that no restrictions on entrepreneurial competition are imposed on the bureaucracy. Section 6.6 drops this assumption and examines the nature and origins of these restrictions. Section 6.7 concludes the chapter.

6.2   Schumpeterian competition

The ordinary model of competition focuses exclusively on price competition. For our purposes, this is an inadequate way to describe the process of competition among bureaus.

The kind of competition that is important in determining which bureaucrats gain greater control over resources and which fall behind is known as *entrepreneurship*. Conventional price theory, however, has emasculated the concept of entrepreneurship to the point where its only function is to limit the size of the firm. This function it performs inadequately, partly because the concept of entrepreneurship has been so emptied of content that it is now simply a name for our ignorance.[2] As is well known, there is no other role for the entrepreneur in conventional price theory because competition is identified in that theory with price-taking behavior: Firms that can sell all they want at the equilibrium price, and nothing at any higher price, obviously have no need for the services of an entrepreneur. Yet, it is well recognized that even perfectly competitive firms do not face an infinitely elastic demand curve once the postulate of perfect information is dropped. If consumers pay a cost to learn the prices charged by different firms, there is clearly a role for entrepreneurship in advertising or disseminating information about prices. If the postulate of perfect homogeneity of products is also dropped, there is a further role for entrepreneurship in terms of quality competition and selection of product lines. And if the technology of production and organization is not fixed and known, the role of entrepreneurship may be expanded to include innovation.

Now, to the layman, advertising and product (policy) differentiation are ways in which firms compete. They are not mere symptoms of imperfect competition, as they tend to be in conventional price theory. Technological innovation is also an important means of competition among firms. But none of these modes of competing are easily treated within the standard model of competition. Consequently, we have turned to a different tradition – the Austrian school of Menger, Hayek, Mises, and Schumpeter, to name only a few of its proponents – in order to model the competition between bureaus.

In that tradition, entrepreneurial competition has always been the epitome of competition. Perhaps the most specific and detailed model of entrepreneurial competition within that tradition is the one put forward by Schumpeter in 1911.[3] In Schumpeter's scheme, the innovators are not the individuals who invent new commodities, technologies, or organizational structures. The innovators are the entrepreneurs who implement new ideas by putting them into production or practice. Typically, the Schumpeterian entrepreneur founds a new firm for this purpose. Initially, when that new firm or organization is put into operation, the entrepreneur is a monopolist and earns monopoly rents. By definition, no other firm is producing his commodity or using his source of supply, technology, or organizational form.

But – and this is where the Austrian concept of competition differs most substantially from that used in conventional price theory – this founding of a monopoly is, in fact, the essence of competition. The new monopolist attracts the customers of other firms. The superiority of the new method of production or the new commodity forces these other firms to respond, that is, to compete or continue to lose business. Their commodities, production techniques, or sources of supply are made obsolete by the competition of the innovator. To Schumpeter, competition is a process of "creative destruction."

As he describes it, entrepreneurial competition is

competition from the new commodity, the new technology, the new source of supply, the new type of organization.

This kind of competition is as much more effective than the other [price competition] as a bombardment is in comparison with forcing a door, and so much more important that it becomes a matter of comparative indifference whether competition in the ordinary sense functions more or less promptly; the powerful lever that in the long-run expands output and brings down prices is in any case made of other stuff.[4]

Entrepreneurial innovation is the driving force in Schumpeterian competition, but it is not the whole process. As a result of innovation, the demand curve facing the entrepreneur shifts outward and the demand curves facing other firms or industries shift inward. The second phase of competition is the emulation of the entrepreneur's innovation by other firms. The result of this "wave of emulation" or second phase of creative destruction is that the entrepreneur's rents are competed away by imitators. So, in Schumpeter's description, competition is essentially an evolutionary process. It is easy to recognize the familiar Darwinian concepts behind the Schumpeterian scheme: innovation (mutation or the occurrence of new genetic combinations), emulation (adaptation), and survival of the fittest (creative destruction).

Schumpeter made brilliant use of the concept of entrepreneurship. He used it to analyze large-scale problems of the dynamics of capitalism – especially the business cycle and the transformation from laissez-faire capitalism to mixed capitalism, a transformation that would ultimately lead, he predicted, to socialism.[5] However, the concept of entrepreneurship is not limited in application to long-run or large-scale problems, nor need it be associated with an evolutionary schema. Other so-called Austrians use it to understand the daily and more mundane workings of competition. Kirzner, for example, defines entrepreneurship as "alertness to new opportunities." In his framework, these range from arbitrage opportunities to buy at lower or sell at higher prices than those that had been previously obtained to production opportunities – in which entrepreneurship implies grasping the opportunity to purchase a number of inputs and transform them into a product that will have a greater value than the costs of the inputs.[6]

In the more general Austrian view, entrepreneurship is not restricted to the innovator but includes the acts of emulators as well. Entrepreneurship encompasses all forms of competitive behavior for the simple reason that in this view, entrepreneurship *is* competition; they are one and the same process.[7] The next section illustrates the application of this principle to the public sector.

6.3   Schumpeterian competition in the public sector

Although it is obvious that competition exists in the public sector – among both political parties and bureaus – it is no less obvious that *price* competition plays a much smaller role there than in the private sector. Even the most educated citizen has no idea of the "prices" of public policies and could not obtain more or less of different policies if he knew their prices. Yet, contemporary public choice theorists have attempted to impose the model of price competition on this setting. This attempt has resulted in many of the sterile fictions of contemporary public choice theory, such as attaching "pseudo" or "tax prices" to individual public policies and modeling the behavior of citizens as movements along price–quantity demand curves.

In much contemporary theorizing about bureaucracy, the same literal transposition of Marshallian economics has led to a view of citizens as having a demand or marginal valuation curve for the services of each bureau, as if each bureau was constitutionally required to produce that particular service. Combine this with the postulates that bureaucrats do not innovate and that citizens' demands for public services are unchanging, and one easily arrives at the conclusion that the growth of bureaucracy must be analyzed in terms of the preferences and power of bureaucrats. In this way, by adhering to the letter of the formal models and the techniques of neoclassical economics, the spirit of that approach is abandoned.

By contrast, to our knowledge, no serious attempt has been made to model competition in the public sector as an entrepreneurial process. Yet some major innovations – or acts of Schumpeterian entrepreneurship – in the public sector in recent years are easy to list: the New Deal, Keynesian demand management to regulate the business cycle, social security, nationalized health and other programs of the welfare state, cost–benefit analysis and planning and program-budgeting (PPB) systems, programs of environmental control, and so on. Of course, the ideas for many of those programs originate neither with the bureaucracy nor with politicians, but from citizens' groups, academics, social critics, the media, and private business. It is not our purpose, however, to argue that new programs, policies, regulations, and techniques of administration are original *inventions* of the bureaucracy. The implementation of new programs, policies, regulations, or techniques of administration are *innovation*, not inventions, to use Schumpeter's distinction, and it is innovation that constitutes entrepreneurship. To repeat, innovation consists of the *implementation* of an idea, not its invention, and in the public sector, policy implementation is typically the work of the bureaucracy.

In many respects, the process of innovation is the same in the public sector, or within organizations generally, as it is in the market sector. For example, major innovations will result in the creation of new branches within bureaus and sometimes in new bureaus, just as in the market sector, Schumpeter depicted the capitalist entrepreneur as setting up a new firm to launch his innovation. And in both sectors, successful innovations are presumably those that seem to meet a real social need or to be a correct response to an administrative problem. Although this aspect of innovation was neglected or perhaps disregarded by Schumpeter, it is explicit in the definition used by other Austrians of entrepreneurship as alertness to opportunities. In their view, the entrepreneur sees or grasps opportunities; he does not create them. To put it differently, consumers do not have preferences for goods that do not exist. Only in their response to new goods do they reveal whether they did or did not need that product. Similarly, citizens' demands that something be done about the environment, the high cost of government, inflation, or unemployment, to use the most obvious contemporary examples, imply that opportunities for entrepreneurship in the public sector are there to be grasped, but they do not reveal what kinds of new policies will be successful.

The concept of entrepreneurship is just as relevant to an understanding of the competition among corporate bureaus as it is to competition among public bureaus. But entrepreneurial competition in public and private bureaucracies does differ from that in the market in the way money is raised to finance innovations. The difference does not originate in the oft-noted fact that public bureaucrats do not finance innovation out of their own pockets; neither does the typical capitalist entrepreneur. As Schumpeter emphasized, the entrepreneur is not the risk taker; in his scheme, innovations are typically financed by bank credit.[8] Competition in a bureaucracy differs from competition in a market mainly in that, in a bureaucracy, the capital market is hierarchically organized. To characterize the bureaucratic process, imagine that the bureaucracy is made up of a number of levels. Bureaucrats at each level are subordinates who compete for resources allocated by their immediate superiors. In the public sector, the superiors (sponsors) are politicians (Ministers) who may also, for some purposes, be considered heads of bureaus, although formally, the heads are Deputy Ministers. In the private sector (corporations), the superiors (sponsors) are usually a company's board of directors.

The next section presents a simple model of the process of resource allocation within a hierarchy. For simplicity, we will describe only resource allocation by sponsors among bureaus. The same principles apply, however, to resource allocation by superiors to subordinates between any two hierarchical levels and, therefore, to resource allocation among branches within a bureau, as well as among bureaus.

6.4 The allocation of resources among bureaus

The principle by which sponsors allocate resources among bureaus is easy to state: In equilibrium, resources will be allocated among different bureaus in such a way that the benefit to sponsors is equalized at the margin. This principle is standard for rational allocation of resources among different uses. However, its application to resource allocation among bureaus – and therefore bureaucratic networks – is complicated by the fact that subordinates may use resources efficiently or inefficiently, and that sponsors cannot be assumed to know or be able to anticipate which strategy is being employed by a bureau's network in a given instance. (To the extent that sponsors can successfully police and discover inefficient behavior, subordinates will never be inefficient.) In the short run, we shall argue that bureaus can compete equally well for resources by being either efficient or inefficient. The allocation of resources is determined by each bureau's *capacity for selective behavior* – loosely speaking, by the strength of its networks. In the long run, however, a bureau cannot continue to be systematically inefficient over a large class of policies without discovery by the sponsors. It will then be in the interest of sponsors to reduce and possibly destroy that bureau's networks, and hence its capacity for selective behavior, by transferring and replacing key personnel or by reorganizing the bureau.

In both the short run and the long run, competition for resources among bureaus always equalizes the marginal capacity for selective behavior among bureaus. Alternatively, competition equalizes the price of informal services across bureaus. This means that, even if mobility of personnel among networks or bureaus is restricted or

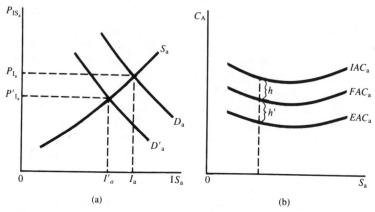

Figure 6.1.

blocked, reallocation ("movement") of resources among bureaus produces the same result of an equal price for informal services across
bureaus – a loose illustration of the factor–price equalization theorem.
This section is devoted to a description of this equilibrium. In the next
section, we shall show how it changes under Schumpeterian competition.

Consider Figure 6.1. Panel (a) depicts the supply and demand for
informal services in bureau A in producing one of that bureau's
policies (S_a). The equilibrium price paid for informal services there is
P_{I_a}. Panel (b) depicts the effect of the use of informal services on the
costs of producing that policy. If the services are used efficiently,
average costs are lowered from FAC_a to EAC_a by the amount h'; if
they are used inefficiently, costs are raised from FAC_a to IAC_a by the
amount h.

Figure 6.2 depicts the informal service market in a second bureau
(B). (There are many bureaus in a bureaucracy, all of which compete
for resources, but the general principle is illustrated by considering
only two bureaus.) In bureau B, as depicted, the initial equilibrium
price for informal services is P_{I_b}; it is lower than the price in bureau A.
The capacity for efficiency or inefficiency is therefore larger in B than
in A. Consequently, the distance k in Figure 6.2b is larger than h in
Figure 6.1b; similarly $k' > h'$. Bureaucrats in B will, therefore, want to
move to the network in A, as discussed in the last chapter; we now
assume that this movement is not possible.

Assume further that no specialized factors, apart from informal
services, are used in the production of the marginal policy in either A
or B. This assumption implies that the formal cost curve associated

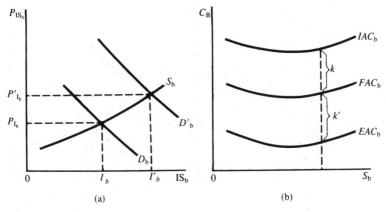

Figure 6.2.

with policy S_a – curve FAC_a in Figure 6.1 – would be unchanged if production of that policy were transferred to bureau B. Similarly, policy S_b, currently being produced in bureau B, could be reallocated to bureau A and produced with the same formal costs (FAC_b). To put it differently, the assumption of no specialized factors implies that the only factors that make costs lower or higher in one bureau as opposed to another are the price and quantity of informal services used in that policy, and whether these services are used efficiently or inefficiently. On this assumption, the analysis explains the size distribution of bureaus as well as the size distribution of networks, as we have already noted.

To proceed, suppose initially that D_a in Figure 6.1 and D_b in Figure 6.2 are the demand curves for informal services in their efficient uses, and that efficient strategies dominate inefficient strategies in both bureaus. If informal services are used efficiently in both bureaus, it follows that bureau B can produce S_b at lower costs than can A, because the price of informal services is lower in B than in A. And bureau B can produce policy S_a at lower costs than can bureau A. If production of S_a is transferred to bureau B and the price of informal services in B does not rise, or does not rise too much, costs of production will be lower there; sponsors will therefore wish to transfer the production of policy S_a to bureau B. Accordingly, the demand curve for informal services in B will shift to the right as policies and resources are transferred to that bureau, and the demand curve in A will shift to the left as sponsors reallocate policies and resources away from that bureau. This movement will continue until the price of informal services – and the marginal capacity to reduce the cost of policies through efficient behavior – are equalized across bureaus. In equilibrium, the demand curve facing bureau A will be D'_a, and that facing B will be D'_b. The prices for informal services in A will be P'_{I_a}, equal to P'_{I_b} in bureau B, and the marginal capacity for efficient behavior will be equal in both bureaus.

Of course, this analysis – and the determination of the equilibrium price of informal services – assumes a predetermined total of resources in the bureaucracy that is to be allocated among bureaus. But this poses no problem. An increase in the size of the bureaucracy would result in a higher price for informal services for all bureaus, and a contraction in its size would result in a lower price. The distribution of resources among bureaus would, however, be unaffected.

It might appear that we have also assumed that sponsors can directly observe the cost curves of different bureaus. For, if they could not, how can they transfer resources from bureaus with higher costs to those with lower costs, as we have assumed they do in the analysis above? Yet an assumption that average costs of policies are observable is obviously false. For most public bureaus – for example, external affairs, defense, finance, health, and welfare – even defining the output of the bureaus – let alone measuring it – presents insurmountable problems. So, whereas the total costs of the bureau's operations are easily known, costs per unit of output are unclear, and these costs cannot be assumed to be known to politicians.

Many writers have seized upon this unmeasurability of output in government bureaus as a characteristic that distinguishes them from private bureaus.[9] We suggest, however, that more careful analysis will show this to be incorrect. The performance of bureaus is difficult to measure in both public and private sectors. One reason is that the costs of the bureaucracy itself are difficult to measure. Consider a single-product firm using no specialized factors, where one can divide the total costs of production by the number of units produced to arrive at average costs. Even in this case, one does not, as Friedman has shown,[10] arrive at a measure of average costs. For if a firm in a competitive industry had average costs that exceeded the price of its product, that firm's equity would tend to be revalued downward in such a way as to make average costs equal to price. Similarly, if the firm's average costs were lower than its price, its equity would be revalued upward by the capital market until, again, average costs equaled price. So one cannot, in principle, obtain a statistical measure of the average costs of a firm that is independent of its revenues.

But this is still not the heart of the matter. To assess the productivity of a bureau within a private firm, the sponsor must know not the firm's average costs, which is just an average figure for all the bureaus in the bureaucracy, but the contribution of that bureau to the firm's profitability. And, as Alchian and Demsetz have emphasized,[11] a measure of the firm's overall profitability is of no help in assessing the contribution of a single bureau to that profit. In order to assess this, one needs a measure of the performance of that particular bureau. The extent to which the performance of the entire organization is or is not measurable is largely irrelevant.

There is, then, no simple measure of costs or efficiency in either private or public bureaus. In both cases, we suggest, performance evaluation is a complex matter involving the use of several indicators of performance and subjective judgment. Alternatively, from the point of view of the bureaus that are competing for resources from sponsors, the fact that there is no simple measure of efficiency implies that entrepreneurial competition will proceed along many different dimensions and take subtle forms.

What difference does all this make to our earlier conclusion that, when all subordinates behave efficiently, resources will tend to be allocated among bureaus in proportion to their capacity for selective behavior? Clearly, so long as the capacity for efficiency and the capacity to compete for resources in the ways suggested are the same, this result will continue to hold, even if the cost curves of bureaus themselves are not directly measurable. That is, if the sponsors' subjective ranking of bureaus according to their performance, although necessarily imperfect and subject to error, does in the long run correspond to their objective capacity for efficiency, then the allocation of resources will be the same as if the cost curves were directly measurable.[12] Now, the capacity for efficiency is determined by the price and quantity of informal services within bureaus. It seems reasonable to suggest that those bureaus whose internal and external networks are most extensive will not only be most efficient but will also have the best capacity to market their policies to sponsors, that is, to *appear* most efficient. When all bureaus are efficient, therefore, we conclude that the unmeasurability of cost curves does not introduce permanent distortions into the allocation of resources among bureaus from the sponsors' point of view.

Let us now consider a case in which informal services are used inefficiently in both bureaus. Let D_a now represent the initial demand curve for services in their inefficient instead of their efficient use, so that the initial price and quantity of informal services are the same as those depicted in Figure 6.1. The cost curve, however, is IAC_a rather than EAC_a. Similarly, let D_b in Figure 6.2 now represent the initial demand curve for services in their inefficient use, so that the initial equilibrium in the informal services market is also as depicted there. The associated cost curve will be IAC_b, and again, because the price of informal services is lower in B than in A, the distance k (or IAC_b − FAC_b) is greater than the distance h (or IAC_b − FAC_b), that is, the marginal capacity for inefficiency is greater in B than in A.

If costs were directly measurable, then, because actual costs are lower in A than in B, the sponsor would transfer resources from B to A. But costs are not measurable, and resources are allocated in proportion to the capacity of bureaus to market their policies to sponsors. Thus, although costs in B are higher than in A, bureaucrats in B – because the internal and external networks in that bureau are more comprehensive and work more smoothly (with lower transaction costs) than those in A – will be *more* successful than bureaucrats in A in marketing their policy to the sponsor. They will produce case studies showing the efficiency of their programs. They will have more contacts and will have accumulated more trust with bureaucrats in monitoring bureaus who are evaluating their programs on behalf of the sponsor, and the evaluation studies produced by these bureaus will also tend to document their efficiency. They may even use contacts in the media and other outside groups to show that any disquieting evidence that their programs are ineffective cannot withstand closer scrutiny. Consequently, the equilibrium when both bureaus are inefficient will be the same as when they are both efficient. Resources will be transferred *from A to B*, and this transfer will continue until the marginal capacity for inefficient behavior is equal in both bureaus.

In short, we suggest that bureaus can compete for more resources by using either efficient or inefficient strategies. The strategy actually chosen depends, for any policy, on the relative heights of the D_i and D_e curves displayed in Figure 3.2. If $D_i > D_e$, the most effective way for a bureau to obtain additional resources is to use inefficient rather than efficient strategies, and vice versa if $D_e > D_i$. But the efficiency – inefficiency decision is entirely separate from the question of resource allocation among bureaus.

To suggest that sponsors must be able to discover inefficient behavior through their own networks or through their ability to police subordinates is to misunderstand the nature of selective behavior. To the extent that sponsors can discover inefficiency in this way and penalize the bureau for it, the D_i curve tends to be below the D_e curve, and subordinates tend to be efficient rather than inefficient. (Recall from our discussion of Chapter 3 that the return to inefficiency depicted by the height of the D_i curve includes the risk of discovery and sanction by sponsors.) In short, the extent to which inefficiency is the most viable strategy for subordinates is the extent to which they can practice inefficiency and get away with it.

So, we conclude that competition for resources among bureaus results in resource allocation in proportion to their marginal capacity for selective behavior, or until there is an equal price for informal services throughout the bureaucracy. This implies that resources are allocated among bureaus so that their value *to the bureaucracy* is largest. If policing was costless, or if trust between sponsors and bureaucrats was perfect, or if cost curves were directly observable, or if superiors could never be entrapped, subordinates would always use their networks efficiently, and the allocation of resources among bureaus that results from competition would also optimize the value of resources to sponsors. But because policing is not costless, trust is not perfect, cost curves are not directly observable, and superiors can be entrapped even knowingly, although not wittingly, subordinates can sometimes obtain more resources by using inefficient rather than efficient behavior.

Does this mean that sponsors are helpless to counter the distortions in resource allocation caused by inefficient subordinates? It does not. It only means that *competition among bureaus* does not reveal to sponsors whether bureaus are efficient or inefficient; it reveals only the capacity for selective behavior. Inefficient behavior can, however, be controlled with other instruments. Direct policing is one such instrument, and we have already discussed its use in monitoring and limiting inefficiency. There is one further weapon that sponsors can use to counter suspected inefficiency; reduce or destroy a bureau's capacity for selective behavior by reorganizing it or taking whatever other steps are necessary to weaken or destroy its networks. We turn now to a discussion of that instrument.

The problem with reorganization from the sponsor's point of view is that it reduces the capacity of subordinates to be efficient as well as inefficient. As a result, we expect it to be used only when the sponsor suspects that a bureau's networks are more often used inefficiently than efficiently, so that their continued existence is detrimental to the achievement of his objectives. Sponsors cannot determine whether networks are used efficiently or inefficiently in any particular instance. But they will gain an impression of the extent to which a bureau is systematically efficient or inefficient over a large number of policies over a period of time. It is possible that this impression will be mistaken, and that a sponsor will continue to reward an inefficient bureau by giving it more resources, or penalize an efficient one by

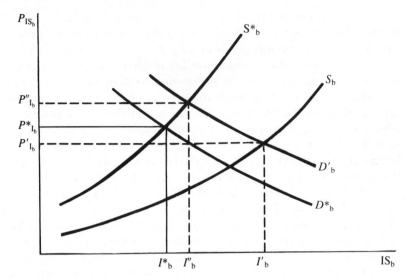

Figure 6.3.

reducing its capacity to compete by forcing it to reorganize. However, it does not seem likely that a bureau can continue to be inefficient year after year over a large number of policies without sponsors discovering this fact.

The analysis of reorganization is straightforward. What sponsors seek to achieve by reorganization is a change in the shape and location of a bureau's supply curve of informal services. If the purpose of the reorganization is to destroy networks, this can be analyzed with the help of Figure 6.3. Suppose that the reorganization is effected in bureau B, whose final equilibrium, shown in Figure 6.2, is reproduced in Figure 6.3: The supply curve is S_b, the demand curve D'_b, causing I'_b of informal services to be purchased at a price P'_{I_b}. The destruction of networks implies an upward shift of the supply curve to $S*_b$, leading to a new equilibrium price of P''_{I_b} on the assumption that the demand curve remains at D'_b. This, however, cannot be a position of final equilibrium, for P''_{I_b} is higher than the price of informal services prevailing elsewhere in the bureaucracy, namely, P'_{I_a} in bureau A (see Figure 6.1), equal to the initial price P'_{I_b} in Figure 6.3. Consequently, the demand curve will shift inward. Its networks reduced, bureau B no longer has the capacity to attract resources that it had before. The demand curve in bureau A (not depicted) will shift to the right, because its capacity to attract resources is now *relatively* greater. The final equilibrium price in bureau B (and in bureau A) will be $P^*_{I_b}$, between the initial price P'_{I_b} and the temporary equilibrium price P''_{I_b}. Consequently, as a result of the destruction of networks in bureau B, the price of informal services will be higher there and the quantity purchased smaller. The capacity of other bureaus for selective behavior is unchanged, but the demand for informal services in other bureaus (such as A) has increased. As a result, the price of informal services prevailing everywhere in the bureaucracy will be higher than the price that prevailed initially.

Whether bureau B will continue to be inefficient after the reorganization cannot be determined by this analysis. That will depend on the amount of trust that can be established between sponsors and bureaucrats after the reorganization versus the amount that will be accumulated among the bureaucrats. What the analysis does suggest is that, at a minimum, sponsors can expect to reduce the bureau's capacity to be either efficient or inefficient and its associated capacity to compete for resources.

There are other types of reorganization whose effects are entirely different from the one just discussed. In particular, bureaus will sometimes be reorganized to *increase* rather than decrease their capacity for selective behavior. Some examples of this type of reorganization will be presented in the next section. But in order to pave the way for that discussion, we must first return to the Schumpeterian notion of entrepreneurial capacity and show how our model provides a precise definition of this concept.

6.5   Entrepreneurial capacity

In the previous section, the equilibrium size distribution of networks, and consequently that of bureaus, was analyzed given the distribution of supply curves of informal services among bureaus. At the end of the section, this assumption was partially relaxed in that we allowed sponsors to affect these supply curves through reorganization. In this section, we go further in this direction and discuss other determinants of the supply of informal services. Some of these were introduced in Chapter 4; they are the factors that allow trust to be created or accumulated at relatively low costs in some bureaus and only at high costs in others. We reexamine these factors in the present context of the theory of the size distribution of bureaus. We then introduce another factor that was implicit in the analysis of Chapter 4 but not discussed, namely, the notion of entrepreneurial capacity.

Consider Figure 6.4, which depicts an initial equilibrium in the

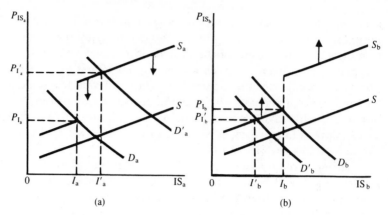

Figure 6.4.

informal services market in a bureaucracy composed, again for simplicity, of two bureaus, A and B. The initial equilibrium allocation of resources between them is given by the curve D_a for bureau A, at which the price paid for informal services is P_{I_a} and the quantity supplied is I_a, and D_b in bureau B, yielding I_b of informal services at a price paid equal to P_{I_b}. The price received by subordinates in both bureaus is not shown, to keep the diagrams simple, but can be obtained by subtracting transaction costs from the price paid. As drawn, the demand curves in both bureaus intersect the supply curves at truncation points. The reason for this construction is given below.

Let us now introduce opportunities for innovation. Opportunities, or at least the size of opportunities, are to a large extent unpredictable and cannot be a feature of equilibrium. If the opportunities are generated by research, then even if the amount of research going on in different bureaus is known, the occasions on which this research turns up an important innovation cannot be predicted. Similarly, although it may be known how rapidly the environment is changing, the occurrence of energy crises, wars, inflation, and other opportunities for bureaucratic innovation and growth obviously cannot be taken into account in the description of equilibrium.

However, although opportunities are necessarily unpredictable, the ability of bureaus to take advantage of opportunities – what we shall call *entrepreneurial capacity* – is something that our model can illuminate. We shall see that it is entrepreneurial capacity and not opportunities for innovation that explains the size distribution of bureaus.

Thus, assume that an opportunity for innovation arises in bureau A. As a result of this opportunity, the demand curve in A shifts to the right from D_a to D'_a. If the total budget of the bureaucracy is to remain fixed, the demand curve in B must shift inward to the left, as sponsors can give more resources to A only by taking them from B. The price paid for informal services therefore rises in A to P'_{I_a}, and the quantity of informal services demanded there rises to I'_a; in bureau B, P_{I_b} falls to P'_{I_b} and I_b to I'_b. For purposes of illustration, we assume that the increase in resources to A is sufficiently large that the superior of that bureau is forced to buy services from subordinates with whom he has accumulated little trust, namely those beyond the point of truncation in Figure 6.4. Consequently, most of the increase in demand results in an increase in the price paid for informal services, and the increase in the supply of informal services is relatively small.

The situation depicted in Figure 6.4 is clearly a disequilibrium one, because the prices paid and received for informal services in bureau A are higher than those in B. If the supply curves in A and B were to remain unchanged, over the long run resources would be transferred back to B until the initial equilibrium was restored. This may not happen, however, because the new opportunity has created a second disequilibrium. This is manifested in the fact that trust will tend to accumulate among bureaucrats in bureau A and to depreciate in bureau B. These accumulations and depreciations will shift the supply curves in both bureaus. This, in turn, will mean that the new *equilibrium* curves D_a and D_b will be different from those prevailing initially.

To understand this, recall Figure 4.1a, which we reproduce as Figure 6.5. This figure shows that as the number of transactions between two parties increases, the amount of trust between them also tends to increase (although, we suspect, at a diminishing rate). It follows that as the entrepreneur in bureau A begins to transact with subordinates beyond the point of truncation (in Figure 6.4) as a result of the increased amount of resources at his disposal, he will tend to build trust with them. Consequently, the supply curve gross-of-transaction costs will tend to fall, as shown by the arrow in Figure 6.4a. The new equilibrium price paid for informal services will be lower, the price received will be higher, and the quantity supplied will increase.

In bureau B, precisely the opposite will take place. The demand curve for informal services having fallen, $(I_b - I'_b)$ of services are no longer demanded. Initially, this will have little effect on the amount of trust between the head of the bureau and those subordinates whose services are no longer being required, but as the situation continues and no transactions occur between them, the trust previously accumulated will begin to depreciate for lack of use. Consequently, a point of

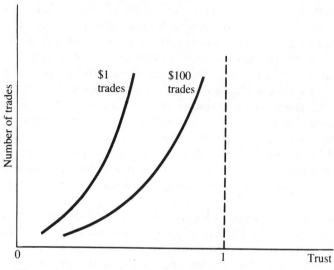

Figure 6.5.

truncation will occur at the new equilibrium. A difference will develop between the costs of transacting with those whose services have remained in demand versus those whose services have not.

In both bureaus, therefore, the point of truncation will tend to shift from the initial equilibrium intersection of the demand and supply curves to the new equilibrium. How far will transaction costs in A fall (how much trust will be developed) as a result of the increase in the frequency of transactions there, and how far will transaction costs in B rise (how much will trust tend to depreciate) as a result of the decrease in the frequency of transactions in that bureau? We have no name for the ability or capacity of an entrepreneur to build trust for a fixed size and number of transactions with a given set of individuals, but in the present context it seems appropriate to call this *entrepreneurial capacity*. For it is clear, from Figure 6.3 and its analysis, that in the long run, the larger this capacity, the more resources a bureau will be able to attract and hold. Consequently, this capacity plays the same role in our model as it does in the traditional analysis. Our analysis differs only in being more precise about the nature of entrepreneurial capacity. In our framework, it is the capacity to build a network, and to transact with its members at relatively low cost with a given amount of resources.

This notion is expressed formally in Figure 6.6, where entrepreneurial capacity is measured by the location of the curve depicting

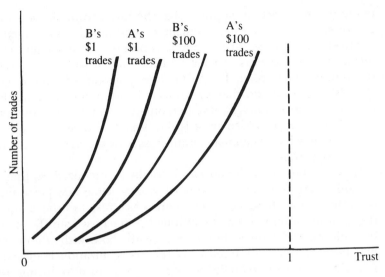

Figure 6.6.

the amount of trust accumulated as the number of transactions of a given size varies. As drawn, individual A has a greater entrepreneurial capacity than B, because the amount of trust he can accumulate is larger for transactions of a given size than it is for B.

In the traditional analysis, entrepreneurial capacity is an attribute of individuals. The reader, recalling the analysis of the production of trust in Chapter 4, will appreciate that this cannot be true in our model, except in a strictly limited sense. We showed there that trust is essentially a joint or collective asset – both A and (say) C will have to invest in order for the asset $_cT_a$, the amount by which C trusts A − to be produced; once produced, the asset is an asset of both A and C. So although one can speak of A's capacity to build trust with other individuals, it must be recognized that this capacity will differ, depending on the individuals with whom trust is being accumulated.

To put it differently, the amount of entrepreneurial capacity that any individual can exhibit depends on his social environment, the characteristics of backgrounds, social cleavages, and other indicators discussed in Chapter 4.[13] Entrepreneurial capacity will also be affected by contract law for individuals operating in markets and, for individuals in organizations, by the formal organization, rules, and procedures, which for each individual are relatively fixed.

The role of both of these factors may be illustrated by looking further at the effects of reorganizations, which we began examining in the previous section. Suppose that the formal organization and the personnel in a bureau have remained substantially unchanged for a relatively long period of time. As a consequence, stable and sharply differentiated patterns of trust and interaction will have developed throughout the bureau. Trust will be very strong between some individuals or groups and sharply truncated with others. Among the latter, casual interaction will have demonstrated a relatively low correlation coefficient on which trust is developed, and more frequent interaction may have been made unnecessary by the structure of tasks in the organization.

Now, suppose that the bureau is totally reorganized, so that some personnel are transferred to other bureaus, some new personnel are brought in, and those who remain are – as a result of the reorganization – brought into new and continued contact with a different set of individuals, and tend to lose contact with those with whom contact had been frequent or intense. If the reorganization is effective in reducing barriers to mobility among networks, or in reducing truncation and the importance of cliques that had developed as a result of truncation, new opportunities for entrepreneurial capacity are created. We expect the bureau to grow more rapidly than before the reorganization.

An illustration of exogenous events in stimulating entrepreneurial capacity is provided by the *displacement effects* analyzed by Peacock and Wiseman.[14] They observed that national crises – especially wars, but also severe depressions such as the Great Depression of the 1930s – tend to result in an initial upsurge of government spending to handle the crisis. Further, once the crisis has ended, the government sector does not return to its former size, but remains permanently above the level it would have reached on the basis of its previous trend. Peacock and Wiseman, however, do not provide a satisfactory theory of this phenomenon. They merely suggest that the population's willingness to be taxed or its tolerance for high taxes would have increased as a result of the high taxation experienced during the crisis. Our analysis does account for the existence of displacement effects in a more satisfactory way: The reorganization of the governmental bureaucracy in response to the crisis stimulates entrepreneurial capacity as new policies and programs are introduced. The ending of the crisis means further reorganization. Although some personnel will leave the bureaucracy entirely, others who have acquired experience and contacts in government during the crisis will remain and be transferred to other bureaus. As a consequence, the entire bureaucracy, and not merely the bureaus whose services were in high demand during the crisis, will tend to be reorganized, and new relationships, networks, and opportunities for entrepreneurial capacity will be stimulated throughout the bureaucracy. The bureaucracy will increase in size because of the stimulation to entrepreneurial capacity provided both by the crisis and the reorganization that follows.

At an even broader level, Mancur Olson's hypothesis that massive dislocations in a country's social structure – caused especially by wars and revolutions – tend to stimulate economic growth, and his extensive empirical evidence for that hypothesis, support the view that entrepreneurial capacity is stimulated by structural reorganization.[15] Olson's theoretical rationale for his evidence is the same as that suggested here: Growth is stimulated by the breakup of unions, cliques, and other restrictive forms of economic organization. Although he does not use the term *entrepreneurial capacity,* some such concept is clearly required to complete his model. After all, what else is restricted prior to the crisis and stimulated by the destruction of monopolistic organizations, and what accounts for the increase in growth rate, if not something like entrepreneurial capacity?

6.6   Restrictions on competition

Restrictions on bureaucratic competition may occur in several ways. They may be imposed on the bureaucracy by sponsors, or may be legally imposed, or may result from union restrictions or civil service rules. In the latter two categories are laws that prohibit the discharge of civil servants except under specific situations; that restrict patronage appointments; that require that departments hire a certain proportion of their employees from specified minority groups; state that jobs must be filled by persons with credentials that meet general civil service requirements and not merely departmental ones, and so on. Union restrictions specifying that tasks must be performed by those with formal qualifications to do the job have the same effect. All of these requirements restrict the free workings of competition and inhibit entrepreneurship within organizations.

Obviously, sponsors may sometimes be forced to accept restrictions on competition within the bureaucracy imposed by law, by unions, or by the civil service. Moreover, some restrictions undoubtedly arise as unintended by-products of measures introduced to police selective behavior, as analyzed in Chapter 3. But other restrictions are deliberately imposed by sponsors on the bureaucracy and require an explanation.

One example of such restrictions are "territorial" restrictions by which functions are assigned to particular bureaus in the public sector or to particular departments or divisions in private firms. To the extent that these quasi-property rights operate, other bureaus are prevented from seeking the resources allocated to these bureaus and competition appears to be muted.

Entrepreneurial competition, however, need not be lessened by such restrictions. Schumpeter, for example, thought that the prospect of at least a temporary monopoly was a necessary stimulus to innovation. Most contemporary evidence favors the *Schumpeterian hypothesis,* as it is now called, that the optimum market structure for maximizing entrepreneurial competition or innovative activity is not perfect competition but some degree of monopoly. On the basis of current evidence, the optimum market structure from this point of view is one of moderate concentration.[16] It is not hard to rationalize this evidence in theory, and some recent contributions do so in a very sophisticated way.[17]

The existence of quasi-property rights within organizations clearly fits into this framework. These rights do exist. They provide some stimulus to entrepreneurial activity in that bureaucrats will obtain the benefits from an increased allocation of resources to their bureau. But they are not inviolable. Responsibility for particular functions is sometimes shared among bureaus, with primary responsibility for functions shifting among them. And functions are often shifted from one bureau to another.[18]

However, we do not suggest that sponsors want to implement a structure that maximizes entrepreneurial competition within the bureaucracy. For one thing, sponsors impose many types of restrictions that limit rather than foster entrepreneurship, such as the common practice of limiting the relative rates of growth or decline of bureaus or departments.

The reasons for such restrictions are easily understood if we start from the Austrian proposition that the essence of competitive behavior is an alertness or willingness to grasp opportunities. Such opportunism[19] has many virtues from a social point of view, as economists have pointed out ever since the work of Adam Smith. However, their wisdom on this point has never been fully accepted. The reason, we believe, is that opportunism may be incompatible with accumulating and maintaining trust. The reader will recall from Chapter 4 that the accumulation of trust is based on foregoing of certain kinds of opportunities: Individual i accumulates the trust of another individual, j, in part by foregoing opportunities to benefit himself at j's expense. On the other hand, if i and j are competing for the same resources, then whatever i gets, j loses; *competition is precisely the reverse of trust accumulation.* So, the more i and j compete, the less they will be able to trust one another, as is clearly revealed by the secrecy and rivalry characteristic of such competition, which are inconsistent with the accumulation of trust between them. Consequently, potential entrepreneurs within the bureaucracy face a trade-off: The more entrepreneur i chooses to compete against j, the less j will trust him.

In the analysis of restrictions on competition originated by Alchian and Kessel,[20] discussed in the last chapter, an individual or organization faces two alternatives: the pursuit of pecuniary income, and perhaps amenities highly correlated with income such as prestige or power, and the pursuit of nonpecuniary goals such as leisure. Competition is associated with the first pursuit and the lack of competition with the second. In Alchian and Kessel's analysis, restrictions on competition, therefore, result in a substitution of nonpecuniary for pecuniary income.

In our model, pecuniary income and associated goals may be attained by two different strategies: by competing or by investing in trust. Consequently, increased restrictions on competition will have two effects: They will lead, as in the Alchian and Kessel analysis, to the substitution of nonpecuniary for pecuniary income, but they will also lead to the substitution of investment in trust for competition in the pursuit of pecuniary income.

Put differently, restrictions on competition foster cooperation rather than competition.[21] Where restrictions are imposed for this purpose by the sponsor, the increased pursuit of nonpecuniary goals such as leisure should be interpreted as the price of encouraging investment in trust. Similarly, if restrictions are reduced in order to promote competition, the volume of trust (or network capital) among bureaus that compete with each other more vigorously than before will tend to depreciate. This reduction in trust and in the associated capacity for supplying efficient informal services are the price of encouraging competition.

To sum up, changes in restrictions on or barriers to competition can be used by sponsors to promote behavior by bureaucrats (subordinates) that is more consonant with their aims. The full battery of instruments for superiors therefore comprises direct policing, reorganization, and alterations in the level of restrictions on competition among bureaus.

The most common way to reorganize and to change the level of restrictions is by manipulating the formal structure of the organization. Our model therefore implies a relationship between an organization's formal and informal structures (network or surrogate market for informal services) and hence between the formal structure and the allocation of resources among bureaus. In other words, even if property rights within bureaucracies are trust-based and not law-based, because the amount and distribution of trust (networks) depend on the organization's formal structure, so will the allocation of resources within bureaucracies.

In the special case in which transaction costs are zero, Coase[22] has shown that legal liability rules (formal structure) have no impact on the allocation of resources in marketlike transactions. Similarly, we can argue that if transaction costs within bureaucracies were zero, alterations in formal structures would have no effect on the allocation of resources among bureaus. One need not rely on Coase's reasoning to get this result. If transaction costs within bureaucracies were zero, there would be perfect trust throughout.[23] Changes in formal structures could obviously not alter the amount or distribution of trust and hence could not alter the allocation of resources among bureaus.

6.7   Conclusion

In this chapter, we have been concerned with entrepreneurial competition, or the competition for resources among bureaus, and the factors that determine how resources are allocated among bureaus by politicians. We showed first that this competition does not reduce the capacity of bureaus for inefficient behavior. It is the capacity for selective behavior, used efficiently or inefficiently, that determines the ability of bureaus to compete for resources. Hence, in equilibrium, resources are allocated so that the marginal capacity for selective behavior is equalized across bureaus.

We then described the forces that determine the capacity of bureaus to behave selectively, elaborating further on the analysis of trust accumulation in Chapter 4. This led to a definition of entrepreneurial capacity as the ability to accumulate trust or networks with given resources within a formal structure. We showed how variations in the formal structure (reorganizations) affected the ability of bureaucrats to compete for resources, and could therefore be used by politicians to change the allocation of resources among bureaus. Finally, we discussed the origin and nature of restrictions on entrepreneurial competition. We showed that the rationale for such restrictions – which are a universal and little understood feature of most organizations – is easily understood in the context of our model: They tend to promote trust and cooperation in organizations.

This chapter completes our theory of bureaucratic behavior. The

labeled *Parkinson's Law*. We try to show that there is a version of Parkinson's Law that makes good economic sense and should be relevant to understanding the behavior of bureaucrats in both public and private organizations.

7.2   Organizational structure and productivity

In this first application, we use our theory of bureaucracy to develop a set of testable hypotheses relating productivity and its growth rate to various aspects of organizational structure. The standard economic theory of the firm describes productivity as a function of technology and the quantity and quality of labor and capital inputs, and the growth rate of productivity as a function of the growth rate of these variables. The factor of organization is often mentioned, but no satisfactory theory exists that explains why some firms are better organized than others, or even what this means.

At the popular level, there is no shortage of answers to this question. There is, and perhaps always will be, a surfeit of books and articles on management techniques, guides to effective problem solving, managing human relations in organizations, and so on. But this literature is seldom given empirical content and has no predictive power.

Our own answer is that organizational structures differ in efficiency primarily because of differences among them in the amount and distribution of trust. The two key variables are the amounts of vertical trust and horizontal trust. The amount of vertical trust (T_V) determines the capacity for efficient behavior, that is, the size of the reduction in the firm's costs when selective behavior is efficient. The amount of horizontal trust (T_H) determines the capacity for inefficient behavior – the size of the increase in costs incurred as a result of inefficient behavior. Finally, as discussed in Chapter 3, the ratio T_V/T_H helps to determine (in addition to monitoring costs) whether selective behavior with respect to any particular policy is efficient or inefficient. Of course, over any class of policies, subordinates will sometimes be efficient and sometimes inefficient. Productivity figures are averages over policies, and "the" ratio T_V/T_H may also be interpreted as an average ratio that determines the *relative frequency* of efficient versus inefficient behavior. Productivity will be higher, *ceteris paribus*, the greater the capacity for efficient behavior, the smaller the capacity for inefficient behavior, and the greater the relative frequency of efficient versus inefficient behavior.

In part, the growth rate of productivity, as with conventional factors, tends to be related to the growth rates of these variables (positively related to the rate of growth of T_V and negatively related to the rate of growth of T_H). The growth rate of productivity will, however, also be related to the *levels* of T_V and T_H because, we suggest, a high level of T_V and a low level of T_H will tend to permit and indeed to be responsible for relatively rapid accumulation of the conventional variables – especially physical and human capital. The reason is that, as has been suggested elsewhere,[1] the main obstacle to employee investments in specific capital is the presence of high transactions costs or mistrust between employee and employer. If T_V is relatively large, so in general is the growth rate of specific human capital. Similarly, the growth rate of physical capital and the rate of adaptation to changes in technology depends on the capacity of the organization to absorb changes in machinery and methods for using it. The larger the amount of T_V, the greater the willingness of employees to absorb these changes. The smaller the amount of T_H, the smaller their capacity to disrupt or block them if they choose to do so.

In our view, these factors are genuine *causes* of growth in productivity. On the other hand, the standard approach, which analyzes growth as a result of X percent of change in capital, Y percent of change in technology, and so on, explains growth in the sense of breaking it up into its constituent parts. However, it does not give a very satisfying explanation of why some firms or countries are able to achieve those changes in capital and knowledge, whereas others are not.[2] Later in this chapter, we shall return to this point and illustrate it by looking at the causes, in our sense of this term, of the extremely rapid growth of Japanese firms since the World War II. Our present task is to develop the predictions of our model of organizational structure on productivity.

The basic problem with trust variables as indicators of productivity is that these variables are not easily measured. The amount or distribution of trust may not be unmeasurable in principle, but it is certainly difficult to imagine how it could be economically measured. However, we need not do so in order to construct adequate predictions or tests from the theory. For T_V and T_H are not exogenous, but are themselves dependent upon a number of factors. As we shall see, these factors include the amount of turnover, the amount of perquisites such as bonuses for subordinates, and the frequency of promotions. These variables are readily measurable. So, one way to test the theory is to correlate productivity – the basic dependent variable, measured by average productivity per man (Q), against those variables that affect the amount and distribution of trust.

To proceed, let us begin by recalling some aspects of the theory of trust initially developed in Chapter 4. We suggested there that trust is a capital good that is accumulated by individuals so that they can trade with each other over time, or in other circumstances where commitments are not self-enforcing. The anticipated net yield to investing in trust will be larger, the larger the anticipated gains from trade between them and the smaller the costs of developing trust between them. The amount of T_V that subordinates want to accumulate will therefore tend to be related to the values of these variables between subordinates and superiors. Similarly, the desired stock of T_H will be related to the values of these variables among subordinates.

To see how such variables as promotions and turnover affect these yields, let P be a subordinate's probability of promotion to the next level, X his probability of quitting, and S the probability that he will remain where he is. Only two of these three variables are independent, because $P + X + S = 1$. So, we can discuss only P (promotions) and X (turnover). Each of these variables is partly the outcome of organizational practices and policies, partly the result of the subordinate's own tastes, and partly outside the direct control of either. For example, the amount of turnover is the joint outcome of the organization's policy on salaries and other amenities, the subordinate's own propensity for mobility, and opportunities available elsewhere.

Consider promotions first. If the frequency of promotions is large, the net yield to forming trust with superiors – who either decide on promotions or whose reports will certainly influence that decision – obviously increases, and subordinates will tend to substitute investments in T_V for those in T_H. So, for this reason alone, $\partial T_V/\partial P > 0$, $\partial T_H/\partial P < 0$. Moreover, the larger the probability of promotion, the larger the anticipated frequency of interaction between a subordinate and his current superiors, and the smaller the anticipated frequency of interaction between him and those at his current level. These effects also imply $\partial T_V/\partial P > 0$ and $\partial T_H/\partial P < 0$.

The effects on behavior and productivity are as follows. Because $\partial T_V/\partial P > 0$, the capacity for efficient behavior is positively related to P, and because $\partial T_H/\partial P < 0$, the capacity for inefficient behavior is negatively related to P. In addition, these two effects unambiguously imply $\partial (T_V/T_H)/\partial P > 0$, so the frequency of efficient behavior is positively related and that of inefficient behavior negatively related to P.

On all these counts, promotions raise productivity, (Q), that is, $\partial Q/\partial P > 0$. But increasing the frequency of promotion is also costly. Promotion usually means a higher salary, and there are other costs as well. For example, if length of tenure at any one job is lower, average costs of on-the-job training will tend to be higher. There will also be extra administrative costs, including the obvious costs of deciding who gets promoted and who does not. For these and possibly other reasons, $\partial C/\partial P > 0$, where C stands for the costs of promotion. If we further assume either diminishing returns to the productivity-augmenting effect of promotion ($\partial^2 Q/\partial P^2 < 0$) or increasing marginal costs of training or administration ($\partial^2 Q/\partial P^2 > 0$), there is a unique optimal level of P, namely, where $\partial Q/\partial P = \partial C/\partial P$.

From this analysis, it follows that promotions will tend to be more frequent in some organizations than others for any one of three possible reasons: (i) the productivity benefits from promotions are higher; (ii) the costs of promotion are lower; or (iii) the level of promotions that maximizes profits (in the case of firms) is not optimal from the point of view of senior bureaucrats in the organization. The last possibility might arise, for example, if the organization is run by a clique who see a threat to their own position in the rapid promotion of certain junior employees. This is an example of selective inefficient behavior by superiors.

One factor that affects the availability or cost of promotions is the growth rate of demand for the organization's output. The cost of offering promotions is obviously smaller when demand and therefore the size of the organization is growing; the more rapid the rate of growth, the smaller the cost. Because an increase in the optimal level of promotions raises productivity, it follows that there is also a positive relationship between the growth rate of demand and productivity.

At high rates of growth, diminishing returns ($\partial^2 Q/\partial P^2 < 0$) imply that the productivity-augmenting effect of promotions becomes progressively smaller. At high rates of growth, moreover, other things – diminishing returns to labor and shortages of complementary factors or bottlenecks – that tend to have a negative impact on productivity may outweigh the positive effect of promotions. But the effect of an increased optimal level of promotions on productivity is always positive.

One interesting implication of the positive association between growth, promotions, and productivity is that average productivity may be procyclical, as suggested by the evidence – evidence that has puzzled economists since the 1930s.[3] Although a number of attempts have been made to reconcile the conventional theory of the firm with this evidence, we know of no other model that implies a strictly positive relationship between productivity and the growth of demand, and therefore *predicts* correctly that productivity would move procyclically.[4]

In addition, we believe that the explanation suggested by our model for the procyclical behavior of productivity is both simple and intuitively appealing: When demand is growing, prospects for promotion are relatively good, and employees will want to maintain or deepen their relationship with their superiors, who will be deciding whom to promote. On the other hand, when demand is falling, prospects for promotion are slim, and the yield to these investments is relatively small. Selective behavior therefore tends (other things equal) to be efficient in periods of growth and inefficient in periods of decline. This change in behavior, which will take place throughout the organization, is reflected in the figures on productivity.

The second variable that our theory points to as important in the explanation of productivity differences is the amount of perquisites (PE) or *perks*, as they are commonly referred to. As we use the term here, perks are payments to employees that are not part of the employees' contractual wage. They may be made in money (such as bonuses, merit pay, or expense accounts) or in kind (the fabled executive washroom privileges, the use of a company golf course, special housing or subsidized housing, medical plans, and so on).

In our theory, the function of perks is simple: They are a means (besides promotions and contractual salary increases) by which superiors may pay subordinates for informal services. Their chief virtue, from the superior's point of view, is that they are more flexible than changes in either contractual salary or formal status. One reason is that the superior need not be limited to criteria set up in the formal compensation scheme in order to find ways to compensate employees for informal services rendered. Second, perks may be relatively flexible in terms of timing: they can be given or taken away on relatively short notice, compared to contractually negotiated forms of compensation.

There are some perks that all employees are automatically entitled to (by custom or implicit contract), whereas others are given on a discretionary basis. Most empirical data do not distinguish discretionary from nondiscretionary perks. The important theoretical variable for our purposes is discretionary perks, and this points to a difficulty for statistical implementation of the theory. However, if the ratio of discretionary to nondiscretionary perks were approximately constant across firms, total perks could serve as an index of discretionary perks.[5] An increase in the amount of discretionary perks available to superiors reduces the transaction costs of making exchanges between superiors and subordinates. The cost of exchange being lower, more vertical exchanges will take place at every quantity of vertical trust. The net yield to T_V formation will fall, because perks are a substitute for T_V, that is, $\partial T_V/\partial PE > 0$, whereas the net yield to T_H will remain unchanged. Productivity will *increase* ($\partial Q/\partial PE > 0$) despite the fall in the net yield to T_V, since the costs of vertical transactions are lower, whereas those of horizontal exchange are unchanged. Subordinates will tend to substitute efficient for inefficient behavior, raising productivity.

Let us now turn to the effects of a third variable – turnover – on the incentives to accumulate T_V and T_H, and therefore on productivity. The relevant theoretical variable is a subordinate's subjective probability that he will leave the organization (X). So, both quits and firings are included. An increase in X reduces both the anticipated number of future trades between the subordinate and his superiors, and between him and other subordinates. So, the incentive to accumulate both T_V and T_H is diminished, that is, $\partial T_H/\partial X$ and $\partial T_V/\partial X$ are both negative, and the capacity for either efficient or inefficient behavior declines. Moreover, the anticipated number of horizontal and vertical trades will both be reduced by the same proportionate amount. So, T_H and T_V decline by the same proportion, the ratio T_V/T_H is unchanged, and the relative frequency of efficient versus inefficient behavior is unchanged.

Whether productivity is increased or reduced by an increase in turnover depends on whether selective behavior, as determined by other variables such as promotions and perks, is primarily efficient or inefficient. If T_V/T_H is high, so that selective behavior is primarily efficient and therefore productivity-enhancing, the reduced capacity for selective behavior as a result of the increased turnover means that productivity will fall, that is, $\partial Q/\partial X < 0$. Conversely, if T_V/T_H is low, selective behavior actually lowers productivity, and a reduction in the capacity for selective behavior will raise productivity, that is, $\partial Q/\partial X > 0$.

The major emphasis of the literature on turnover in labor economics is on the costs of turnover.[6] These include an increase in administration costs and in expenditures on training and a reduction in employee incentives to accumulate firm-specific capital. In that literature, turn-over always reduces productivity. If it could be prevented without cost, the optimum amount of turnover would always be zero. In our framework, as we have just seen, this is true only when T_V/T_H is high and selective behavior is efficient. If T_V/T_H is low, so that selective behavior is mostly inefficient, an increase in turnover raises productivity.

What accounts for this divergence between our approach and that taken in the literature on turnover? In that literature, as mentioned above, the basic difficulty with turnover is that it wastes or reduces the incentives to accumulate human capital that is specific to the firm. Because this human capital is always productivity-enhancing, an increase in turnover is always detrimental to productivity. Our theory of trust can be fitted into this framework, because trust is also a form of human capital. It is also specific not to the firm but to the individuals who jointly accumulate it. So, in this respect there is no essential difference between our model and that developed in the labor economics literature.

Our theory breaks with this literature in emphasizing that not all of the capital accumulated by subordinates is productivity-enhancing. The standard theory assumes that it is. So there is no place in the standard literature for cliques – networks that reduce the efficiency of the firm; for informal practices such as work-to-rule – deliberately slowing down an assembly line in order to raise piece rates; for stodgy middle-management groups who collude to alter or withhold information from upper management that does not reflect well on their performance; or for top management groups who sometimes see in fast-rising subordinates a potential threat to their position and collude to remove or reduce that threat. All of these examples of selective inefficiency are made possible only by investments in specific (trust) capital. And all reduce productivity. It may very well be that on balance, the negative contribution made to productivity and to its rate of growth by these capital investments is less than the positive contribution made by other investments in specific capital, including investments in T_V. However, we believe the opposite possibility should also be considered.

A related variable of interest is the amount of turnover at senior bureaucratic levels in the organization – turnover among superiors (X_A). This increase in turnover will lower the net yield from investing in T_V between superiors and subordinates, just as an increase in turnover among subordinates does, so that $\partial T_V / \partial X_A < 0$. On the other hand, the possibility of the formation of non-profit-maximizing cliques among superiors is also reduced, that is, $\partial T_{H_A} / \partial X_A < 0$. So, the analysis of turnover among superiors is the same as that for turnover among subordinates. The capacity for either efficient or inefficient selective behavior will be reduced, whereas the relative frequency of efficient and inefficient behaviors is unchanged. So, if behavior is primarily efficient, $\partial Q / \partial X_A < 0$, that is, the increase in turnover reduces productivity, and if behavior is mainly inefficient, $\partial Q / \partial X_A > 0$.

One interesting application of these results is to the hypothesis that instability in the political system – that is, frequent changes in government – implies that policy-making power will tend to fall into the hands of the bureaucracy. This hypothesis has been advanced to describe the behavior of the French bureaucracy under the Third and Fourth Republics.[7]

Our analysis says that the instability (high turnover) at the sponsor level will reduce the yield to and therefore the amount of trust between sponsors and bureaucrats. This implies a reduction both in the capacity for and frequency of efficient behavior by the bureaucracy. Second, the *relative* yield to network capital among bureaucrats will be larger (although the absolute yield is unchanged), and consequently the capacity for and frequency of inefficient behavior will increase. The policy-making power of the bureaucracy is not necessarily increased as a result, but the output of the public sector will reflect the interests of bureaucrats more, and those of sponsors less, than it would if the political system were more stable. So, our analysis agrees with the spirit of the hypothesis and differs from it mainly in being more precise.

A fifth variable is the numerical ratio of superiors to subordinates (the inverse of the span of control). This affects the amount and distribution of trust in two ways. First, if the ratio is high, the extent of monitoring of subordinates' activities is relatively large, and the yield to T_H formation will be relatively small because selectively inefficient behavior will rarely be profitable. In addition, if the ratio is high, the frequency of vertical contact and therefore the net yield to T_V formation is also high. So, an increase in the ratio of superiors to subordinates increases T_V and lowers T_H. Therefore, it increases the capacity for efficient behavior diminishes the capacity for inefficient behavior, and increases the relative frequency of efficient versus inefficient behavior.

These five variables – promotions, turnover among subordinates, turnover among sponsors, perks, and the ratio of superiors to subordinates – complete our basic theory of the relationship between organization structure and productivity. The next section illustrates this theory by looking at the role played by each of these variables in the large Japanese firm. We also use that illustration to expand on the theory itself in a number of ways. These are outlined at the beginning of the next section.

7.3   The Japanese firm: an ideal bureaucracy?

The results in the preceding section can be used to explain the functioning and notable success of the organizational structure of the

Table 7.1 *Millions of man-days lost in disputes*

	Japan	United States
1968	2.8	49.0
1969	3.6	42.9
1970	3.9	66.4
1971	6.0	47.6

Source: Data from Ministry of Labor, Year Book of Labor Statistics, 1972, p. 326, and Statistical Abstract of the United States, 1973, p. 251. Table reproduced with permission from N. Glazer, "Social and Cultural Factors in Japanese Economic Growth", in H. Patrick and H. Rosovsky, eds., *Asia's New Giant: How the Japanese Economy Works* (Brookings, 1976), p. 883. Copyright © 1976 by the Brookings Institution.

modern Japanese corporation. There are two reasons for looking at the organization of the Japanese firm. First, in many respects, it appears to be an ideal bureaucracy from the point of view of maximizing efficient behavior by subordinates, although this is hardly the way it is viewed in the literature. Many features of the Japanese system, especially the practice of lifetime employment and the importance of seniority in determining pay, tend to be viewed either as necessary adaptations to traditional culture[8] or as a forced response to tight labor market conditions.[9] Some writers recognize the efficiency of these practices[10] but miss the point that these factors are also important in determining the efficiency of Western firms, because they have no model of efficiency based on the possibility of vertical and horizontal exchanges.

Second, examination of the Japanese firm is a convenient way to illustrate some organizational practices that do act as important incentives to subordinates to accumulate T_V, but that are not easily quantifiable, and so were left out of our discussion above.

We begin by mentioning some aspects of the Japanese firm that illustrate the importance of T_V in raising productivity. A quantitative illustration is provided by the sets of figures in Table 7.1, which compare the millions of man-days lost in disputes in Japan and the United States over a recent period and are self-explanatory.

Another quantitative illustration of the role of T_V in raising productivity is given by M. Hashimoto, who emphasizes the importance of low transaction costs between employer and employee in the Japanese firm in allowing for wage adjustments over the course of the business cycle.[11] Wage decreases may reduce employee incentives to accumulate firm-specific capital. The difficulty stems "from the suspicion that one party is trying to appropriate a portion of the other party's return to the investment or from mutual mistrust in the accuracy of their measurements of productivity."[12] The greater the amount of T_V, the easier it is to negotiate changes in wages. The existence of low transaction costs in Japanese firms, however, is taken as given by the author, and their source is not analyzed. The model is supported by evidence from cross-sectional multiple regressions using the flexibility of wages (measured by the ratio of bonuses to earnings) as the dependent variable, and variables that are highly correlated with investments in specific capital, such as education, firm size, and years of experience in the current firm, as the independent variables.

These examples illustrate specific ways in which T_V raises productivity. They are far from exhaustive, and they do not provide a measure of its overall importance. Another way to appreciate how T_V increases productivity is to look at some of the institutions and practices by which investments in T_V are encouraged and investments in T_H discouraged in the Japanese firm. First, we shall discuss the variables mentioned in the preceding section and then turn to other factors that are less easy to quantify but may also be important.

The first variable is opportunities for promotion. We have no aggregate numbers, but Ronald Dore's comparison between the size of those opportunities in a Japanese electronics firm (Hitachi) and a British factory (English Electric) is instructive.[13] In the British firm, opportunities for promotion are very limited. In the Japanese firm, there are no less than 16 grades of personnel, ranging from managerial workers at the top level to three different kinds of "specially titled workers," three classes of foremen, and eight grades of "skilled workers and administration workers."[14] Even more interesting is the fact that, as Dore points out, "with the exception of those in the foreman category, these grades have *no functional connotation whatsoever*. Promotion from grade to grade simply means more status and a higher level of annual salary increases."[15] Because promotions have no functional connotation, the costs of this instrument as an incentive are considerably reduced. Thus, Dore continues,

[Promotion in the Japanese firm] is not, in other words, a seniority promotion system of the kind found in British railways or blast furnaces; promotion does not depend on someone retiring, leaving his shoes to be stepped into. It is a scale of "person-related payments" – as opposed to "job-related payments" – to use the everyday language of Japanese wage lore.[16]

What determines who gets promoted and who does not? Again, according to Dore, "The seniority principle requires that everybody goes up a notch every year of some minimal proportions. The merit assessment is two-fold – first in determining how quickly a man shall be promoted to the next highest grade; second, in determining whether his annual rise shall be higher, lower, or the same as, the average for workers in his grade."[17]

So, everyone who joins Hitachi can look forward to a continuous series of promotions if he stays with the firm – the seniority principle. On the other hand, merit plays a considerable role. For example, by the age of thirty-five, the fast-moving worker can be earning one and a half times as much as another worker of the same age and with the same experience.[18]

The effectiveness of the system in promoting T_V is obvious. And its effectiveness in minimizing T_H should not be discounted. On this point, the comments of another Western observer are revealing:

In Japan, once minimum standards of seniority and skill are met, worker competition often is decided by a worker's vertical relationship to his superiors. Great emphasis is placed on impressing superiors, on flattery, and behind-the-door deals. It increases friction among workers and makes it difficult to develop deep horizontal friendships and worker solidarity.[19]

Let us now turn to perquisites. In the Japanese firm there is, first of all, a system of bonus payments. Here, aggregate figures are available. These show that the ratio of special payments – mainly bonuses – to total cash earnings for workers in firms employing at least 30 workers is large and has been steadily increasing over the postwar period, ranging from 13.6 percent in 1951 to 26.6 percent in 1975.[20]

In addition to bonuses, which are discretionary, there is a wide range of social welfare expenditures, most of which are available to all employees (i.e., are nondiscretionary). These range from subsidized mortgages or rents to special hostels for employees, health care programs, and company-sponsored social facilities and trips. To illustrate the magnitude of the expenditures involved, Hitachi's total outlays on social welfare, *excluding* sick pay, amounted to 8.5 percent of total labor costs. The corresponding figures for English Electric were not available, but in another study of English firms, the median figure was 2.5 percent, *including* sick pay.[21]

In addition, there are the legendary Japanese expense accounts for those at senior levels and the system of lump-sum retirement gratuities (based on grade, length of service, and final salary). The importance of the latter is enhanced when one remembers that the typical age of "retirement" in Japan is fifty-five, and that after official retirement, many employees continue to work; either for their old firm (at a lower salary) or for one of its subsidiaries or subcontractors.

Turnover is also relatively low in the large Japanese firm, the system of employment often being referred to as *lifetime employment*. Workers cannot be *legally* dismissed in ordinary circumstances.[22] Comparative figures for the United States and Japan confirm that labor turnover for large firms in Japan is lower, mobility is smaller, and the average number of years of tenure on the current job is larger.[23] Figures on turnover at the sponsor level are not available, so far as we know, but one important related difference between boards of directors in Japan and those in Western countries is that in Japan, a very large percentage of directors arrive at that position after a lifetime of work in the firm.[24]

Many observers appear to believe that the large role played by seniority in the wage system of the Japanese firm is uneconomic. Yet if promotion opportunities were equally large, but based solely on merit rather than on a combination of merit and seniority, it is hard to imagine that turnover could be kept as low as it has been without paying significantly higher average wages. Otherwise, the initial losers in the promotion game would surely be tempted to go elsewhere.

Our fifth variable is the ratio of superiors to subordinates, or the density of supervision. Illustrative figures are again provided by the comparison between Hitachi and English Electric. At Hitachi, there is one supervisor for every 16 workers, whereas at English Electric, the ratio is 1 to 35.[25]

So, on all of these counts – promotions, turnover, perks, and density of supervision – the Japanese firm appears to provide much larger incentives to accumulate T_V and smaller incentives for T_H than its Western counterpart.

Let us now turn to other aspects of the Japanese system that affect the amount and distribution of trust. One aspect of Japanese industry with obvious consequences for the accumulation of T_H and T_V is the importance in Japan of the local or branch union, which normally is coterminous with the enterprise, as opposed to the more national craft or skill-based unions of most Western countries. Another is the practice of layoffs in the Japanese firm. Regular employees are rarely laid off in large firms;[26] when they are, they are still paid most of their salary during this period.[27] Finally, when layoffs occur, it is not only the workers at lower levels who are affected, but those at middle levels as well.[28] This practice is advantageous not only because it is seen to be fair, but also because it reduces the development of T_H among lower-level employees.

Other egalitarian aspects of the Japanese firm, with similar advantages, are these: (i) all employees are paid exactly the same way; (ii) there is usually only one company cafeteria for all employees, rather than separate ones for management and workers; and (iii) all personnel use the same sports clubs and vacation resorts.[29] Glazer sums up these aspects as follows:

It is not playing with words to say that rank and level are important [in the Japanese firm] and class is not. Class, after all, refers not to a number or a grade and the specific rewards attached to it; rather, it refers to a complex of key elements in life that serve to mark off one stratum from another. Obviously distinctions of rank can also be distinctions of class – as when, to reach a certain rank, a person must be of a certain social class, or when certain ranks form a new privileged class. In general, this is not the situation that prevails in the Japanese factory.[30]

Are all of these practices and the *nenko* wage system itself – as the system of lifetime employment, with promotion and wages depending on years of tenure, is sometimes called – merely a reflection of the Japanese social structure? Undoubtedly that plays an important role. However, it is hardly the whole story. First, the *nenko* system exists only in the large Japanese firm, and even there it is restricted to permanent employees. None of the practices described above are used in the smaller firms, where a large fraction of production still takes place in Japan. And they do not apply to temporary employees in the large firms. Second, although there is considerable disagreement over the origins of the *nenko* system – as mentioned above, some emphasize the role of traditional culture, whereas others give more weight to the role of labor market conditions – there seems to be basic agreement that the *nenko* practices were widely adopted only after World War II.[31]

If the *nenko* system is not just a reflection of social structure, would it operate equally well in other societies? This question is too complex to address here, but an answer should be forthcoming. The Japanese seem to be introducing their system elsewhere,[32] and it may also be spreading through imitation.

In any case, there is no doubt about the success of the system in Japan. Although average productivity levels there are still lower than in the United States, it is well to recall that in 1952 the GNP per capita in Japan was less than one-tenth that of the United States. From 1953 to 1972, productivity grew at an annual rate of 8.8 percent, so that by 1972 the GNP per capita was about one-half that of the United States.[33]

Many factors have contributed to that growth. But an explanation of growth solely in terms of conventional factors seems to miss the point. For example, one analysis[34] explains Japanese economic growth as the result of five factors. In order of importance, they are:

capital accumulation; advances in knowledge (catching up with Western technology); the achievement of economies of scale; a fourth factor called *components of labor input except education,* which include changes in hours worked and in the composition of the labor force by age and sex; and the reduction of the work force inefficiently used in agriculture.[35]

Now, these factors undoubtedly explain, or at least help to explain, how the Japanese economy grew so fast. That is the authors' stated purpose. But they do not explain *why* the Japanese economy grew so fast over this period or why the Indian economy, for example, did not. What enabled the Japanese to accumulate capital (nonresidential structures and equipment) throughout the postwar (1953–71) period at an average annual rate of 9.2 percent?[36] Why did the Japanese, and not the Indians, catch up to and surpass[37] Western technology?

The problem with standard explanations of growth is that, as Denison and Chung admit, "we found no way to bring into the measures [of labor inputs] the special talents of management, people, procedures for selecting them, or the effects of competition or its absence on management performance."[38] Nor, we might add, is there any way of bringing into them any other elements of the internal organization of firms or institutional or social structures. That, in our opinion, is missing a good deal, and in this application, we have tried to help fill the gap.

7.4   Income and price controls[39]

Our goal in this section is to show that the theory of selective behavior can explain two sets of facts that at first appear difficult to reconcile. First, over the last 25 years, governments in democratic countries have often resorted to wage and price controls as a way of dealing with inflation. This policy has been implemented with increasing frequency. Second, over the same 25 years, these controls have not generally been successful in stabilizing prices. Despite sometimes sympathetic and serious efforts by several policy analysts to show that controls have worked, the record seems clear: Controls have been ineffective in any but the shortest time frames in stabilizing prices.[40]

Why, then, do governing political parties, which must be assumed to be as rational as consumers and business entrepreneurs, use an instrument that does not seem capable of achieving its purpose? Two or three trials could be explained as searches to discover the value of a new policy tool or as errors, but after numerous unsuccessful attempts, a different explanation is required.

One explanation might be the desire of governing political parties to be reelected and therefore in the utility derived by a majority of citizens from wage and price control programs. There are three objections to this analysis. First, it implies that electorates never learn that the instrument does not deliver what it promises. If this assumption is rejected, then second, it could be assumed that electorates derive satisfaction from policy instruments themselves and not from the successful attainment of a goal. Although this possibility cannot be logically ruled out, it must be demonstrated, not assumed. Such a demonstration seems difficult to provide generally and for this case in particular.

Third, empirical evidence although not conclusive, does not indicate that electorates want controls, even if they want price stability. We have two kinds of evidence. The first is the outcome of elections. Two cases can be mentioned. In 1974, Edward Heath, then Prime Minister of the United Kingdom, called an early election to be given a mandate to pursue the program of controls that his government had earlier implemented; his party was defeated. Also in 1974, Pierre-Elliot Trudeau, Prime Minister of Canada, was reelected after campaigning strongly against wage and price controls in a campaign in which that was essentially the only issue discussed.[41] The second kind of evidence derives from a 1975 survey of the Canadian population. It indicates that whereas 86.9 percent stated that inflation was Canada's most important problem, only 38.4 percent favored income and price controls as a way of dealing with it.[42]

We therefore assume that the demand for income and price controls does not originate with the electorate. Then if, and to the extent that, politicians and political parties mirror the preferences of the electorate, the demand for controls does not originate there either. This assumption is stronger than we need, but because a weaker assumption would not materially affect our results, we adopt this strong version.

We suggest that the demand for controls originates in the bureaucracy. Interestingly, the analysis of the forces and mechanisms that bureaucrats set in motion to translate their notional demand for controls into an effective demand provides us with a partial hypothesis of why controls fail. We examine this below.

In the next subsection, we make explicit a distinction about the locus of macro-economic instability that is only implict in the literature. In Subsection 7.4.2, we suggest a hypothesis for the origin of the demand for controls, and in Subsection 7.4.3, we examine how bureaucrats elicit political support for them. In that subsection, we focus on the selective behavior of bureaucrats.

7.4.1   *The sources of economic instability*

We believe that macroeconomic instability, that is, variations around long-term trends in price, output, and employment levels, can originate either in the private or public sectors.

When the activities of governments are very limited, public budgets are small and variations in the supply of money are largely the result of accidental events, it is reasonable to impute instability in prices and employment to variations originating in the private sector: to such things as variations in gold discoveries, in the "animal spirits" of entrepreneurs, or, for smaller open economies, in "shocks" imparted by changes originating in other countries.

Once the size of public budgets becomes equal to 40 percent or more of the GNP, and once the money supply becomes managed, it is more difficult always to impute economic instability to agents in the private sector. Some instability can still originate there as a result of changes in the "animal spirits" of entrepreneurs, in substantial crop failures, in the formation of cartels in some basic commodity, in abrupt alterations in the birth rate, and so on, but changes in public expenditures, public revenues, money supply, the composition of the national debt, and so on can also cause instability. One must therefore adopt the view that the origin of macroeconomic instability is sometimes private and sometimes public.

This assumption, coupled with the recognition that governments and public bodies generally are endogenous to the socioeconomic system, mean that it is often difficult, at least when a new variation around a trend begins, to pinpoint the source of the instability. Only after the scope of the phenomenon is known can its origin be located. We suggest that whereas agents in the private sector do not care whether or not they are responsible for instability when it originates with them, agents in the public sector do not want to be blamed when they are responsible. This desire to avoid blame provides the initial fillip to a demand for controls.

7.4.2   *The demand for controls*

Suppose that an economy with more or less stable prices and full employment is subjected to an exogenous shock such as a large increase in the price of crude oil following the formation of a cartel by oil-producing countries, or a large increase in the price of grains following substantial crop failures. Assume, further, that these relative price increases are transformed into absolute price increases by an increase in the money supply. This last increase, in turn, could result from a belief by the authorities that the elasticity of demand for oil (or grain) at the price in the initial equilibrium is so small (in absolute terms) that expenditures on oil and oil-derived products (or grain and grain-derived products) would increase substantially and also that, in the short run at least, the prices of the goods from which demand expenditures are shifting are inflexible downward, so that without an increase in the money supply – to "validate" the higher price of oil (or grain) – unemployment would rise.

For a time after the exogenous shock and the increase in the money supply, it is possible for politicians, advised by bureaucrats, to believe that the inflation is the result of outside forces. However, as time passes and the effects of the exogenous shock recede, as the public forms expectations of further inflation, and as additional increases in the supply of money, again to forestall unemployment, validate inflationary expectations, it becomes more and more difficult to hold external forces responsible.

To put it differently, as time passes, the perceived responsibility for inflation shifts from outside forces to the government and, within the government, to the bureaucrats, who are asked by their superiors to account for the situation. In other words, the perceived origins of inflation shift from the private sector to the public sector. At the same time, bureaucrats are pressured to account for what is going on.

What are the consequences of this changing locus of responsibility for inflation? First and very important, it erodes the confidence and trust that politicians have in their advisors, the senior bureaucrats. Moreover, as inflation persists and accelerates, that erosion becomes more significant.[43] The reader will recall that the position of the D_e curve – the curve reflecting the demand for efficient services by superiors, in this case politicians – relative to the exogenously given D curve in Figure 3.2 (reproduced with slight modification as Figure 7.1) is determined by the amount of trust between superiors and subordinates. The consequence of inflation, and of transfer of responsibility from outside to inside forces that its continuation induces, is to shift the D_e curve leftward, as indicated by the arrows in the diagram.

In other words, beginning with an equilibrium situation in which efficient informal services are supplied, as indicated by the fact that the D_e curve is to the right of the D_i curve in Figure 7.1, the persistence of inflation, by eroding the trust between politicians and bureaucrats, shifts the D_e curve leftward. The shift may be large enough to induce a withdrawal of efficient services and the delivery of inefficient ones, but this need not be.

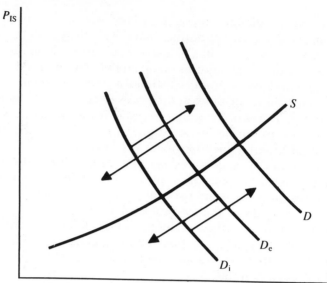

Figure 7.1.

However, inflation will also induce a rightward shift in D_i, so that eventually the type of informal services supplied will be reversed. Why will the D_i curve shift rightward? From the theory of selective behavior, we know that such a shift can result from changes in the amount of trust among bureaucrats and/or changes in the extent of policing.

In this case, the D_i curve will shift to the right as a result of an increase in trust among bureaucrats. How is this brought about? By a consideration of the "virtues" – from the point of view of bureaucrats – of income and price controls. From their point of view, there are two benefits. First, controls always fail; second, failure cannot be imputed to anyone in particular. For these reasons, they are wanted by bureaucrats. Let us look at each of these "virtues" in turn.

Bureaucrats know that controls will fail. It is because they can assume such failure that they want them. After controls have failed, it will be possible to demonstrate that the reason for failure, not only of controls but of all macro-economic management policies, lies not with them but with others.

This retransfer of responsibility for economic mismanagement that bureaucrats are able to achieve by implementing a policy doomed to failure rests on two grounds. First, control programs fail because they are always opposed by some groups in society. This is inevitable. Because the costs of policing a control scheme vary among groups and industries, it will be implemented with more vigor in some sectors than in others. Before implementation even begins, those groups that are more easily policed will oppose controls. As soon as opposition appears, it is easy for bureaucrats to blame these groups for the failure of controls and, by implication, for the results of general economic mismanagement.

The second ground is equally obvious. A control program is nothing but the substitution for numerous institutions that adjust more or less automatically to their environment by a subset of administrative rules. Because the set of all possible control rules must be very large, and because there is no known subset that dominates all others in efficiency and equity, the subset selected and implemented is bound to be largely arbitrary. It will therefore be easy for bureaucrats, as the failure of the control program becomes evident, to argue that although they favored controls, they did not favor the particular subset of rules chosen. Therefore, they will argue, they cannot be held responsible for the resulting fiasco.[44]

Bureaucrats favor controls for a second reason: Their implementation consists of substituting a policy whose outcome depends jointly on the inputs of several different groups (business, labor, federal and provincial governments), and in which the contribution of each group is difficult to ascertain and measure, for a policy whose responsibility lies with the government and hence with the bureaucracy. There are two consequences. First, responsibility for the outcome of the policy is never clear. Therefore, the possibilities for strategic behavior in taking credit for successes and shifting blame for failures are greatly increased. Second, because the contribution of each input is unclear, that is, because the marginal product or contribution is hard to measure, factors tend to be paid (judged) on an input measure such as administrative skills. It is therefore possible for the controls program to fail completely and at the same time for a number of bureaucrats to make their reputation on the basis of the skill with which they handled themselves, their smoothness in negotiating, their ability to sit through long, tedious meetings, and so on.

For these reasons, the prospect of income and price controls engenders a feeling of solidarity among all bureaucrats responsible for economic management. That leads to trust and to a rightward shift in the D_i curve. If inflation is severe enough, the D_i curve will cross over the D_e curve (which is moving leftward on its own), and instead of efficient services, subordinates will now supply inefficient ones.

7.4.3   *The acquiescence of politicians*

So far, we have assumed or established the following: The public and hence the politicians do not have a strong or even a weak demand for controls. Bureaucrats, however, want them, and if that demand becomes strong enough – portrayed by a crossover of the D_i and D_e curves in Figure 7.1 – they will attempt to get them.

How will they achieve this? The formal answer is that they will be inefficient. But what does that mean in this particular context? It means that bureaucrats will set out to convince their superiors, the politicians, that controls are needed. One need not assume Machiavellian behavior, deceit, or dishonesty on the part of bureaucrats, because in all likelihood the pursuit of their own interest will be, as it is for everyone else, veiled in a self-perception of dedication and altruism. However, discussion of controls, once absent, will become pervasive. The attacks on macroeconomic theory, hitherto veiled and disguised, will become overt and strident ("macroeconomic theory is outmoded and inapplicable"). Economists who had led a richly deserved life of obscurity in policy formation because they favored controls will be brought forward, read, and quoted.

The internal forecasts that had once shown that inflation was transitory and would shortly be under control will begin to emphasize that it cannot be licked except with drastic medicine. One will hear more and more frequently that if controls did not work at other times and places, it was because of "special" factors.

In addition, controls will now be advocated in public by many types of people. Often they are former bureaucrats or are close to bureaucratic circles. The political media[45] will also become clamorous for controls, not only editorially but through a systematic slanting of the news by reporters. Because the various protagonists are *mutatis mutandis* engaged in the same kind of activity, it may be instructive to focus on one of them to understand the behavior of all. We concentrate on the role of the political media (or media, for short), because there is much about them that is interesting in itself, but also because they are a fair reflection of the behavior of all nonbureaucratic protagonists.

Immediately before the introduction of income and price controls, there is a concerted demand for them by the media. This may appear to contradict the notion that the media are profit- or utility-maximizing organizations that present the news and even slant it according to the preference of the public, which we are assuming has a weak or even nonexistent demand for controls.

This contradiction is only apparent and is easily disposed of. The media must have access to information about what is going on, and much of that information is obtained from bureaucrats. Bureaucrats and media people, in other words, transact with each other in networks. Several aspects of this exchange relationship should be underlined. First, to reduce or even prevent opposition to a controls program, bureaucrats can threaten to withhold information about what is going on in the government. Second, bureaucrats can and usually will feed distorted information to the media, that is, information that exaggerates both the problem of inflation and the ability of controls to deal with it. Third, the media will promote controls only to the extent necessary to obtain from bureaucrats the information necessary to pursue their own affairs. Fourth, as soon as controls are announced, the media – like the bureaucrats – will begin to explain that the scheme implemented is not the one they favored. In other words, the media and the bureaucrats will drop their commitment to any controls program.

In this process, one can see why, in part, controls usually fail. Other things being equal, their success depends on public support. This support will, to some extent, be denied by the desire of bureaucrats and the political media to oversell the policy in the first place, and then to back off from it once implemented. In this connection, it is interesting to note that the success of controls during war-time is generally assumed. Why should that be? Partly, we conjecture, because either the threat or the existence of censorship causes bureaucrats and the media to resist opposition to a program once it has been implemented.

The above interpretation is not restricted to the media. It applies to all those in society who rely directly on information from bureaucrats for their business if they are consultants or advisors – as many former bureaucrats are – or for their status if they are economic forecasters. When bureaucrats are agitating for controls, some of these individuals will recommend them. It is the price they have to pay not to be cut off from the flow of information that ensures their livelihood or their social status in society. Once the program is implemented, they will have to change their minds and statements for the same reasons.

This network activity, that is, this trading in information between bureaucrats and the media, exists for one purpose: to pressure politicians to agree to controls program. All this activity – the manifestation of (selective) inefficient behavior – will convince some politicians that controls are needed, and they will then vote for them. Others may remain unconvinced, but entrapped by skilled and able bureaucrats, they will have no other alternative but to vote for the program.

This point is of some importance, because it reveals much about the nature of inefficient informal services. Those to whom these services are supplied may or may not be annoyed with them, may or may not resent their delivery, may or may not even be aware that they are inefficient. Inefficient services, as the foregoing application illustrates, further the interests of bureaucrats and may be strongly adverse to those of politicians. However, if the bureaucrats are successful, they will convince the politicians – possibly not all of them, but many – that by implementing a policy that is costing them votes, they are behaving as true statesmen. That is the real test of successful inefficient informal services.

7.5   Parkinson's Law[46]

> Work expands to fill the time available for its completion.
>
> *C. N. Parkinson*

The ideas of C. Northcote Parkinson[47] have had considerable influence on contemporary thinking about public administration. The Parkinsonian notion that bureaucrats can expand their empires and simultaneously reduce their workloads, so that the typical public servant heads a large staff that does very little, is probably the most popular view among ordinary citizens of what goes on in the public sector. Moreover, as suggested earlier (see especially Chapter 3), the dominant approach in public choice theory is the Parkinsonian idea that bureaucrats are essentially empire builders, or, in more precise language, that bureaucrats maximize the size of the bureau under their control. Other Parkinsonian notions have also been influential. For example, Milton Friedman has promoted the notion – which in the following discussion we label the *strong* version of Parkinson's Law – that when bureaucrats expand their empires, they actually *reduce* the level of services they provide to the public.[48] According to this version of the law, one can cut government spending and get more government services or, at worst (best?), suffer no reduction in them. In an age when both scholars and the general public are concerned that governments may have grown too large, Parkinson's Law certainly makes good reading.

For all these reasons, we thought it worthwhile to take this law seriously and to see if it were true that, as is sometimes asserted, it makes good economic sense as well.

Our argument is organized as follows. Because there are many different versions of Parkinson's Law, both in Parkinson and in interpretations of his writings, Subsection 7.5.1 presents several alternatives and then isolates one version that we believe captures the essence of Parkinsonian thinking. Previous explanations of the law are then discussed. We conclude that these explanations – Friedman's monopoly model of the public sector and Niskanen's model of a budget-maximizing bureau – cannot account for the law in a satisfactory way. In Subsection 7.5.2, we offer an explanation of Parkinson's Law based on our own model. Subsection 7.5.3 concludes this section.

7.5.1   The strong version of Parkinson's Law

There are a number of alternative hypotheses that have at one time or another been referred to as Parkinson's Law. To consider them, one must first divide the work force of any organization into two components: an administrative component (A) and a direct labor component (L). These two are commonly distinguished in the statistics on private firms. In government, the distinction is often less clear, but sometimes it is easy to make. For example, in military organizations, the L's are the ones who do the actual fighting; the A's are those who do not.

Three possible alternative Parkinsonian hypotheses with respect to the behavior of A have or can be made:

1. A expands by a constant factor over time.
2. The A/L ratio increases over time.
3. A sometimes expands at the same time that both L and the output of the organization decline.

The first version is roughly true, at least for recent history, but unremarkable. This is because L has also expanded, and the growth in administrators may be explained by the growth of the economy. The second version is more impressive and also true. However, there is evidence that the growth in the A/L ratio has been most pronounced in chemical and engineering firms, by all accounts among the most dynamic and technically progressive sectors of the economy.[49] Seen in this light, the standard explanation of the increase in A/L in terms of changes in the productivity of administrative tasks such as coordination appears more promising than one of bureaucratic expansionism.

The third hypothesis is the most striking, arguably the one that most captures the spirit of Parkinson's thought, and is henceforth our subject. It is the one we label the *strong* version of Parkinson's Law. Parkinson illustrated this hypothesis with the case of the British navy. He observed that from 1914 to 1928 the number of ships in the navy *declined* by 67 percent and the number of officers and men by 31.5 percent, but that the admiralty (the A's) *increased* over this period by 78 percent, providing, as Parkinson notes, "a magnificent navy on land."[50]

Later, in a series of lectures entitled *The Essential Parkinson,* Parkinson described another (so far as we know, fictitious) case of a German industrial group with a headquarters staff of 2,000 whose factories were destroyed by enemy action. However, he reports: "It was then discovered that the administrative staff were working just as hard as ever, even when there was nothing left to administer. Here was gratifying proof, in practice, of what I had described in theory."[51]

To Parkinson, a top-heavy administration is associated with the decline of an organization or a state. Looked at this way, the third hypothesis is an implication of the first combined with the occurrence of some other event that causes the organization to decline. Thus, if administrations are bound to multiply, and continue to do so even when there is an exogenous decline in the size of the direct labor force, we will observe an increase in A at the same time that both L and output decline.

This interpretation, in which bureaucracies play an essentially passive role in organizational decline (because all they do is to keep on multiplying, like rabbits), is not the only one possible. Milton Friedman has popularized an alternative explanation (first proposed by the physician Max Gammon) in which the growth of the bureaucracy is the cause of the organization's decline. Gammon summarizes his *theory of bureaucratic displacement* as follows:

In a bureaucratic system . . . increase in expenditure will be matched by fall in production. . . . Such systems will act rather like black holes in the economic universe, simultaneously sucking in resources, and shrinking in terms of "emitted" production.[52]

In Friedman's words, in a bureaucratic system, "useless work drives out useful work."[53]

As examples of this process, Friedman cites the British National Health Service over the period 1965–73, the subject of Gammon's analysis. He also refers to the U.S. educational system from 1971–72 to 1976–77 and, as a case of Parkinson's Law operating in reverse, New York City's government from 1976 to 1977, when cuts in the number of public employees allegedly resulted in better service.

We do not mention these examples as serious evidence of Parkinson's Law. The reason for citing them may become clearer if we consider black holes in physics. Physicists sometimes postulate the existence of a phenomenon not on the basis of observation, but because it is required by their theory. The existence of black holes was initially predicted by theoreticians but doubted by the majority of physicists. Subsequently, their existence was confirmed by observation, and this fact added to confidence in the entire theory.

Interpreted as an economic black hole, Parkinson's Law, far from being required by neoclassical economic theory, is inconsistent with it. The contradiction is easily established. The basic postulate of economic theory is that of rational behavior. Applied to the standard model of the production of goods and services, with two factors, labor and capital, this leads to the definition of a region of production that is uneconomic. In this region, the quantity of one factor, for example labor, is so large relative to that of the other factor, that it is counterproductive; its marginal productivity is negative. A reduction in labor will both lower costs (because labor has a positive price) and raise output. As long as the organization has a goal other than the growth of its own bureaucracy, no rational manager will continue to operate with these factor proportions. Hence the standard prediction that production in this region will never be observed.

In the strong version of Parkinson's Law, the administration has become so large relative to direct labor that the organization is operating in an uneconomic region. This is why officials who expand their staff find themselves working harder than ever to accomplish the same task as before. On these theoretical grounds, economists therefore deny the relevance of Parkinson's Law to private organizations.

With respect to public organizations, a curious phenomenon occurs. Many economists accept Parkinson-type observations on the flimsiest evidence as a standard example of how the public sector works. Friedman's article is a case in point.

The difference, it is said, is that the public sector is organized monopolistically, whereas the private sector is competitive. For purposes of argument, assume that this is the case: Democracies, despite appearances, are really dictatorships. *We would still not expect to observe the operation of Parkinson's Law.* The theorem that organizations do not operate in the unproductive region is a consequence not of competition but of rational behavior. Why would a dictator have so many administrators that they are counterproductive? If he were a perfect dictator, that is, if the public sector were operated entirely for his benefit, why should he both pay more for his administration and have fewer things accomplished for him than he could have otherwise?

We conclude that Friedman's government monopoly model cannot account for Parkinson's Law. Only if the monopoly power in the government is held entirely by the bureaucracy, and the bureaucracy cares only about its size, does this explanation of Parkinson's Law appear plausible. This is essentially Niskanen's model of bureaucracy, Can this model account for the strong version of Parkinson's Law? The model makes no distinction between administrators and direct

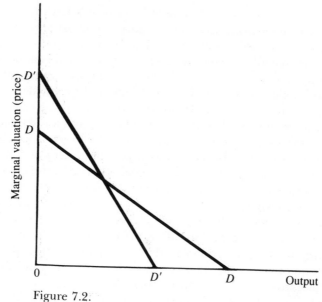

Figure 7.2.

labor. However, one can still ask whether, in that model, the size or budget of the bureau can increase at the same time that its output declines. This will indeed happen, Niskanen shows,[54] if the elasticity of demand for the bureau's services falls. In Figure 7.2 the demand curve for the bureau's output changes from DD to $D'D'$, implying that the bureau provides a smaller output of OD' in exchange for a larger budget.

However, although this prediction is plausible in theory, it does not account for Parkinson's observations. Recall that the period in which the number of ships and officers of the British navy declined, while the admiralty increased, is 1914–28. It can scarcely be argued that the need for defense and therefore for the navy was larger after the end of the war than at its inception. Yet this would have to be Niskanen's proposition.

7.5.2   Selective behavior and Parkinson's Law

To provide a rationale for the strong version of Parkinson's Law within our theory of selective behavior, we first divide the organization into three levels: sponsors, senior bureaucrats or heads of bureaus (the A's), and their subordinates (the L's).[55] Some of the L's will be members of networks operated by bureau heads. Of these, some will have performed informal services in the past without repayment, so that bureau heads will be indebted to them.

Let us now assume an exogenous fall in the demand for the organization's output, leading to a reduction in its work force. Assume also that administrators (the A's) have one characteristic not remarked by Parkinson, namely, that they possess skills that are organization-specific[56] and are consequently less likely to be dismissed when demand is low. In this case, cuts in the work force have to come from among the L's (not the A's) and would presumably be made throughout the organization on some formal basis, such as seniority.

Subordinates who are members of networks with senior bureaucrats will be aware that if they are dismissed, they will never be repaid for the trust they accumulated in the past and for the loans extended. To avoid taking a capital loss on the investment and debts, they will "call in their loans" and demand to be promoted.

The bureau head or other senior bureaucrats who are in debt to some L's must be aware that dismissal of L's on an objective basis would not discriminate between L's who are in their networks and those who are not. If they do not promote the L's in their network, they suffer a double loss: (i) they lose the L's in their network; and (ii) those who remain in the organization will observe that network membership did not, in the end, turn out to be worth much. Hence, the senior bureaucrats' future promises will be immediately discounted, and their ability to rebuild their networks permanently impaired, in the same way that anyone who fails to repay his obligations will have difficulty getting a loan in the future. Hence they too will want to promote the L's who are in their networks.

At the same time, promoting the L's to administrative levels increases the costs of output and presumably frustrates the wishes of the sponsor. The dilemma faced by senior bureaucrats is acute. They can maintain their networks with subordinates and their capacity to develop and use them only by being inefficient vis-à-vis their sponsor. If they are discovered, the value of their network connection with the sponsor will be reduced. In short, a decline in demand implies either that the trust between sponsors and senior bureaucrats and/or between senior bureaucrat and subordinates cannot be maintained at its former level. One or both must be reduced.

However unpleasant the dilemma from the bureau head's point of view, the strategy involved is clear. The bureau head will seek to promote the number of L's to A rank that minimizes his total capital loss.

Surprisingly, it is not possible to say whether the promotion of L's to A rank will be associated with efficient or inefficient strategies. If trust is relatively large between the sponsor and the senior bureaucrats, the sponsor will be willing to allow the promotion of many L's to A rank. Here, preserving the bureau head's networks, although increasing costs in the present, is in the sponsor's own long-run interest. In that case, promotion will be associated with efficient behavior. On the other hand, if trust is relatively large among senior bureaucrats and between them and subordinates, the former will want to promote many of the latter to A rank against the wishes of the sponsor. In that case, promotions will be associated with inefficient behavior.

Nor does the number promoted depend on monitoring costs. When these costs are low, the number promoted under an inefficient strategy will obviously be low (although it will not be zero unless policing costs are zero), because the bureau head will not be able to "take" a larger number of promotions for his subordinates without discovery by the sponsor. The number promoted under an efficient strategy will also be low, because if costs of policing are low, the sponsor will not wish to see a larger number promoted, and the bureau head in this case is pursuing his sponsor's interest.

In all cases, however, a decline in demand produces the same qualitative result: an absolute decline in the number of L's, a decline in output, and an absolute increase in the number of A's. That is the strong version of Parkinson's Law.

If our explanation seems contrived, we hasten to point out that our academic readers can probably see the process at work in their own organizations. We first observed it when we inquired why, given the strong demand for economics and business courses despite the general decline in enrollments, no funds were available to hire new staff in these departments. One reason suggested was that the departments where the demand was weakest had seen the writing on the wall and prematurely promoted their untenured professors to tenured positions to make them immune from dismissal.

Several other aspects of Parkinson's Law call for more detailed comment. As the above example illustrates, the process has a definite end point, namely, when all debts have been repaid. Unlike Parkinson's version, therefore, our model does not predict a continuous expansion in the A ranks, but rather a one-time increase. Second, the process need not be exactly as described above; it can take many alternative institutional forms. The basic problem is to discriminate between L's in networks and those not in networks; one obvious way to do this is to reorganize the bureau. Whatever other functions reorganization permits during a period of declining demand,[57] it permits this discrimination by creating new slots among the A's for L's from networks and eliminating the positions of other L's. Reorganization is thus, in part, a means of repaying debts and settling accounts within an organization.

Parkinson's example of the British navy is a simple case. The L's who were still alive after the war were presumably promoted to A rank not to avoid dismissal but as a reward for loyal service. The L ranks were not reexpanded to their former strength because so large a force was no longer required after the war. We would expect all military organizations to go through the same process, that is, to become top-heavy after a major war.

Most organizations reduce their output by dismissing their employees, not because of death in wartime. For them, the fuller analysis given here is necessary. If Parkinson's Law were considered relevant only for military organizations, that analysis would not be needed. But there is no reason why the strong version of the law should not apply to all organizations, private as well as public. Bureaucrats in private firms are no less concerned with accumulating networks than their public counterparts, because networks are no less important for obtaining power and influence over the policies of private organizations.

Parkinson himself was surprised at the reaction of businessmen to his theory:

I originally supposed that this administrative burden was peculiar to governments. It had existed, I knew, in the later phases of Roman and Moghul Empires. But the publication of *Parkinson's Law* brought me a stream of correspondence, much of it from people engaged in commerce and industry. Writing from a variety of offices in the most distant and various countries, they all wrote, in effect, "How did you come to know about *our* organization?"[58]

7.5.3 Conclusion

Our basic question in closing is this: If we have succeeded in rehabilitating Parkinson's Law, need we accept the policy implications drawn from it by Friedman and others? Can a cut in government spending possibly result in increased output?

If the argument of this section is correct, the answer is clearly no. A top-heavy administration, in our framework, is a symptom of decline, not its cause. We have shown that neither top-heavy administration nor decline need result from or be associated with bureaucratic expansionism. To put it differently, the cut in expenditures or the decline in demand results in a top-heavy administration, not the reverse. The reason is that bureaucrats will seek to implement cuts in ways that are least damaging to their long-run capacity for selective behavior.

CHAPTER 8

Concluding observations and agenda

8.1   Departures

In the preceding chapters, we presented a theory of bureaucracy that is logically self-contained and capable of predictions, and that, we believe, explains a good deal of bureaucratic conduct. Although it is also a fairly simple theory, it departs from accepted models and views of bureaucracy in a number of ways that we will mention as a way of summing up.

Our most important departure from conventional theories of bureaucracy is this: We do not model the relationship between superiors and subordinates as relations of authority, but instead as relations of exchange based on trust.[1] In our view, bureaucracies should, at least in part, be conceived as sets of networks (surrogate markets) in which bureaucrats – superiors and subordinates at all levels – trade with each other. It is true that when inefficient services are supplied by subordinates, superiors acquire something they do not want. However, this does not mean that the relationship is not one of exchange, any more than having a transmission replaced in a car that needs a new gasket implies that one has left the world of market exchange.

One could say that our analysis of network trading – in which buyers sometimes get what they want but at other times get something quite different – is applicable to a wide range of transactions in the markets of everyday life, where one generally gets what one expects, but sometimes not. The difference is that network trading is mainly supported by trust, whereas market trading is mainly supported by contracts. But that difference should not be exaggerated, because trust also plays a role in many market transactions.

There is some resemblance between the theory of selective behavior and recent theories of market adjustment that emphasize asymmetries in information between buyers and sellers, asymmetries that lead to adverse selection.[2] However, in those models, either the problem is resolved by an exogenous institutional device such as guarantees,

162

licenses, or liability laws in whose presence markets may function efficiently, or the problem remains unresolved and these markets "fail."

Our model pertains to organizations and not to market behavior. In it, the existence of trust – the analog of guarantees and liability laws in adverse selection models, except endogenized – does not imply that buyers always get what they want. The theory of selective behavior is concerned with situations in which buyers sometimes get what they want, but sometimes do not. We have suggested conditions, related to the distribution of trust and the cost of monitoring, under which each of these outcomes obtains. We suspect that analogous theorems could be developed for market trading.

We also depart from generally accepted models of bureaucracy in our treatment of competition. Other models of bureaucracy in the public sector are models of monopoly. There are models of bureaucracy in the private sector that stress competition within organizations, but they also use the principle of competition to argue that bureaucratic behavior is unimportant. We have sought to develop a model in which both competition and bureaucratic behavior play important roles in the outcome, because we are convinced that this model is an accurate reflection of the world. In it, competition does not eliminate selective behavior, whether efficient or inefficient. This accounts for our emphasis on and explanation of the use of direct monitoring, reorganization, and regulation by sponsors to combat inefficient behavior. We ask the reader who believes we are right in emphasizing competition, but who thinks that competition ensures that only efficiency rises to the top, to explain why sponsors in both public and private bureaucracies continually use these instruments. And we ask the reader who rejects our emphasis on competition, but believes in the importance of bureaucratic behavior, to explain the struggles for power and influence, shifting alliances, mobility, and the constant stream of proposals for new policies or modifications of old ones, all of which are characteristic of bureaucracy everywhere.

We depart from currently popular models in other ways. We do not suggest that subordinates are always inefficient, nor do we assume that they are always efficient. Bureaucrats behave selectively in our model, and we make no statements about absolute efficiency. At the same time, we do derive a set of testable hypotheses about the comparative efficiency or productivity of organizational structures or bureaus under different exogenous conditions such as rates of demand growth, turnover, and the extent of regulation.

The question of whether bureaucracies are efficient is separate and distinct from whether bureaucrats are efficient. The first question pertains to the allocation of resources (including income distribution, because redistribution is a government policy) and cannot be answered without a theory of demand for public and private policies and a theory of how supply and demand adjust to each other. The second question – the efficiency of bureaucrats – pertains to the relationship between superiors and subordinates. This is the question we have addressed in this book.

Finally, in contrast to conventional views, we do not propose one theory of bureaucracy in the public sector and another in the private sector. We have sought to demonstrate that the theory of bureaucracy suggested above is applicable to all bureaucracies, whether public or private.

Only time and detailed empirical work will tell us whether our approach is correct. Meanwhile, we hope that the applications of the model in Chapter 7 to economic issues in both private and public organizations indicate that our approach is worth pursuing further.

8.2   The way ahead

It is not our intention to outline the orientation of future research. Instead, we point to certain areas that should be understood more fully before we can analyze in a more general framework the central economic question of resource allocation.

We believe that the theory of bureaucratic conduct developed in the foregoing chapters is applicable to all bureaus and bureaucracies, whether public, private, or in that vast intermediate domain that is neither fully public or private and that some call the *voluntary sector*. If we have been successful, the next question is, are all bureaucrats, bureaus, and bureaucracies effectively competing against each other? To put it differently, what are the nature and properties of the relationship – and the competition, if that is the right term – between bureaus in the private, public, and voluntary sectors?

This is not an easy question to answer or one that, to our knowledge, has been addressed in the terms in which we conceive it. But it has received attention. The prevalent, largely implicit, view in neoclassical economics is that bureaucrats, bureaus, and bureaucracies in the public, private, and voluntary sectors are largely independent of each other. True, some links are made. Public bureaus will (should?) move in to repair market failures (including unemployment and inflation) and to correct the distribution of income. But otherwise, their lives are (should be?) separate.

At a less formal level, there is a neoclassical–neo-Marxist view that private bureaus and bureaucracies are usually successful in "capturing" public ones and inducing them to produce and supply the public policies that the private sector wants. At the limit – and in some models, the limit has been reached – public bureaus and bureaucracies are only the instruments of private ones, sometimes colluding in pressure groups and lobbies. These groups and lobbies extract from governments regulatory policies, direct changes in the distribution of wealth and income via programs favoring certain groups, unemployment via policies that prevent money wages from flexing downward, and inflation via policies that lead to deficit spending.

We will not pursue either of these views, which appear to be far removed from the forces underscored by neoclassical economics. We do not deny that these views contain some truth, but given the weakness of the theoretical infrastructure, we believe that only a few implications can ever be generated from them. We believe a new approach is needed and suggest that modeling the competition between bureaus in the private and public sectors is a possible starting point.

A second research area concerns the demand for public output. The theory of the demand for private output is well developed and credible. In contrast, when considering the demand for public output, one immediately encounters such abstractions as tax prices or pseudo prices, variables that, in general, have no empirical counterparts. Individuals pay taxes based on their incomes, purchases, assets, and so on, which are then used to produce public output, not to regulate demand. In other words, it is difficult to know when the price of international diplomacy or the price of family allowances has gone up or down for individual citizens. Clearly, a better paradigm is needed.

That, however, would be only an intermediate step. What we ultimately need is a theory of the interaction of supply and demand for private, public, and voluntary output. The dominant "auctioneer" model is a rough first approximation for the theory of private markets, but clearly it cannot fill even that almost pretheoretic role for adjustments in the public sector. Yet, that is often what we resort to in the literature of public choice.

This book presents a theory of supply in bureaucratic organizations – nothing more. Consequently, we have not and cannot address such central problems as why governmental or corporate bureaucracies grow or decline. Our theory of supply does contain elements of answers to such questions, but a theory of the relative growth of the public, private, and voluntary sectors will be able to weigh each element properly only when a good theory of demand and a theory of the interaction between supply and demand are available. Until that time, economists address such questions at their peril, for it is difficult, using only a fraction of a model, to avoid the pitfalls of ideology.

The use of the neoclassical paradigm to encompass more than market behavior is a formidable challenge that may never be successfully met. The problems to be resolved are numerous and important. But if the challenge is met, economists and others will understand better why resources are allocated as they are and will presumably be in a better position to recommend improvements.

Notes

Preface

1 A. Breton and R. Wintrobe, "The Equilibrium Size of a Budget-Maximizing Bureau: A Note on Niskanen's Theory of Bureaucracy," *Journal of Political Economy* (Vol. 83, No. 1, February 1975), pp. 195–207.
2 The rationale for and the use of these instruments was first discussed by Anthony Downs. See his *Inside Bureaucracy* (Boston: Little, Brown, 1967).
3 R. Wintrobe, *The Economics of Bureaucratic Organization* (Toronto: University of Toronto, unpublished doctoral dissertation, 1976). A revised version of Chapters 3 and 4 is contained in R. Wintrobe, "The Optimal Level of Bureaucratization Within a Firm," *Canadian Journal of Economics* (Vol. XV, No. 3, August 1982).
4 G. Tullock, *The Politics of Bureaucracy*. Washington, D.C.: Public Affairs Press, 1965.

1 Preliminary survey

1 F. H. Knight, *Risk, Uncertainty and Profit* (New York: Houghton Mifflin, 1921, reissued by The London School of Economics, 1948); R. H. Coase, "The Nature of the Firm," in K. E. Boulding and G. J. Stigler, eds., *Readings in Price Theory*, (Homewood, Ill.: Richard D. Irwin, 1952). See also H. A. Simon, *Administrative Behavior* (New York: Macmillan, 1957), and O. E. Williamson, *Markets and Hierarchies* (New York: Macmillan, 1975).
2 The *locus classicus* of this view is found in Chester I. Barnard, *The Functions of the Executive* (Cambridge, Mass.: Harvard University Press, 1938).
3 A representative sample of that literature includes R. Wilson, "The Theory of Syndicates," *Econometrica* (Vol. 36, No. 1, January 1968) pp. 119–32; M. Spence and R. Zeckhauser, "Insurance, Information, and Individual Action," *American Economic Review* (Vol. 61, No. 2, May 1971) pp. 380–7; S. A. Ross, "The Economic Theory of Agency: The Principal's Problem," *American Economic Review* (Vol. 63, No. 2, May 1973) pp. 134–9; and J. E. Stiglitz, "Incentives, Risk, and Information: Notes Toward a Theory of Hierarchy," *Bell Journal of Economics* (Vol. 6, No. 2, Autumn 1975), pp. 552–79.
4 K. J. Lancaster, "A New Approach to Consumer Theory," *Journal of Political Economy* (Vol. 74, No. 2, April 1966), pp. 132–57.

2 Public and private policies

1 The concept of production as related to public policies is analyzed in Section 2.4. For the present, the reader should assume that production is measured in terms of flows per time period.

2 P. A. Samuelson, "The Pure Theory of Public Expenditures," *Review of Economics and Statistics* (Vol. 36, No. 4, November 1954), p. 387.

3 Such a consideration had already governed Breton's approach in *The Economic Theory of Representative Government* (Chicago: Aldine, 1974), Chap. 2.

4 It is interesting to note that in the Toronto market, when a switchover from an all-sizes to a small-medium-large classification was initiated for rubber overshoes, it was done almost simultaneously by all suppliers, implying a virtually synchronous recognition of the altered character of the median buyer! The same thing happened when men's shirts became available in sleeve lengths of 30–32, 32–34, and so on, instead of the previously available classification of 30, 31, 32, and so on.

5 The literature on median voter (buyer) models is extensive. For a good survey, the reader is referred to W. H. Riker and P. C. Ordeshook, *Introduction to Positive Political Theory* (Englewood Cliffs, N.J., Prentice-Hall, 1973).

6 The degree of latitude that bureaucrats – public and private – have in combining characteristics is the subject of the next chapter.

7 See, for example, K. J. Lancaster, "A New Approach to Consumer Theory," *Journal of Political Economy* (Vol. 74, No. 2, April 1966), pp. 132–57, and G. S. Becker, "A Theory of the Allocation of Time," *Economic Journal* (Vol. 75, No. 299, September 1965), pp. 493–517. In that analysis, consumers effectively produce the commodities they consume, so that consumption and production are simultaneous. We are not offering a theory of demand in this book; consequently we follow the new approach in only a limited way.

8 E. H. Chamberlin, *The Theory of Monopolistic Competition*, 6th ed. (Cambridge, Mass.: Harvard University Press, 1950).

9 The literature on public bureaucrats is replete with lofty ideals deemed to be pursued in the public interest. The literature on the social responsibility of business indicates that the pursuit of the public good is a perquisite of corporate bureaucrats.

10 G. S. Becker, *The Economics of Discrimination* (Chicago: University of Chicago Press, 1957); A. A. Alchian and R. A. Kessel, "Competition, Monopoly, and the Pursuit of Pecuniary Gains," in H. G. Lewis, *Aspects of Labor Economics* (Princeton, N.J.: Princeton University Press, 1962); O. E. Williamson, "Managerial Discretion and Business Behavior," *American Economic Review* (Vol. 53, No. 5, December 1963), pp. 1032–57; J.-L. Migué and G. Bélanger, "Towards a General Theory of Managerial Discretion," *Public Choice* (Vol. 17, Spring 1974), pp. 27–43; and M. C. Jensen and W. H. Meckling, "Theory of the Firm: Managerial Behavior,

Agency Costs and Ownership Structure," *Journal of Financial Economics* (Vol. 3, No. 4, October 1976), pp. 305-60.

11 E. Hehner, "Growth of Discretions – Decline of Accountability" in W. D. K. Kernaghan, *Bureaucracy in Canadian Government* (Toronto: Methuen, 1969), p. 153. The broad generality of this question can be appreciated by considering the diversity of areas in which it has been diagnosed and analyzed. See, for example, T. J. Lowi, *The End of Liberalism; Ideology, Policy and the Crisis of Public Authority* (New York: Norton, 1969); G. Tullock, *The Logic of the Law* (New York: Basic Books, 1971); and I. Ehrlich and R. A. Posner, "An Economic Analysis of Legal Rulemaking," *The Journal of Legal Studies* (Vol. 3, No. 1, January 1974), pp. 257-86.

12 L. M. Bezeau, "Complexity as a Characteristic of Policies in Albert Breton's Economic Theory of Representative Government," *Public Choice* (Vol. 34, Issue 3-4, 1979), pp. 493-8.

13 A full-page advertisement by Bethlehem Steel in *The New York Times* notes that the U.S. government has guaranteed loans to private businesses of $360.5 billion. What is the true cost of such guarantees to the government, that is, by how much should the budget of the U.S. government be increased because of these loan guarantees? See *The New York Times*, Aug. 27, 1980.

14 One of the best examples of this is Galbraith's notion of *social balance*, which is based on definitions of public and private expenditures that are not commensurable, for the reasons given in the text. See J. K. Galbraith, *The Affluent Society* (Boston: Houghton Mifflin, 1958).

15 Earlier, Breton [see his "Economics of Representative Democracy" in *The Economics of Politics* (London: The Institute of Economic Affairs, 1978)] assumed that politicians and bureaucrats were usually complementary factors in producing S_i, namely, that $\partial^2 S_i / \partial T_p \partial T_B > 0$. That view was hasty. It derives from too narrow a stress on the decision-making process associated with designing policies and with parliamentary proceedings and neglects the subsequent implementation of producers.

16 R. E. Park, "The Possibility of a Social Welfare Function: Comment," *American Economic Review* (Vol. 57, No. 5, December 1967), pp. 1300-4.

17 We assume competition, but as will become clear in Chapter 4, we do not always assume perfect competition. See, in particular, our analysis of network truncation in that chapter.

18 We are not the first to assume an internal surrogate competitive market. Such an assumption is made explicitly, for example, by Alchian, Alchian and Demsetz, Leibenstein, Jensen, and Meckling and again recently by Fama. See A. A. Alchian, "Corporate Management and Property Rights" in H. Manne, ed., *Economic Policy and the Regulation of Securities* (Washington, D.C.: American Enterprise Institute, 1969), pp. 337-60, reprinted in E. G. Furubotn and S. Pejovich, *The Economics of Property Rights* (Cambridge, Mass.: Ballinger, 1974); A. A. Alchian and H. Demsetz, "Production, Information Costs, and Economic Organization," *American Economic Review* (Vol. 62, No. 5, December 1972), pp. 777-96; H.

Leibenstein, "Aspects of the X-Efficiency Theory of the Firm," *The Bell Journal of Economics* (Vol. 6, No. 2, Autumn 1975), pp. 580–606; M. C. Jensen and W. H. Meckling, "Theory of the Firm: Managerial Behavior, Agency Costs and Ownership Structure," *Journal of Financial Economics* (October 1976), pp. 305–60; and E. F. Fama, "Agency Problems and the Theory of the Firm," *Journal of Political Economy* (Vol. 88, No. 2, April 1980), pp. 288–307.

19 These services are defined at length in the next chapter.

20 Some characteristics are like public goods in that when they are produced by any one person or group, they are available in more or less the same quantity to all. We do not insist that such characteristics cannot serve as currency in surrogate markets. Because they will be expected freely if supplied, they cannot elicit the delivery of anything, not even informal labor services. Pure public-goods characteristics induce failure of surrogate markets, as of other competitive markets if exclusion cannot be implemented.

21 We assume that all supply functions, like demand functions, are utility-based.

22 W. A. Niskanen, Jr., *Bureaucracy and Representative Government* (Chicago: Aldine-Atherton, 1971).

23 J.-L. Migué and G. Bélanger, "Towards a General Theory of Managerial Discretion," *Public Choice* (Vol. 17, Spring 1974), pp. 27–43.

24 J. F. Chant and K. Acheson, "The Choice of Monetary Instruments and the Theory of Bureaucracy," *Public Choice* (Vol. 12, Spring 1972), pp. 13–34, and in many other papers using the same idea.

25 G. Tullock, *The Politics of Bureaucracy* (Washington, D.C.: Public Affairs Press, 1965).

26 It is also the case for Breton's work on treasuries. See "Modeling the Behaviour of Exchequers" in L. H. Officer and L. B. Smith, *Issues in Canadian Economics* (Toronto: McGraw-Hill Ryerson, 1974).

27 A good example is G. Brennan and J. M. Buchanan, "Towards a Tax Constitution for Leviathan," *Journal of Public Economics* (Vol. 8, No. 3, December 1977), pp. 255–74.

28 To understand the meaning of making specific assumptions about objectives for bureaucrats, the reader should imagine the state of demand theory if specific targets had been assumed for consumers.

3 A theory of selective behavior

1 A notable exception is Gordon Tullock. See his *The Politics of Bureaucracy* (Washington, D.C.: Public Affairs Press, 1965).

2 The extension to $N > 3$ levels is straightforward. We therefore restrict ourselves to three tiers without loss of generality.

3 W. A. Niskanen, Jr., *Bureaucracy and Representative Government* (Chicago: Aldine-Atherton, 1971).

4 M. Weber, *The Theory of Social and Economic Organization* (Edinburgh: W. Hodge, 1947).

5 P. Doeringer and M. Piore, *Internal Labor Markets and Manpower Analysis* (Lexington, Mass.: Heath, 1971).

6 See especially the symposium on the economics of internal organization in the *Bell Journal of Economics* (Vol. 6, Nos. 1 and 2, Spring and Autumn, 1975), pp. 163-278, 552-606.

7 The behavior of these formal cost curves, as well as their interrelationships to the cost curves associated with the informal structure, are examined in more detail in Section 3.6.

8 These codes, rules, and procedures are not givens, but evolve in unspecified ways. The argument in the paragraph is based on the documented view that formal structures almost always depart from optimum efficiency.

9 The ideas adumbrated in this paragraph are developed in Section 6.6, where the equilibrium amount of restrictions is determined.

10 The classic statement of that view is presented in Weber, *The Theory of Social and Economic Organization*. For summaries, see R. Bendix, "Bureaucracy," *International Encyclopedia of the Social Sciences*, Vol. 2 (New York: Macmillan and the Free Press, 1968). See also R. K. Merton, *Social Theory and Social Structure* (Glencoe, Ill.: Free Press, 1957), Chaps. 6 and 7; and T. Parsons, *The Structure of Social Action* (New York: McGraw-Hill, 1937), pp. 506ff.

11 Weber, *The Theory of Social and Economic Organization*, p. 311.

12 J. K. Galbraith, *The New Industrial State* (Boston: Houghton Mifflin, 1967). Ironically, although Galbraith asserts that "there is no name for all who participate in group decision-making or the organization which they form" and proposes "to call this organization the Technostructure" (p. 71), there can be no doubt that the view of corporate bureaucracy he (unknowingly?) espouses is Weberian.

13 Most of the academics we know are Weberians in evaluating the bureaucracy they work in – the university – in that efficiency is evaluated by reference to the quality of inputs (faculty and students). In recent years, however, without much regard for consistency, many have shifted tradition in the evaluation of governmental bureaus, although not of their own.

14 Statements that "knowledge is power" or that "information is power" are meaningless unless one also indicates how that knowledge or information is or can be used.

15 See M. Weber, "Parliament and Government in a Reconstructed Germany" in G. Roth and C. Wittick, eds., *Max Weber: Economy and Society*, Appendix II (Berkeley: University of California Press, 1978). The piece was originally published in S. Hellmann, ed., *Die Innere Politik* (Munich and Leipzig: Duncker and Humbolt, 1918).

16 The *Dictionnaire de Littré*, which stresses the origin of words as well as their ancient usages, notes that the word *bureaucrat* "se dit par ironie."

17 Bendix, "Bureaucracy," p. 206.

18 C. N. Parkinson, *Parkinson's Law and Other Studies in Administration* (Boston: Houghton Mifflin, 1962).

19 G. Tullock, *The Politics of Bureaucracy* (Washington, D.C.: Public Affairs Press, 1965).
20 J.-L. Migué and G. Bélanger, "Towards a General Theory of Managerial Discretion," *Public Choice* (Vol. 17, Spring, 1974), pp. 27–43.
21 W. A. Niskanen, *Bureaucracy and Representative Government* (Chicago: Aldine-Altherton, 1971), and "Bureaucrats and Politicians," *Journal of Law and Economics* (Vol. 18, No. 3, December 1975), pp. 617–44.
22 It would serve no purpose to list all contributions to this growing literature. Although a complete bibliography is not available, a good selection of relevant research up to 1965 can be found in A. Downs, *Inside Bureaucracy* (Boston: Little, Brown, 1967), pp. 281–6, and in the Migué-Bélanger and Niskanen papers for more recent work.
23 A. Breton and R. Wintrobe, "The Equilibrium Size of a Budget-maximizing Bureau: A Note on Niskanen's Theory of Bureaucracy," *Journal of Political Economy* (Vol. 83, No. 1, February 1975), pp. 195–207.
24 Niskanen, "Bureaucrats and Politicians," pp. 623–9.
25 To avoid undue repetition, we restrict our argument to the case of budget maximization. For the issue at hand, the imputation of other specific goals (see the discussion in Section 2.5) makes no difference.
26 In particular, neither the median-voter model – a hallmark of the Virginia school – developed by Bowen and Black [H. R. Bowen, "The Interpretation of Voting in the Allocation of Economic Resources," *Quarterly Journal of Economics* (Vol. 58, No. 1, November 1943), pp. 27–49 and D. Black, *The Theory of Committees and Elections* (Cambridge, Mass.: Cambridge University Press, 1958)]; nor the government-as-monopoly model of Knight [F. H. Knight, *The Ethics of Competition and Other Essays* (London: Allen and Unwin, 1935)]; nor the minimum-coalition model developed by Riker [W. H. Riker, *The Theory of Political Coalitions* (New Haven, Conn.: Yale University Press, 1962)]; nor the Downsian competition model [A. Downs, *An Economic Theory of Democracy* (New York: Harper & Row, 1957)]; nor the wealth-redistribution model of Director, Stigler, and Peltzman [(G. J. Stigler, "Director's Law of Public Income Redistribution," *The Journal of Law and Economics* (Vol. 13, No. 1, April 1970), pp. 1–10, "The Theory of Economic Regulation," *The Bell Journal of Economics and Management Science* (Vol. 2, No. 1, Spring 1971), pp. 3–21, and S. Peltzman, "The Growth of Government," *Journal of Law and Economics* (Vol. 23, No. 2, October 1980) pp. 209–79] can support that view of government and hence of bureaucracy.
27 See Breton and Wintrobe, "Budget-maximizing Bureau," pp. 198–9.
28 In his review of Niskanen's book, Earl Thompson [*Journal of Economic Literature* (Vol. 11, No. 3, September 1973), pp. 950–3] argued that the process assumed by Niskanen was "simply implausible" (p. 951). Without postulating a form of selective behavior, the activities required of bureaucrats to reverse the slope of cost curves are implausible.
29 Recall that in place of *budget*, such words as *discretion, secrecy,* and *prestige* can be substituted.

30 See H. Kaufman, *Are Government Organizations Immortal?* (Washington, D.C.: The Brookings Institution, 1977).

31 J. M. Buchanan and G. Tullock, "The Expanding Public Sector: Wagner Squared," *Public Choice* (Vol. 31, Fall 1977), pp. 147–50. See also G. Brennan and J. M. Buchanan, "Towards a Tax Constitution for Leviathan," *Journal of Public Economics* (Vol. 8, No. 3, December 1977), pp. 255–74 and T. E. Borcherding, *Budgets and Bureaucrats: The Sources of Government Growth* (Durham, N.C.: Duke University Press, 1977).

32 See, in particular, J. E. Meade, "Is 'The New Industrial State' Inevitable?" *Economic Journal* (Vol. 78, No. 310, June 1968), pp. 372–92, and R. M. Solow, "The New Industrial State or Son of Affluence," *The Public Interest* (No. 9, Fall 1967), pp. 100–8.

33 We are aware that all behavior is selective. That fact notwithstanding, we have opted for this expression to characterize bureaucratic behavior, because we have been unable to find a better one.

34 Tullock, *The Politics of Bureaucracy.*

35 O. E. Williamson, "Hierarchical Control and Optimum Firm Size," *Journal of Political Economy* (Vol. 75, No. 2, April 1967), pp. 123–38.

36 We return to this question, and to some of the problems it raises, in the next section. In particular, we address the problem of enforcement and information costs.

37 We address this question in Chapter 6.

38 Recently, one such glimpse, and one that is probably biased, was provided by J. P. Wright, *On a Clear Day You Can See General Motors* (New York: Avon Books, 1980).

39 See, among others, R. G. Evans, E. M. A. Parish, and F. Sully, "Medical Productivity, Scale Effects and Demand Generation," *Canadian Journal of Economics,* (Vol. 6, No. 3, August 1973), pp. 376–93. See also A. Blomquist, *The Health Care Business* (Vancouver: The Fraser Institute, 1979).

40 See, for example, C. R. Plott and M. E. Levine, "A Model of Agenda Influence on Committee Decisions," *American Economic Review* (Vol. 68, No. 1, March 1978), pp. 146–60; and T. Romer and H. Rosenthal, "Political Resource Allocation, Controlled Agendas, and the Status Quo," *Public Choice,* (Vol. 33, No. 4, 1978), pp. 27–43.

41 The interested reader is referred to the excellent account of the Coyne affair in R. Bothwell, I. Drummond, and J. English, *Canada Since 1945: Power, Politics, and Provincialism* (Toronto: University of Toronto Press, 1981), Chap. 23. See also P. C. Newman, *Renegade in Power: The Diefenbaker Years* (Toronto: McClelland and Stewart, Carleton Library Series No. 70, 1973), Chap. 21

42 Bothwell, Drummond, and English, *Canada since 1945,* pp. 223–4.

43 These tasks were fulfilled in the last chapter. See Sections 2.4 and 2.5.

44 We postpone our discussion of the position of the demand curve until Chapter 6.

45 Let S and B stand for sponsors and bureaucrats, respectively; B is then assumed to be somehow divided in two, B_1 and B_2. The assumption in

the text is that trust between S and B is zero, whereas that between B$_1$ and B$_2$ is positive.

46 The competitive paradigm cannot account for vindictive, vengeful, and retaliative behavior. That is one of its weaknesses. If we thought that bureaucratic relations were of that nature, we would have proceeded along different lines.

47 This point has already been made, although with a difference, by Kenneth Arrow. See *The Limits of Organization* (New York: Norton, 1974), p. 26.

48 They are more like transportation costs than a tax, because they measure a flow of real resources absorbed in the act of trading, just as a transportation cost measures real resources absorbed in the act of changing location.

49 For a derivation of certainty-equivalent utility functions, see M. Friedman and L. J. Savage, "The Utility Analysis of Choices Involving Risk," *The Journal of Political Economy* (Vol. 56, August 1948), pp. 279–304.

50 The reader should bear in mind that in bureaucracies, monitoring or policing is a bureaucratic activity and therefore subject to selective behavior. Because of this, the cost of policing can be higher or lower than the formal costs. See the discussion of the next section. The bureaucratic nature of monitoring has already been noted by Arrow, *The Limits of Organization*, p. 72.

51 The entire discussion could be based on an alterative diagram, such as Figure 3.2*. This diagram plots alternative supply curves instead of demand curves. As drawn, inefficient services would be supplied because the price received by subordinates for inefficient services (P_i) is larger than the price for efficient services (P_e). Measures of transaction costs can be read off as they were in Figure 3.2.

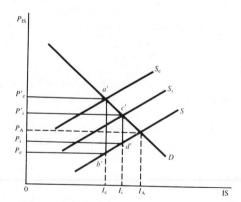

Figure 3.2*

52 We have derived a model of optimal policing for the simple case of the budget-maximizing bureau elsewhere. See Breton and Wintrobe, "Budget-maximizing Bureau," pp. 199–204. We generalize this approach here. For a general derivation of production function for monitoring, see G. S. Becker, "Crime and Punishment: An Economic Approach," *The Journal of Political Economy* (Vol. 76, No. 2, March–April 1968), pp. 169–217; also R. Wintrobe, "The Economics of Bureaucracy" (unpublished Ph.D. dissertation, University of Toronto, 1976).

53 See, in particular, H. Leibenstein, "Allocative Efficiency vs X-Efficiency," *American Economic Review* (Vol. 56, No. 3, June 1966), pp. 392–415; "Competition and X-Efficiency: Reply," *Journal of Political Economy*, (Vol. 81, No. 3, May–June 1973), pp. 765–77; "Aspects of the X-Efficiency Theory of the Firm," *Bell Journal of Economics* (Vol. 6, No. 2, Autumn 1975), pp. 580–606; and "X-Inefficiency Xists: Reply to an Xorcist," *American Economic Review* (Vol. 68, No. 1, March 1978), pp. 203–11.

54 These denials are somewhat weakened (negated?) by the use, in diagrams, of tangency solutions to describe individual adjustment. These solutions reflect nothing but maxima (assuming the appropriate second-order conditions that are also inscribed in all the relevant curves and diagrams) and hence rational behavior. See, in particular, the *Journal of Political Economy* and *Bell Journal of Economics* papers listed in the previous footnote.

55 Leibenstein, "Aspects of the X-Efficiency Theory," p. 582.

56 Leibenstein, "Competition and X-Efficiency," p. 766.

57 These "inert areas" describe nonadjustment by individuals. They exist only because the constraints are improperly specified. If adjustment (or transaction) costs were incorporated in them, as they should be, the inert areas would reduce to points, but not inert points.

58 Nowhere is this better stated than in the long paragraph in the middle of p. 771 of Leibenstein's reply to Schwartzman in the *Journal of Political Economy* (1973), although earlier in that same paper (p. 766) the notion of X-efficiency is associated with "efficiency in the engineering sense" – two views that are never reconciled.

59 Among many articles, see Leibenstein, "Allocative Efficiency vs X-Efficiency"; J. P. Shelton, "Allocative Efficiency vs 'X-Efficiency,'" *American Economic Review* (Vol. 57, No. 5, December 1967), pp. 1252–8; W. G. Sheppard, "The Elements of Market Structure," *Review of Economics and Statistics* (Vol. 54, No. 1, February 1972), pp. 25–37; and W. J. Primeaux, "An Assessment of X-Efficiency Gained through Competition," *Review of Economics and Statistics* (Vol. 59, No. 1, February 1977), pp. 105–7.

60 See note 58 for the reference.

61 Here we will not discuss whether X-inefficiency can persist in the long run under competitive conditions; our focus is the single bureau or firm. For a discussion of this question, see Chapter 6.

62 O. E. Williamson, *Markets and Hierarchies* (Glencoe, Ill.: Free Press, 1975).
63 O. E. Williamson, "Hierarchical Control and Optimum Firm Size," *Journal of Political Economy* (Vol. 75, No. 2, April 1967), pp. 123–38. The concept, which originated in the psychological literature [see F. C. Bartlett, *Remembering* (New York: Cambridge University Press, 1932], was first applied to bureaucracies by Tullock in *The Politics of Bureaucracy*.
64 Williamson, "Hierarchical Control."
65 R. Wilson, "Informational Economies of Scale," *Bell Journal of Economics* (Vol. 6, No. 1, Spring 1975), pp. 184–95.
66 The argument would be unaffected if that curve were falling throughout.
67 For a graphic derivation of these curves, the reader is referred to G. J. Stigler, *The Theory of Price*, (New York: Macmillan, 3rd ed. 1966), pp. 166–8.

4 The accumulation of trust

1 This assumption is further examined and supported in Section 4.6.
2 One of the best discussions of property rights and their relationship to markets is still J. H. Dales, *Pollution, Property and Prices* (Toronto: University of Toronto Press, 1968), Chap. 5.
3 Two notable exceptions are H. Demsetz, "Towards a Theory of Property Rights," *American Economic Review* (Vol. 57, No. 2, May 1967), pp. 347–59, and R. A. Posner, *Economic Analysis of Law*, 2nd ed. (Boston: Little, Brown, 1977).
4 The question implies that the only alternative to laws is trust. To simplify an already complicated analysis, we hold to this view throughout this book. (See, however, the discussion of Section 4.4). Our discussion of trust is unaffected by restricting the alternatives to two.
5 This circumstance has been analyzed in J. C. McManus, "The Costs of Alternative Economic Organizations," *Canadian Journal of Economics* (Vol. 8, No. 3, August 1975), pp. 334–50.
6 Posner's primitive society is characterized by many barter exchanges in the sense adopted here. In all cases, he notes the "lack of contract-enforcement mechanisms" (p. 9). See R. A. Posner, "A Theory of Primitive Society, with Special Reference to Primitive Law," *The Journal of Law and Economics* (Vol. 23, No. 1, April 1980), pp. 1–54.
7 The extension to other contexts and other types of transactions is generally simple and straightforward. The reader will be able to verify this for himself, and we shall indicate this below.
8 Arrow, *The Limits of Organization,* p. 23.
9 For example, A. M. Spence, *Market Signaling: Information Transfer in Hiring and Related Screening Processes* (Cambridge, Mass.: Harvard University Press, 1974). In addition to the two papers by Akerlof quoted below, see his "The Economics of 'Tagging' as Applied to the Optimal Income Tax, Welfare Programs, and Manpower Planning," *American Economic Review* (Vol. 68, No. 1, March 1978), pp. 8–19.

10 The use of indicators by anthropologists is also very much to the point of our argument. See, for example, E. Colson, *Tradition and Contract* (Chicago: Aldine, 1974).

11 Some individuals are not trustful personalities, whereas others are; this explains the different interpretations given and significance attached to different indicators or traits by different individuals. On some of the factors conditioning trustfulness, see E. H. Erikson, *Childhood and Society* (New York: Norton, 1963), and *Identity and the Life Cycle* (New York: Norton, 1980).

12 The possibility of sanctions further complicates A's communication problem. We address this question below.

13 No one has more powerfully analyzed that aspect of sanctions than Dostoyevsky. For dramatic treatments, the reader is directed especially to Raskolnikov in *Crime and Punishment* and to Dmitry Karamazov in *The Brothers Karamazov* (Penguin Classics, 1951 and 1958).

14 Another dimension is discussed immediately below.

15 H. G. Johnson, "An Economic Theory of Protectionism, Tariff Bargaining, and the Formation of Customs Unions," *Journal of Political Economy* (Vol. 73, No. 3, June 1965), pp. 256–83, and C. A. Cooper and B. F. Massell, "Toward a General Theory of Customs Unions for Developing Countries," *Journal of Political Economy* (Vol. 73, No. 5, October 1965), pp. 461–76.

16 By "net," we mean that the costs of setting up and operating the alternative system have been taken into account.

17 K. J. Arrow, "Political and Economic Evaluation of Social Effects and Externalities" in J. Margolis, ed., *The Analysis of Public Output* (New York: Columbia University Press and National Bureau of Economic Research, 1970), p. 20.

18 V. L. Smith, "The Primitive Hunter Culture, Pleistocene Extinction, and the Rise of Agriculture," *Journal of Political Economy* (Vol. 83, No. 4, August 1975), pp. 727–56.

19 O. E. Williamson, M. L. Wachter, and J. E. Harris, "Understanding the Employment Relation: The Analysis of Idiosyncratic Exchange," *Bell Journal of Economics* (Vol. 6, No. 1, Spring 1975), p. 270.

20 R. N. McKean, "Economics of Trust, Altruism, and Corporate Responsibility" in E. S. Phelps, ed., *Altruism, Morality and Economic Theory* (New York: Russell Sage Foundation, 1975).

21 M. Kurz, "Altruistic Equilibrium" in B. Belassa and R. Nelson, eds., *Economic Progress, Private Values, and Public Policy* (Amsterdam: North-Holland, 1977).

22 These assets are collective in the sense of being collectively owned, whether collectively or privately produced. On the private production of collective rules, see W. M. Landes and R. A. Posner, "Adjudication as a Private Good," *Journal of Legal Studies* (Vol. 8, No. 2, March 1979), pp. 235–84, as well as the other papers in that issue.

23 In two important papers, Akerlof has suggested models of how some

collective capital assets – social customs – can be maintained and destroyed. The models assume the prior existence of social customs and therefore are not helpful in understanding why they arise in the first place. See G. Akerlof, "The Economics of Caste and of the Rat Race and Other Woeful Tales," *Quarterly Journal of Economics* (Vol. 90, No. 4, November 1976), pp. 599–618; and "A Theory of Social Custom, of which Unemployment May Be One Consequence," *Quarterly Journal of Economics* (Vol. 94, No. 4, June 1980), pp. 749–76.

24 For reference to these last two, see G. S. Becker and G. J. Stigler, "Law Enforcement, Malfeasance, and Compensation of Enforcers," *Journal of Legal Studies* (Vol. 3, No. 1, January 1974), pp. 3, 4.

25 Arrow in "Political and Economic Evaluation," p. 20, and in *The Limits of Organization,* pp. 23 and 26, seems unable to decide whether trust can be augmented by purposive action by economic agents. Becker and Stigler, "Law Enforcement," p. 11, use a definition of trust that implies that it can be increased, but they do not develop the idea. Strangely enough, this is also true of Hirschman's treatment, even though his book contains a chapter on "A Theory of Loyalty." In any case, Hirschman uses his concept of loyalty to describe a relationship between an individual and an organization. Our notion of trust is different. See A. O. Hirschman, *Exit, Voice and Loyalty* (Cambridge, Mass.: Harvard University Press, 1970).

26 The standard reference is R. D. Luce and H. Raiffa, *Games and Decisions* (New York: Wiley, 1957). For recent expositions, see L. G. Telser, "A Theory of Self-Enforcing Agreements," *Journal of Business* (Vol. 53, No. 1, January 1980), pp. 27–44, and J. Hirshleifer, "Evolutionary Models in Economics and Law: Cooperation versus Conflict Strategies," *Research in Law and Economics* (forthcoming).

27 What we call cheating here and elsewhere in this discussion is the same as inefficient behavior in a bureaucratic context.

28 See M. R. Darby and E. Karni, "Free Competition and the Optimal Amount of Fraud," *Journal of Law and Economics* (Vol. 16, No. 1, April 1973), pp. 67–88.

29 Luce and Raiffa, *Games and Decisions.*

30 C. Geertz, "The Bazaar Economy: Information and Search in Peasant Marketing," *American Economic Review* (Vol. 68, No. 2, May 1978), pp. 28–32.

31 Posner, "A Theory of Primitive Society."

32 In Posner's model, legally enforceable property rights – until primitive law appears – are explicitly ruled out; in Geertz's model, that assumption is only implicit.

33 Posner is very careful not to commit himself irrevocably to the high-information-cost model, sensing problems. He seems to have chosen it *faute de mieux.* Posner, "A Theory of Primitive Society," p. 8.

34 Geertz, "The Bazaar Economy," p. 31; italics supplied.

35 Posner "A Theory of Primitive Society," p. 5.

36 As our discussion in section 4.3 on how trust is produced has made clear, that production poses an information problem; indeed, it poses a number

of information problems related to the interpretation by the borrower (B) of the signal given by the lender (A), an interpretation that is made more difficult by the existence of sanctions and the communication of the significance to be placed on their withdrawal. We suggest that the practices of clientization and of focused bargaining in bazaar economies, and of gift giving, overpayment of sellers, and generosity in primitive economies, can be interpreted as efforts to resolve the above-listed information problems in the process of producing a nonlegal support to property rights that will make trade possible.

37 Posner, "A Theory of Primitive Society," p. 10.

38 Posner, "A Theory of Primitive Society," p. 11.

39 C. M. Turnbull, *The Mountain People* (New York: Simon & Schuster, 1972).

40 For example, see Gary Becker's "A Theory of Social Interactions," *Journal of Political Economy* (Vol. 82, No. 6, November–December 1974), pp. 1063–94, and his "Altruism, Egoism, and Genetic Fitness," *Journal of Economic Literature* (Vol. 14, No. 3, September 1976), pp. 817–26. The confusion is important in that it results in falsely attributing a productivity to caring that is actually a yield on trust. Other writers, notably Arrow and McKean – though the latter asserts the opposite ("Economics of Trust," p. 29) – lump trust and altruism together and consider them as a single phenomenon. This view is partly responsible for the general belief that trust, like love or caring, must be treated as outside rational decision making. See K. J. Arrow, "Gifts and Exchanges," *Philosophy and Public Affairs* (Vol. 1, No. 4, Summer 1974), reprinted in Phelps, ed., *Altruism, Morality and Economic Theory*, and McKean, "Economics of Trust." The nature of the problem is discussed in R. S. Wintrobe, "It Pays to Do Good, But Not to Do More Good Than It Pays: A Note on the Survival of Altruism," *Journal of Economic Behaviour and Organization*, forthcoming.

41 A. Breton and R. Wintrobe, "A Theory of 'Moral' Suasion," *The Canadian Journal of Economics* (Vol. 11, No. 2, May 1978), p. 210–19.

42 H. Heclo, *A Government of Strangers* (Washington, D.C.: The Brookings Institution, 1977), and H. Heclo and A. Wildavsky, *The Private Government of Public Money* (London: Macmillan, 1974).

43 Although the language is different and no theory of "social collusions" (networks) is offered, the role played by such rules in P. A. Samuelson, "An Exact Consumption-Loan Model of Interest with or without the Social Contrivance of Money" [in J. E. Stiglitz, ed., *The Collected Scientific Papers of Paul A. Samuelson* (Cambridge, Mass.: MIT Press, 1966), Vol. 1, pp. 232–4] is the same as it is here, although in a slightly different context.

44 See J. Landa, *The Economics of the Ethnically-Homogeneous Chinese Middleman Group: A Property Rights-Public Choice Approach* (unpublished Ph.D. dissertation, Blacksburg, Va.: Virginia Polytechnic Institute and State University, June 1978).

45 R. Breton and D. Stasiulis, "Linguistic Boundaries and the Cohesion of Canada" in R. Breton, J. G. Reitz, and V. Valentine, *Cultural Boundaries and the Cohesion of Canada* (Montreal: Institute for Research on Public

Policy, 1980), and A. Breton and R. Breton, *Why Disunity? An Analysis of Linguistic and Regional Cleavages in Canada* (Montreal: Institute for Research on Public Policy, 1980).

46 K. J. Arrow, "Models of Job Discrimination" in A. H. Pascal, ed., *Racial Discrimination in Economic Life* (Lexington, Mass.: Heath, 1972); E. S. Phelps, "The Statistical Theory of Racism and Sexism," *American Economic Review* (Vol. 62, No. 4, September 1972), pp. 659–61.

47 M. D. Sahlins, "On the Sociology of Primitive Exchange" in M. Banton, ed., *The Relevance of Models for Social Anthropology* (London: Tavistock, 1965).

48 O. E. Williamson, *Corporate Control and Business Behavior* (Englewood Cliffs, N.J.: Prentice-Hall, 1970).

49 For a good analysis of how recruitment into Canada's federal bureaucracy was affected by the Public Service Act and how truncation was reduced by the virtual elimination of francophones, see C. Beattie, J. Désy, and S. Longstaff, *Bureaucratic Careers: Anglophones and Francophones in the Canadian Public Service,* (Ottawa: Information Canada, 1972).

50 J. Landa, "A Theory of the Ethnically Homogeneous Middleman Group: An Institutional Alternative to Contract Law," *Journal of Legal Studies* (Vol. 10, No. 2, June 1981), pp. 349–62.

51 K. J. Arrow, "Political and Economic Evaluation of Social Effects and Externalities" in Margolis, *The Analysis of Public Output,* p. 15.

52 Geertz, "The Bazaar Economy," p. 30.

53 Williamson, Wachter, and Harris, "Understanding the Employment Relation," pp. 258–60.

5 The compensation of bureaucrats

1 R. Marris, "Is the Corporate Economy a Corporate State?", *American Economic Review* (Vol. 62, No. 2, May 1972), pp. 103–15.

2 A. A. Alchian, "Corporate Management and Property Rights" in H. Manne, ed., *Economic Policy and the Regulation of Corporate Securities* (Washington, D.C.: American Enterprise Institute, 1969); E. F. Fama, "Agency Problems and the Theory of the Firm," *Journal of Political Economy* (Vol. 88, No. 2, April 1980), pp. 288–307.

3 See W. A. Niskanen, Jr., "The Peculiar Economics of Bureaucracy," *American Economic Review* (Vol. 58, No. 2, May 1968), pp. 293–305; *Bureaucracy and Representative Government* (Chicago: Aldine-Atherton, 1971), *Bureaucracy: Servant or Master?* (Hobart Paper No. 5, London: Institute of Economic Affairs, 1973); "Bureaucrats and Politicians," *Journal of Law and Economics* (Vol. 18, No. 3, December 1975), pp. 617–43. This assumption seems to have been modified somewhat in Niskanen's more recent writing. See "Competition Among Government Bureaus" in *The Economics of Politics,* (Reading No. 18, London: Institute of Economic Affairs, 1978).

4 J. Migué and G. Bélanger, "Towards a General Theory of Managerial Discretion," *Public Choice* (Vol. 17, Spring 1974), pp. 27–43.

5 J. F. Chant and K. Acheson, "Bureaucratic Theory and the Choice of Central Bank Goals: The Case of the Bank of Canada," *Journal of Money, Credit, and Banking* (Vol. 5, No. 2, May 1973), pp. 637–55.

6 Alchian, "Corporate Management and Property Rights."

7 M. Friedman, "Gammon's Black Holes," *Newsweek* (November 7, 1977).

8 A. Downs, *Inside Bureaucracy* (Boston: Little, Brown, 1967).

9 See J. R. Hicks, "Annual Survey of Economic Theory: The Theory of Monopoly," reprinted in G. J. Stigler and K. E. Boulding, *Readings in Price Theory* (Homewood, Ill.: Irwin, 1952), where one can read the often-quoted sentence, "the best of all monopoly profits is a quiet life" (p. 369).

10 T. E. Borcherding, "Towards a Positive Theory of Public Sector Supply Arrangements" (Vancouver, B.C.: Simon Fraser University: Department of Economics and Commerce Discussion Paper Series).

11 A. A. Berle, Jr., and G. C. Means, *The Modern Corporation and Private Property* (New York: Macmillan, 1934).

12 J. K. Galbraith, *The New Industrial State* (Boston: Houghton Mifflin, 1967).

13 Alchian, "Corporate Management and Property Rights."

14 Borcherding, "Public Sector Supply Arrangements," p. 58.

15 A. A. Alchian and R. A. Kessel, "Competition, Monopoly, and the Pursuit of Pecuniary Gain," in H. G. Lewis, ed., *Aspects of Labor Economics* (Princeton, N.J.: Princeton University Press, 1962).

16 The argument *could* apply to government corporations or nationalized industries – to that part of the public sector that sells goods and services to consumers for a price.

17 See Alchian, "Corporate Management and Property Rights."

18 In Chapter 7, we suggest that this is partly the reason why private firms may be more efficient than government bureaus.

19 Berle and Means, *The Modern Corporation and Private Property.*

20 Compare R. Marris, *The Economic Theory of "Managerial" Capitalism,* (London: Macmillan, 1964), Chap. 2, on the motives of managers, with Niskanen, *Bureaucracy and Representative Government,* Chap. 4, on the goals of government bureaucrats.

21 O. E. Williamson, *The Economics of Discretionary Behaviour: Managerial Objectives in the Theory of the Firm* (Englewood Cliffs, N.J.: Prentice-Hall, 1964).

22 Alchian, "Corporate Management and Property Rights."

23 M. C. Jensen and W. H. Meckling, "Theory of the Firm: Managerial Behavior, Agency Costs and Ownership Structure," *Journal of Financial Economics* (Vol. 3, No. 4, October 1976), pp. 305–60; and Fama, "Agency Problems and the Theory of the Firm."

24 Fama, "Agency Problems and the Theory of the Firm," pp. 296ff.

25 Especially Marris, *"Managerial" Capitalism,* and Williamson, *The Economics of Discretionary Behaviour.*

26 See, however, our discussion in Section 5.5.

27 There is evidence that mobility among public-sector managers is higher than among executives in private industry. See the discussion in J. Margolis, "Comment" (on Niskanen's "Bureaucrats and Politicians"), *Journal*

of Law and Economics (Vol. 18, No. 3, December 1975) p. 648, and the references cited there.

28 See pp. 93–4.

29 The assessments that have been attempted are rather unfavorable. See B. Hindley, "Separation of Ownership and Control in the Modern Corporation," *Journal of Law and Economics* (Vol. 13, April 1970), pp. 185–221, and R. Smiley, "Tender Offers, Transactions Costs, and the Theory of the Firm," *Review of Economics and Statistics* (Vol. 58, No. 1, February 1976), pp. 22–32.

30 Tullock argues that this structure is a rational response to barriers to entry into politics. See G. Tullock, "Entry Barriers in Politics," *American Economic Review* (Vol. 55, No. 2, May 1965), pp. 458–66.

31 See Tullock, "Entry Barriers in Politics," and A. Breton, *The Economic Theory of Representative Government* (Chicago: Aldine, 1974).

32 J. A. Schumpeter, *Capitalism, Socialism, and Democracy* (London: Allen and Unwin, 1943); A. Downs, *An Economic Theory of Democracy* (New York: Harper & Row, 1957); G. S. Becker, "Competition and Democracy," *Journal of Law and Economics* (Vol. 1, October 1958), pp. 105–9; and Breton, *Representative Government.*

33 A. Breton and R. Wintrobe, "The Equilibrium Size of a Budget-maximizing Bureau: A Note on Niskanen's Theory of Bureaucracy," *Journal of Political Economy* (Vol. 83, No. 1, February 1975), pp. 195–207.

34 Marris bases his case that corporation managers maximize growth on the fact that mobility of executives among corporations is difficult. See Marris, *"Managerial" Capitalism,* Chap. 2.

35 See Breton and Wintrobe, "Budget-maximizing Bureau," where the argument that politicians can reduce the excess budget of a budget-maximizing bureau was initially developed, and Chapter 3, where this model is generalized to bureaus with other objectives.

36 We doubt, however, that networks are always or even usually bureau-specific. See, in particular, the description of multibureau networks in the British civil service in H. Heclo and A. W. Wildavsky, *The Private Government of Public Money* (London: Macmillan, 1973).

37 The forces that cause this shift are discussed in the next chapter.

38 In this case, however, the effects of the increase in price and the increase in quantity of informal services on the cost curve are offsetting: The increase in the quantity of informal services tends to lower the EAC, whereas the increase in price tends to raise it. The statement in the text assumes that the effect of the increase in quantity is dominant.

39 See Chapter 4. Also, because trust cannot be bought, outsiders cannot bribe insiders to produce trust jointly with them.

6 The size distribution of bureaus

1 A neoclassical model of growth and decline of bureaucracy would require, in addition to a theory of supply such as the one suggested in this book, a theory of demand and a theory of the interaction of supply and demand.

2 See M. Friedman, *Price Theory: A Provisional Text* (Chicago: Aldine, 1976), pp. 104–5.

3 See J. A. Schumpeter, *The Theory of Economic Development* (Cambridge, Mass.: Harvard University Press, 1955), and *Capitalism, Socialism and Democracy* (New York: Harper & Row, 1975).

4 J. A. Schumpeter, *Capitalism, Socialism, and Democracy*, pp. 84–5.

5 Ibid.

6 See I. Kirzner, *Competition and Entrepreneurship* (Chicago: University of Chicago Press, 1973), p. 43.

7 See especially Kirzner, *Competition and Entrepreneurship*, p. 94.

8 J. A. Schumpeter, *The Theory of Economic Development* (Cambridge, Mass.: Harvard University Press, 1955).

9 M. Olson, Jr., "Evaluating Performance in the Public Sector" in M. Moss, ed., *The Measurement of Economic and Social Performance* (New York: Columbia University Press, 1973).

10 M. Friedman, "Comment" on C. Smith, "Survey of Empirical Evidence on Economics of Scale" in *Business Concentration and Price Policy* (Princeton, N.J.: Princeton University Press, 1955), reprinted in Friedman, *Price Theory*, Chap. 6.

11 A. Alchian and H. Demsetz, "Production, Information Costs, and Economic Organization," *American Economic Review* (Vol. 62, No. 5, December 1972), pp. 777–95.

12 In this connection, Lazear and Rosen have shown that it makes little difference whether factors are paid according to their measured marginal products or on the basis of a ranking of their performance, provided rank and productivity are correlated. See E. Lazear and S. Rosen, "Rank-Order Tournaments as Optimal Labour Contracts," *Journal of Political Economy* (Vol. 89, No. 5, October 1981), pp. 841–864.

13 Lack of entrepreneurial capacity is sometimes cited in the literature on underdeveloped economies as a major cause of backwardness. Our analysis shows that this deficiency may be rooted in a country's social structure, a point that is sometimes made in that literature but never satisfactorily explained.

14 A. Peacock and J. Wiseman, *The Growth of Public Expenditure in the United Kingdom* (Princeton, N.J.: Princeton University Press, 1961).

15 M. Olson, Jr., *The Political Economy of Comparative Growth Rates* (mimeo, 1978).

16 The evidence is summarized in F. M. Scherer, *Industrial Market Structure and Economic Performance*, 2nd ed. (Chicago: Rand McNally, 1972), Chap. 15; and in M. Kamien and N. Schwartz, "Market Structure and Innovation: A Survey," *Journal of Economic Literature*, (Vol. 13, No. 1, March 1975), pp. 1–37.

17 See C. Futia, "Schumpeterian Competition," *Quarterly Journal of Economics* (Vol. 94, No. 4, June 1980), pp. 675–96; and P. Dasgupta and J. E. Stiglitz, "Uncertainty, Industrial Structure and the Speed of R & D," *Bell Journal of Economics* (Vol. 11, No. 1, Spring 1980), pp. 1–28.

18 Some cases of such shifts in the Canadian government are discussed in R.

W. Phidd and G. B. Doern, *The Politics and Management of Canadian Economic Policy* (Toronto: Macmillan, 1978).

19 The word *opportunism* is not meant here in its pejorative sense, but simply refers to the grasping of opportunities. Sometimes this is socially beneficial, sometimes not. In popular usage, there is a negative connotation to *opportunism,* as in the work of Oliver Williamson [*Markets and Hierarchies* (New York: Free Press, 1975)], who uses the term to mean "self-seeking with guile."

20 A. A. Alchian and R. Kessel, "Competition, Monopoly, and the Pursuit of Pecuniary Gain" in H. G. Lewis, ed., *Aspects of Labor Economics* (Princeton, N.J.: Princeton University Press, 1962).

21 Becker has presented an analysis of restrictions on competition in families that is similar to ours in some respects; in both his analysis and ours, competition is restricted in order to promote cooperation. In Becker's analysis, however, the restrictions are an accidental by-product of love or caring between family members and are not deliberately imposed in order to foster cooperation. Moreover, in the absence of caring, the restrictions – which, in Becker's model, take the form of redistribution of income among family members – would not exist, despite their productivity in increasing family welfare. So, the productivity of restrictions – the greater cooperation made possible by them – is in this way attributed to love or caring. Our analysis shows that this attribution is unnecessary. See G. S. Becker, "A Theory of Social Interactions," *Journal of Political Economy* (Vol. 82, No. 6, December 1974), pp. 1063-93. Our analysis is more in the spirit of Alchian and Demsetz's "Production, Information, and Economic Organization," *American Economic Review* (Vol. 62, No. 5, December 1972), pp. 777-95 in which organizations seek to encourage "team spirit" and "loyalty." For this purpose, however, Alchian and Demsetz require the concept of "team production," a highly restrictive concept that we neither use nor require.

22 R. H. Coase, "The Problem of Social Cost," *Journal of Law and Economics* (Vol. 1, October 1958), pp. 1-44.

23 Alternatively, one can say that, in that case, trust would be an unnecessary investment even at a zero cost, the maximum amount of it being supplied free.

7 Some applications

1 See M. Hashimato, "Bonus Payments, on-the-Job Training, and Lifetime Employment in Japan," *Journal of Political Economy* (Vol. 87, No. 5, Part 1, October 1979), pp. 1086-1104.

2 On this score, we find Mancur Olson's approach in *The Political Economy of Comparative Growth Rates* (mimeo, 1978) more satisfying, although we do not necessarily agree with the substance of his theory.

3 The literature up to the end of the 1960s is reviewed and the evidence reexamined in R. G. Bodkin, "Real Wages and Cyclical Variations in Em-

ployment: A Re-examination of the Evidence," *Canadian Journal of Economics* (Vol. 2, No. 3, August 1969), pp. 353–74. Important attempts to rationalize the evidence are contained in R. E. Lucas, Jr., "Capacity, Overtime, and Empirical Production Functions," *American Economic Review* (Vol. 60, No. 2, May 1970), pp. 23-7, and R. Barro and H. Grossman, "A General Disequilibrium Model of Income and Employment," *American Economic Review* (Vol. 61, March 1971), pp. 82–93.

4 The contributions by Lucas, and by Barro and Grossman cited in the previous footnote, both show that productivity *may* be procyclical, but they do not imply or predict this result.

5 Nondiscretionary perks, such as social welfare expenditures, may also be important in building trust with employees collectively rather than on an individual basis.

6 A sample of this literature includes B. Jovanovic, "Job Matching and the Theory of Turnover," *Journal of Political Economy* (Vol. 87, No. 5, Part 1, October 1979), pp. 972–90; D. O. Parsons, "Specific Human Capital: An Application to Quit Rates and Layoff Rates," *Journal of Political Economy* (Vol. 80, No. 6, November–December 1972), pp. 1120–43; and R. E. Hall, "Turnover in the Labor Force," *Brookings Papers on Economic Activity,* Vol. 3, (Washington, D.C.: The Brookings Institution, 1972), pp. 709–64.

7 See, among others, Herbert Luethy, *France Against Herself* (New York: Meridian Books, 1959); Lawrence Scheinman, *Atomic Energy Policy in France Under the Fourth Republic* (Princeton, N.J.: Princeton University Press, 1965). E. N. Suleiman, in his excellent *Politics, Power and Bureaucracy in France* (Princeton, N.J.: Princeton University Press, 1974), argues that the hypothesis is not necessarily correct, although he documents (pp. 165-6) that it is widely believed among French civil servants.

8 The most famous exponent of this view is James Abegglen. See his *The Japanese Factory* (Glencoe, Ill.: Free Press, 1958).

9 This is the view put forward by K. Taira, *Economic Development and the Labor Market in Japan* (New York: Columbia University Press, 1970).

10 W. Galenson and K. Odaka, "The Japanese Labor Market" in H. Patrick and H. Rosovsky, eds., *Asia's New Giant: How the Japanese Economy Works* (Washington, D.C.: The Brookings Institution, 1976).

11 Hashimoto, "Bonus Payments."

12 Ibid., p. 1092.

13 Ronald Dore, *British Factory – Japanese Factory: The Origins of National Diversity in Industrial Relations* (Berkeley, Calif.: University of California Press, 1973).

14 Ibid., Table 3.6, p. 100.

15 Ibid., p. 99.

16 Ibid.

17 Ibid.

18 Ibid., p. 112.

19 R. E. Cole, *Japanese Blue Collar: The Changing Tradition* (Berkeley: University of California Press, 1971), pp. 165-6.

20 Hashimoto, "Bonus Payments," Table 1, p. 1088.
21 Dore, *British Factory – Japanese Factory*, p. 283.
22 Hashimoto, "Bonus Payments," footnote 5, p. 1088.
23 Ibid., Table 2, p. 1089.
24 M. Yoshino, *Japan's Managerial System: Tradition and Innovation* (Cambridge, Mass.: MIT Press, 1968).
25 Dore, *British Factory – Japanese Factory*, p. 260.
26 Galenson and Odaka, in Patrick and Rosovsky, *Asia's New Giant*, p. 633.
27 Ibid.
28 We owe this point to a personal conversation with Harry Nishio.
29 Glazer, "Japanese Economic Growth," pp. 884ff.
30 Ibid., p. 887.
31 Hashimoto, "Bonus Payments," p. 1090.
32 According to one report (*Time*, March 30, 1981), the Japanese use the same *nenko* practices in their newly opened factories in the United States.
33 H. Patrick and H. Rosovsky, "Japan's Economic Performance: An Overview," in Patrick and Rosovsky, *Asia's New Giant*, p. 4.
34 E. F. Denison and William K. Chung, *How the Japanese Economy Grew So Fast* (Washington, D.C.: The Brookings Institution, 1976). Similar analyses are presented in D. W. Jorgenson and M. Nishimizu, "U.S. and Japanese Economic Growth 1952–1974: An International Comparison," *Economic Journal* (Vol. 88, No. 352, (December 1978), pp. 707–26, and in R. E. Caves and M. Uehusa, *Industrial Organization in Japan* (Washington, D.C.: The Brookings Institution, 1976).
35 Denison and Chung, *Japanese Economy*, pp. 48ff.
36 Denison and Chung, *Japanese Economy*, p. 49.
37 According to Jorgenson and Nishimizu, the level of Japanese technology surpassed that of the U.S. in 1974. See Jorgenson and Nishimizu, "U.S. and Japanese Economic Growth," p. 723.
38 Denison and Chung, *Japanese Economy*, p. 83.
39 Some of the ideas presented below were first elaborated in conversations with Anthony Scott of the University of British Columbia. We are grateful to him, although accepting full responsibility for the configuration given here.
40 See D. Smith, *Income Policies: Some Foreign Experiences and Their Relevance for Canada* (Ottawa: Queen's Printer, 1966); also L. Ulman and R. J. Flanagan, *A Study of Income Policies in Western Europe* (Berkeley: University of California Press, 1971).
41 One should mention as possible counterevidence the fact that in 1972 Richard Nixon was reelected President of the United States after the implementation of controls, but after an election campaign in which controls were not an issue.
42 *The Globe and Mail* (Toronto, October 10, 1975), p. B-1. The results are from a survey conducted by the Elliot Research Corp. and analyzed by the International Business Studies Research Unit of the University of

Windsor. They are based on a nationalwide quota sample of 5,000 respondents.

43 In a way, trust is eroded because advisors are unable to explain what is going on. From the point of view of their superiors, they appear to be cheating.

44 This strategy is not unique to bureaucrats. It is – and in the recent experience of controls in Canada was – practiced with great skill by most, if not all, of those who agitated for controls and then "altered" (?) their view.

45 The term *political media* is used to distinguish among the various forms of the mass media. In addition to the political media, there are sports, financial, fashion, and other media.

46 Much of this section is drawn from our previously published paper "Bureaucracy and State Intervention: Parkinson's Law?," *Canadian Journal of Public Administration* (Vol. 2, No. 2, Summer 1979), pp. 208–225.

47 These are to be found in *Parkinson's Law and Other Studies in Administration* (New York: Ballantine, 1957) and in *The Essential Parkinson* (New Delhi: Federation House, 1970).

48 M. Friedman, "Gammon's Black Holes," *Newsweek* (November 7, 1977), p. 84. The first discussion of the black holes is to be found in M. Gammon, *Health and Security: Report on the Public Provision for Medical Care in Great Britain* (London: St. Michael's Organization, December, 1976), p. 27.

49 See, for example, R. E. Chester, *A Study of Post-War Growth in Management Organizations* (Paris: Organization for European Economic Cooperation, 1961).

50 Parkinson, *Parkinson's Law and Other Studies*, p. 7.

51 Parkinson, *The Essential Parkinson*, p. 26.

52 Gammon, *Health and Security*, p. 27.

53 Friedman, "Gammon's Black Holes," p. 84.

54 W. A. Niskanen, Jr., *Bureaucracy and Representative Government* (Chicago: Aldine-Atherton, 1971).

55 An alternative division would result if we partitioned subordinates à la Parkinson into an administrative component (the A's) and a direct labor component (the L's). Any form of subdivision can be used depending on the problem.

56 For a discussion of specific capital, see G. S. Becker, *Human Capital*, 2nd ed. (New York: Columbia University Press, 1975).

57 See the discussion of reorganization in the previous chapter.

58 Parkinson, *The Essential Parkinson*, p. 26.

8 Concluding observations and agenda

1 Obviously, if trust does not exist, trade will not take place, and the relationship between superiors and subordinates will be one of authority. In a way, one could say that the standard theory of bureaucracy is one in which trust is assumed too costly to produce.

2 The seminal paper on that question is by George Akerlof. See his "The Market for 'Lemons': Quality Uncertainty and the Market Mechanism," *Quarterly Journal of Economics* (Vol. 84, No. 3, August 1970), pp. 488–500. An important recent contribution to that literature is H. E. Leland, "Quacks, Lemons, and Licensing: A Theory of Minimum Quality Standards," *Journal of Political Economy* (Vol. 87, No. 6, December 1979), pp. 1328–46.

Index

Acheson, K., 27, 28, 89
administration, 33; top-heavy, 155–61
administrative overload, 57–8; *see also* managers
Akerlof, G., 177n23
Alchian, A. A., 90, 93, 114, 129; on competition, 95, 99, 100, 103, 104
altruism, caring: relation of trust to, 78
Area Development Incentives Act (Canada), 20
Arrow, K. J., 69, 73–4, 177n25, 178n40; *The Limits of Organization*, 64
authority, 3, 4, 58, 162; *see also* formal structure

Bank of Canada, 28
banks, central, 79
bargaining, 24, 72; focused, 77; *see also* exchange, trade
barriers: to network entry, 105; to trust, 80, 82–5, 86, 87
barter economy, 63–4
bazaar economy, 76–8, 88
Becker, G. S., 19, 177n25, 183n21
Bélanger, G., 27, 34, 89
Bendix, R., 34
Berle, A. A., 95
Bezeau, L. M., 20
Black, D., 172n26
Borcherding, T. E., 92, 93
Bothwell, R., 45
Bowen, H. R., 172n26
budgets, 34–5; as goal of bureaucrats, 27, 28; maximization of, 34–6, 98, 99, 154, 155; public sector, 17, 20–2, 28, 97, 98–9, 148
bureaucracies, 164; budget-maximizing, 154, 155; currency of exchange in, 26–7, 29; demand for wage and price controls originates in, 147, 150–3; growth of, and organization decline, 156–61; Japanese firm as ideal, 140–6; mode of operation of, 29; models of, 3–4; monopoly model of, 4, 89, 90, 91–4, 105–6; rationality of,

16, 33, 56, 157; *see also* government bureaucracy
bureaucratic theory, 4, 27–8, 30, 111; departures from, 162–4; literature re, 32–7; monopoly assumption in, 4, 89, 90, 91–4; research needs in, 164–6
bureaucratic theory, model of, 4–11, 29, 42; applications of, 11–12, 132–61, 164–5; *see also* selective behavior
bureaucrats, 28, 140; budget-maximization by, 34, 35, 36; capacity for selective behavior, 6–8, 9, 32, 152–3, 164; compensation of, 9, 89–106; decisions re supply of informal services, 46–54; dual role of, 2–3, 30–1; as empire builders, 154; inefficient behavior of, 92–3, 152–4; instruments used in selective behavior, 32, 34–5, 36, 37–41; monopoly power of, 91–2, 97–9; neutrality of, 34; objective function of, 17, 26–9, 35; "quiet life" of, 90, 92–3, 154; schools for, 86; ties to outside people, 79; *see also* exchange, trade; subordinates; trust, between sponsors and bureaucrats
bureaus: competition among, 8, 10, 25–6; competition within, 8, 10–11; inefficient behavior in, 42–3, 45–6; production in, 31; relationships among, 164–5; size distribution of, 27, 37, 107–31, 154

Canada: Coyne affair, 45–6
capital, 31, 134, 139
capital assets, 74; collective, 177n23; trust as, 78–9
career promotion, 27
Categorical Imperative, 83
Chamberlain, E. H., 19
Chant, J. F., 27, 28, 89
characteristics: and goals, 28; policies as, 9, 17–20, 26–7, 29
cheating, 65, 66–7, 74, 75, 76; costs of, 70–1
Chung, William K., 146

189

clientization, 76, 77, 88
Coase, R. H., 130
codes of honor, 4, 74
commands, 4, 41–2; distortion of, 7,
    38–40, 58
Commons, John R., 74
Company manager supervision (CM), 57
compensation, 9, 31, 89–106, 129; see
    also nonpecuniary gains; perquisites
competition, 3, 4, 8–11, 30, 47, 49,
    97–9, 163, 165; among bureaus, 8,
    10, 25–6; among bureaus in various
    sectors, 164–5; equalizes price for in-
    formal services, 115–17, 119; in ex-
    change process, 24–5; internal, 26,
    89–91, 97–108; in presence of small
    numbers, 87, 88; process of "creative
    destruction," 110; for resources,
    107–8, 113; restrictions on, 127–30;
    Schumpeterian theory, 108–15; selec-
    tive behavior and, 90, 99–106
complexity, 20, 27
conflicts, bureaucratic, 8
Confucian code of ethics, 83
constraint concern (concept), 56
contracts, 63, 74, 162; contingent, 61, 88
control, see policing, monitoring
control loss, 7, 39, 58
cooperation, 74–6, 129; see also networks
corporate sector: growth of, 89; litera-
    ture on, 89, 95; managerial monopoly
    in, 90, 94–9; output of, 13, 14, 17; see
    also private policies
cost–benefit analysis, 111
cost curves, 36; formal and efficient,
    31–2, 54–60; and network truncation,
    86–7
costs, 4, 93; of cheating, 70–1; effect of
    selective behavior on, 10, 99–105,
    133; of network membership, 6,
    101–2, 105; of policing and monitor-
    ing, 6, 51, 81–2, 95, 96, 98, 119; price
    and quantity of informal services,
    116–19; production, 113–14; of pro-
    motion, 137–8; of public policies,
    54–60; of sanctions, 71–2; of turn-
    over, 138; see also transaction costs
Coyne, James, 45–6
credit, 63

decision making, see policy decisions,
    technical decisions
demand: and inefficient market behav-
    ior, 43–6; for informal services, 46–7,
    49–50, 85, 86; and productivity, 138;

for public output, 165; theory of, 1;
    see also supply/demand
demand management, 111
Demsetz, M., 114
Denison, E. F., 146
discretion, 20, 27, 35; managerial, 34,
    95, 96–7
displacement effects, 126–7
Doeringer, P., 31
Dore, Ronald, 142–3
Downs, A., 91, 172n26
Downsian competition model, 172n26
Drummond, I., 45

earnings, 99–101, 103–4; see also
    compensation
economic instability, 148–9
economic theory, 12; Austrian school of,
    8, 10–11, 108–11, 112; neoclassical,
    1–3, 4, 26, 157, 165
economies of scale, 14, 16; in informa-
    tion collection, 58
Edgeworth, F. Y., 63
efficiency, efficient behavior, 33–4, 114,
    164; and cost curve, 55–6; demand
    for, 46, 47; depends on trust ratio,
    52; impact of competition on, 99,
    100–1; and instruments of selective
    behavior, 38–9, 41; maximization of,
    in Japanese firm, 141; must be paid
    for, 42; relation with monopoly, 92–5;
    and trust, 82, 133–4; see also selective
    behavior
elections, 147
emulation, 110–11
English, J., 45
English Electric (firm), 142, 143, 144
entrapment, 43, 44–6, 52
entrepreneurial capacity, 121–7,
    130
entrepreneurship, 10–11, 108–11; in
    public sector, 111–15; and restrictions
    on competition, 127–30
entropy, information and command,
    38–40
environmental control, 111
exchange, trade, 7–8, 10, 135; between
    bureaucrats and media, 153; currency
    of, 26–7, 29; in networks, 48, 63–4,
    85–6, 88, 162; and optimal size of
    firm, 60; in production of public pol-
    icies, 24–6; and property rights, 4–5,
    62–4; selective behavior is embodi-
    ment of, 41; in superior/subordinate
    relationship, 3, 4–5 (see also superior/

subordinate relationship); trust in, 73–8
externalities, 61–2; market failure in presence of, 87, 88; trust as, 69

factor-price equalization theorem, 115
Fama, E. F., 95
featherbedding, 43
firms, 3, 4; optimal, 12, 56, 57–60; production, 31; theory of, 133, 135; *see also* corporate sector; private sector
formal structure, 5, 6, 31–2, 87; and cost curves, 54–5, 58–60; efficient operation of, 32; and instruments of selective behavior, 40–1; and resource allocation, 129–30
franchise ownership (FO), 57
Friedman, Milton, 114; monopoly model of public sector, 154, 155, 156, 157, 161

Galbraith, J. K., 33, 37, 169n14
game theory, 24
Gammon, Max, 156
Geertz, C., 76–7, 88
Glazer, N., 145
Golden Rule, 83
government-as-monopoly model, 172n26
government bureaucracy: competition in, 4, 97–9; literature re, 89; production of, 13–14, 17, 20; *see also* public policies; public sector
Great Britain: civil service, 80; National Health Service, 156; navy, 155, 158, 161
Great Depression, 126

Harris, J. E., 74
Hashimoto, M., 141
Hayek, F. A., 8, 109
Heath, Edward, 147
Hehner, Eric, 20
Hicks, J. R., 93
hierarchy, 2–3, 6; competition and, 112–13; incentives in, 87, 88; levels of, 30–1; and optimal size of firm, 57–8; policy production and, 23–5
Hirschman, A. O., 177n25
Hitachi (firm), 142, 143, 144

Ik tribe, 77–8
incentive(s), 87, 88, 94
indicators, 82–4; in trust production, 69–70, 73, 125

inefficiency, inefficient behavior, 34–7, 42–6, 92–3, 152–4; and cost curve, 55–6; demand for, 46–7; impact of competition on, 99–100; and instruments of selective behavior, 38–40, 41, 129, 163; in public bureaus, 42–3, 45–6
inert areas (concept), 56
inflation, 146, 147, 165; responsibility for, 149, 150–1, 152
informal labor services, 10, 31–2, 82; asymmetrical supply of, 46–52, 85, 86; determination of supply of, 121–7; effect of bureau size on price of, 59–60; efficient or inefficient, 46–52, 154; equilibrium volume of, 86; as object traded in networks, 64; paid for by perquisites, 135–6; price and quantity of, 7–8, 88, 115–19, 122–3; supply/demand, 107–8, 113, 115–21; surrogate markets for, 26–7 (*see also* networks); traded for policy characteristics, 26, 29, 41, 60; volume of, 52–4
informal structure, 5–6, 31–2, 57; and cost curve, 54–5; *see also* organization theory
information, 139; distortion of, 7, 37–8, 39–40, 58, 98, 153; lack, cost of in primitive economies, 76–7, 78; leakages and plants, 7, 38, 40
innovation, 109–10, 122–3, 128; in public sector, 112–13
insurance principle, 76, 77

Japanese firm, 11, 132, 140–6; productivity of, 132, 134, 145–6
Jensen, M. C., 95
Johnson, Harry, 72

Kant, I., 83
Kessel, R. A., 93, 129
Keynesian economics, 111
Kirzner, I., 110–11
Knight, F. H., 172n26
Kurz, Mordecai, 74

labor services, 26, 31; *see also* informal labor services
Lancaster, K. J., 9, 19
law and law enforcement, 4, 5, 125; *see also* property rights, law-based; property rights, trust
Lazear, E., 183n12

Leibenstein, H., 12; X-(in)efficiency,
    56–7
leisure, 27, 92, 93, 95, 129
"Leviathan models," 28
lifetime employment, 141, 144
Limits of Organization, The (Arrow), 64
logrolling theory, 24

McKean, R. N., 74, 178n40
managers, 30–1; competition among, 8,
    90–1; lethargy, 93 (*see also* bureau-
    crats, "quiet life" of); literature re, 95;
    monopoly theory re, 90, 94–9;
    selective behavior and (model),
    99–106
market(s), 162–3; competitive, 16, 88;
    distinct from firm, 3; efficiency of, 88,
    96–7; failure of, 87, 88; inefficient,
    42–5; networks as surrogates of, 6,
    41, 47–8, 49, 55–6, 59, 60, 61, 84, 88,
    162
Marris, R., 182n34
Marshall, A., 63
Means, G. C., 95
Meckling, W. H., 95
media, political, 152–3
median-voter model, 172n26
medical services: demand generation
    and, 43–4
Menger, C., 109
merit, 143, 144
Migué, J.-L., 27, 34, 89
minimum-coalition model, 172n26
mobility, 95, 96–7, 126, 182n34; costs
    of, 101–5, 108, 115; in Japanese firm,
    144
money supply, managed, 148, 149
monitoring; *see* policing, monitoring
monopoly: as competition, 109–10, 128;
    of knowledge, 33; power of govern-
    ment, 157
monopoly models (bureaucracy), 4, 89,
    90, 91–4, 105–6
moral codes, 74
moral hazard, 61, 87, 88
motivation, 95
mystification, 43–4, 45, 52

national crises, 126–7
nenko wage system, 145
network truncation, 82–7, 123–4, 126
networks, 5, 10, 11; of bureaucrats with
    media, 153; and competition, 8, 90,
    99–106; defined, 78; equilibrium in,
    55–6, 78–87; exchange in, 7–8, 63–4,

85–6, 88, 162; failure of, 48, 51–2;
    and instruments of selective behavior,
    41–2, 159–60; internal/external, 79;
    are production instructions, 79–80;
    and productivity, 139; size distribution
    of, 82, 107; strength of, and resource
    allocation, 115–21; as surrogate mar-
    kets, 6, 41, 47–8, 49, 55–6, 59, 60, 61,
    84, 88, 162; weakening, destruction
    of, 119–21
Neumann–Morgenstern utility function,
    27
New Deal, 111
New York City: public employees, 156
Niskanen, W. A., Jr., 27, 28, 30, 34,
    35–6; model of bureaucratic theory,
    89, 91–2, 95, 98, 99, 155, 157–8
Nixon, Richard, 186n41
nonpecuniary gains, 93, 94, 95, 129
norms of behavior, 4, 74; *see also* rules
"norms of socialization," 74

obsolescence, planned, 43
Olson, Mancur, 127
opportunism, 88, 110–11, 128–9
organization(s): decline of, 156; expan-
    sion of administrative component in,
    154–61; multidivisional, 86
organization theory, 5, 31–2
organizational slack, 95
organizational structure: and competi-
    tion, 129–30; and productivity, 132,
    133–40; *see also* formal structure; in-
    formal structure
output, 4, 7, 29, 31; difficulty measur-
    ing, 52, 114; effect of selective behav-
    ior on, 10; restriction of, 43; *see also*
    private policies; public policies

Parkinson, C. Northcote, 6, 132, 154;
    The Essential Parkinson, 156; tradition
    of bureaucracy, 34–7
Parkinson's Law, 12, 133, 154–61
patronage, internal, 27
Peacock, A., 126
perquisites, 11, 26; in Japanese firm,
    143; as policy characteristics, 19; and
    productivity, 134, 135–6, 140
Piore, M., 31
planning and program-budgeting (PPB)
    system, 111
policing, monitoring, 4, 39, 48, 52, 129,
    140, 150, 163; costs of, 6, 8, 51, 81–2,
    95, 96, 98, 119; desired level of,
    53–4; wage and price controls, 151

policy characteristics, 9, 17–21, 31; as currency of exchange, 26–7, 64
policy decisions, 9, 13, 19; illustration of term, 14–16; *see also* private policies; public policies
policy implementation, 20, 22–3, 25–6, 38, 40–1, 42; as innovation, 112
political instability, 132, 140
political parties, 146–7
politicians, 30–1, 41–2, 97, 113; exploited by bureaucrats, 91–2; trust relationship with bureaucrats, 149–50; and wage and price controls, 147, 152–3
Posner, R. A., 76, 77
power, 8, 27, 33, 34, 89; competition and, 104–5, 106
price(s), 4, 88; *see also* cost curves
price theory, 3, 108–9, 111
primitive economies, 10, 63, 76–8
prisoner's dilemma (game), 74–5
"private collective action," 74
private policies, 2, 13–29, 164
private sector, 1; competition in, 112–13; and macroeconomic stability, 148–9; relation with bureaus in other sectors, 164–5; *see also* corporate sector
product differentiation: policy decisions re, 15–17
productivity, 4, 114, 157; organizational structure and, 132, 133–40; is procyclical, 132, 135, 138; is related to amount and distribution of trust, 11; *see also* selective behavior
profits, 93–4, 138
promotion, 11; in face of organizational decline, 159–60; frequency of, 134, 135, 137–8, 140, 144; in Japanese firm, 142–3
property rights, 4–5, 48, 94; law-based, 61–4, 74, 87–8, 124; quasi-, 128; trust-based, 61, 62–4, 73–4, 87–8, 130
public budgets, 17, 28, 97, 98–9, 148; economic/official accounting, 20–2
public choice, 1, 154
public goods, 13–14
public policies, 13–29, 164; controlled by private sector, 165; cost of, 54–60; production of, 17, 20–2, 22–6
public sector, 1, 35; and macroeconomic instability, 148–9; market for managers in, 96–7; monopoly models of, 91–4, 97–9, 105–6, 163; Parkinson's

Law operating in, 157; relationship with bureaus in other sectors, 164–5; Schumpeterian competition in, 111–15; size and growth of, 21–2, 97, 126–7

quid pro quo, 26, 42, 64; as money taken by supplier, 45, 47
quotas, 85–6

red tape, 7, 40
regulatory policies, 17, 20–1, 28, 165; *see also* public budgets
rents, 10, 91, 95, 96; monopoly, 91–2; and selective behavior, 101, 103, 104, 105, 106
reorganization, 119–21, 125–7, 129–30, 163
resource allocation, 10–11, 37, 107–8, 113–15, 164; model of, 115–21; and organizational structure, 130; and restrictions on competition, 128
rewards, 51; *see also* compensation; nonpecuniary gains; perquisites
Riker, W. H., 172n26
risk and responsibility, 27, 32
risks, penalties, 47, 48, 50, 51–2; *see also* policing, monitoring
Rosen, S., 183n12
rules, 4, 31, 40–1, 125

salaries, *see* compensation
Samuelson, P. A., 14
sanctions, 67, 70–2, 73, 77; social, 74
Schumpeter, J. A., 1, 8, 10–11, 109, 128; competition theory, 108–15, 128
secrecy, 27, 36
security, 27, 28
selective behavior, 6–8, 9; and allocation of resources, 107–8, 115–21; capacity for, 10–11, 130; decisions in, 46–54, 82; defined, 37; efficient in growth, inefficient in decline, 135, 136–7, 140; illustration of, 37–42; and Parkinson's Law, 158–61; reduced by network truncation, 87; theory of, 9–10, 30–60, 90, 99–106, 162–4 (*see also* efficiency, efficient behavior; inefficiency, inefficient behavior); and wage and price controls, 11–12, 146–54
selective rationality (concept), 56
self-preservation, 27, 35, 36
seniority, 141, 143, 144
service and repair sector, 43

Selton, J. P., 57
slowdowns, 7, 40–1
Smith, Adam, 128
Smith, Vernon, 74
social balance, 85–6, 169n14
social boundaries, 84
social cleavages, 84–5
social customs, 4, 74, 177n23
social security, 111
sponsors, 30–1, 113; and cooperation of
  bureaucrats, 41–2; demand for effi-
  cient/inefficient services by, 46–7, 48,
  50, 115, 118–21; instruments used to
  control inefficient behavior, 38–40,
  41, 129, 163; selective behavior by,
  138; turnover among, 139–40, 144;
  see also superior/subordinate relationship; trust, between sponsors and
  bureaucrats
Stigler, G. J., 172n26, 177n25
structured labor market (concept), 31
subordinates, 2–3, 6–8, 31; relations
  among, 3, 8, 50, 51, 52–3; see also
  bureaucrats; superior/subordinate
  relationship
superior/subordinate ratio, 140, 144
superior/subordinate relationship, 1–3;
  within bureau, 30–60; classical economic views of, 6–7; formal structure
  and, 6; and productivity, 135; and
  selective behavior, 162, 164; see also
  exchange, trade; trust, between sponsors and bureaucrats
supply/demand: competitive, 24–5; for
  informal services, 46–52, 107–8, 113,
  115–27; need for theory of, for private, public, and voluntary output,
  165–6; theory of, 1–2, 35–7, 164

tariffs, 22–3, 72
technical decisions, 13, 14
technology, 109, 134
Thompson, Earl, 172n28
trade, see exchange, trade
transaction costs, 50, 51, 130; Japanese
  firm, 141–2; network, 84–5; in production of trust, 66–8; in trust accumulation, 123–4
Trudeau, Pierre-Elliot, 147
trust, 4–6, 9, 63, 68, 82; amount and
  distribution of, 11, 133–46; as basis of
  superior/subordinate relation, 57, 162,
  163; as capital asset, 64, 73; and competition, 90, 99, 101; and cost curve,

59; defined, 65; disinvestment in, 73,
  74; equilibrium volume of, 68–9,
  78–87; investment in, 73, 75–6, 80–4,
  135 (see also trust accumulation);
  jointly produced and consumed, 69,
  73; literature re, 73–8; mutality of,
  69, 72, 73, 78; in networks, 8, 11, 41,
  42 (see also networks); in primitive
  economies, 76–8; production of
  (model), 64–73, 125; in quasi-public
  good, 69; between sponsors and bureaucrats, 47–50, 51, 52, 57, 59, 82,
  121, 123–4, 134, 140, 149–50,
  159–60, 162, 163; among subordinates, 50, 51, 52–3
trust accumulation, 5, 10, 61–88, 141,
  177n25; and competition, 128–9, 130;
  cost of, 102, 103–4, 121
Tullock, G., 28, 34, 39
Turnbull, Colin, 77–8
turnover, 11; effect on productivity,
  134, 136, 137, 138–40; Japanese firm,
  143–4

United States: federal civil service, 80;
  productivity, 145
U.S. Department of Defense, 28, 91
U.S. Department of State, 91
U.S. Department of Treasury, 91
U.S. National Security Council, 91
U.S. Post Office, 91
utility function: maximization of, 27,
  28–9, 56
utility interdependence: relation of trust
  to, 78

voluntary exchange and transaction, 3
voluntary sector, 164–5
Von Mises, L., 6, 8, 109

Wachter, J. L., 74
wage adjustments (Japanese firm),
  141–2
wage and price controls, 132, 146–54;
  demand for, 12, 148–51; as entrapment, 46; failure of, 150–1, 153
Walras, L., 63
Walras's Law, 26
wars, 126, 127
wealth-redistribution model, 165,
  172n26
Weber, Max, 6, 31, 33, 34; tradition of
  bureaucratic theory, 33–4, 37
Williamson, O. E., 39, 57–8, 74

Wilson, Robert, 58
Wiseman, J., 126
work force: administration/labor ratio in, 155–61
work-to-rule, 7, 40, 43, 139

X-(in)efficiency, 12, 56–7

zero enforcement, 42
zero information costs, 42, 44